Everyone is capable of com!̶ ̶̶ ̶ ̶̶ ̶ with a good marketable 'idea'
that could earn them a fortun

This book is written in a ̶ ̶ ̶ ̶ ̶ ̶ ̶ ̶ ̶ ̶ ̶ ̶ ̶ ̶ ̶ ̶ ̶ l is a
practical, step by step guic̶ ̶ ̶ ̶ ̶ ̶ ̶ ̶ ̶ ̶ ̶ ̶ ̶ ̶ ̶ ̶ ɔceed
beyond the 'idea stage' in ̶ ̶ ̶ ̶ ̶ ̶ ̶ ̶ ̶ ̶ ̶ ̶ ̶ ̶ ̶ ̶ l their
concept.

LEARN ̶

- File a patent or design application
- Assess the market value of your concept
- Safeguard your idea
- Negotiate contracts, licences and royalties
- File for trade and service marks
- Avoid being 'ripped off'
- Develop commercial awareness
- Get financial assistance
- Obtain government assistance
- Check for originality
- Deal with professionals –
  lawyers, accountants and patent agents
- Consider franchising
- Deal with copyright infringement
- Become streetwise and stay in the game!
- Deal with transfer agents
- Use Government Innovative Centres

If you've got the idea, but lack the know-how, then look no further:
IDEAS OR INVENTIONS CAN MAKE FORTUNES has all the
advice and information you'll need to help you on the way to your
success!

FOR ALL

Innovators
Businesspersons
Manufacturers
Managers

To Kevin

I hope that maybe you
believe one or two of them

Best Wishes

March 1996

IDEAS OR INVENTIONS CAN MAKE FORTUNES

HOW TO MAKE YOURS!

BY

HARRY COLE

Owl Publishers (Jersey) Ltd

First published in the Channel Islands
by:

Owl Publishers (Jersey) Ltd.
P.O. Box No. 609
St. Helier
JERSEY JE4 8YB
Channel Islands
FAX: (0534) 32556

British Library Cataloguing in Publication Data:
    Cole, Harry
        Ideas or inventions can make fortunes: how
        to make yours!
        I. Title
        608.742

        ISBN 0951809016 Paperback
        ISBN 0951809008 Hardback

Typeset and printed in Great Britain by
The Guernsey Press Co Ltd.

Contents

Chapter 15
ARE PATENT AGENTS WORTH THEIR SALT?

Chapter 16
NON-DISCLOSURE OF CONFIDENTIAL INFORMATION

Chapter 17
BECOME STREETWISE AND STAY IN THE GAME – WHERE TO GET HELP

- Build yourself a prototype or working model
- Project a good business-like image
- Consider franchising your concept
- Government Innovative Centres and assistance
- Private innovative centres and assistance
- Government Small Firms Centres
- Technology Transfer Agents
- How to assess your royalty payments
- Prestigious awards

Chapter 18
WHAT IS SOMEONE ELSE'S OPINION WORTH?

- Is a professional opinion worth much?

Chapter 19
GET YOURSELF AN ACCOUNTANT

- Let them 'cook your books'

Acknowledgements

My sincere thanks to the many who kindly assisted me in preparing this book: anyone who helped me, but not mentioned is purely accidental, but also get my thanks!

Mr Ron Hickman for your gracious 'foreword' . . . Ron, just give a thought to the possible twenty-five million ruined chairs had you not invented your famous '**WORKMATE**'. But let's give our sympathy to all the chair manufacturers who lost out!

The staff of the Patent Office, who were so helpful and gave me every possible assistance.

Her Majesty's Stationery Office for granting me approval to use many extracts of their varied publications without which, this book would not have been possible.

Mary-Jane Perks for providing an excellent editorial service . . . I know of a surgeon who could use a good 'scalpel' . . . You certainly sliced my words and grammar into shape, and I am thankful that you did!

Julie Van Der Vliet . . . With a name like that I detect some 'Dutch' extraction and because you gave me a wonderful typing- service I'm showing my gratitude by sending you a well-deserved bunch of Tulips!

Alan Copp for designing my book jacket . . . Alan, I bow to your professionalism.

David Le Brocq: for producing my photograph on the cover of this book. David . . . You'll be hearing from my lawyer in due course!

And finally:

My Psychiatrist. . . I'll visit you when you are on the road to recovery!

Dedication

To:

My loving wife Patricia. I've yet to meet a lady who looks after her man so well as you do. I am so lucky and proud to be that man.

Mum, dad, brother Richard and sister Jacqueline. My sons Terry, Gary and Lee. I care for you all!

In Memory:

Of my dear stepfather Bob . . . You loved and cared for my mother so well that I am eternally grateful.

Little Gems

Some of the little gems that are featured preceding each Chapter are my own axioms which filtered through my mind whilst compiling the book.

The rest are drawn from a selection I have gathered over the years. The meaning of those gems will become obvious and may serve to awaken your own inspiration and guide you in the right direction, as they did for me.

HC 1991

'If you don't have a purpose in life
. . . invent one!'

HC

Introduction

Since the evolution of the world, *Homo-Sapiens* have utilized their superior brain power over the animal kingdom to develop an innovative planet that most of us take for granted.

Our modern society demands rapid changes and new products to support the market place which is the lifeblood and main artery to our social and economic well-being.

The purpose of this book is not to enlighten you on any specific invention or inventor, but to offer practical support and much-needed guidance to the many innovators who are forever thinking up great, marketable ideas, but often do not have the business acumen, expertise or information to proceed beyond their idea. Unfortunately, there are countless innovators who are being ripped off simply because they expose their ideas or concepts without first taking any necessary precautions to safeguard their Intellectual Property Rights. This book outlines the procedures to take, and explains, in simple language, the methods of exploiting your concepts, so that you are receiving the benefits due to you.

The book introduces, step by step, a host of issues and aspects of the business world you will need to know about if you're one of those people who has a brilliant idea and are wondering what to do next. It clearly explains:

- how to assess the value of your idea;
- how to obtain maximum protection by filing a patent application, obtaining copyright, or registering a design – with up-to-date information on time and costs involved;
- the do's and don't's of formulating contracts, selling your idea and negotiating the best possible deal;

- tips on how to develop commercial awareness and a realistic business sense;
- how to see through company images and weigh up their effects;
- how to base your decisions on sound judgements not pipe dreams;
- when to consider calling in the professionals – patent agents, lawyers, accountants, market researchers;
- what sources of finance and support are available to help you develop your idea into a marketable and successful product.

In fact, it is a complete guide, from the moment you dream up your idea, to the day you are either fortunate in selling it or decide to 'call quits' and abandon your project in favour of the next!

However, this book should only be treated as an invaluable guide: it is *not* a short cut to your success. There are no short cuts to anyone's success. In this game, you either follow the correct 'rules', or you suffer the consequences. Brilliant ideas may only come to you once in your entire lifetime. Therefore, when they do, don't lose out to others – know how to protect your rights and carry your plans through to their conclusion.

All ideas have some kind of intrinsical value to someone. Search out that someone and persuade them to buy your idea, then you are in business. It's as simple as that. Or so it would seem, but, as we shall see, there's a lot more involved. If you've pretensions to owning a chateau in France and several BMW motorcars, then hold on! Be prepared for some gruelling work and tough negotiations ahead. Knowing the system is the first step; abiding by it and using it to your advantage is the next. Therefore, it may be to your benefit to read on, if only to safeguard against selling your idea or concept for less than it is worth.

Everyone is capable of dreaming up a good marketable idea and the many innovators who have become millionaires through devising 'simple' ideas do not necessarily possess any exceptional marketing talents. What they *do* have, however, apart from their 'great idea', is the confidence to believe in themselves, along with the sheer perseverance and strength of character to want to succeed. A simple idea on its own can go a long way. If you believe it can make you a fortune, then go for it – this book shows you how.

The language used in this book is extremely 'down to earth', with the patent, design and copyright system written in a style that can easily be understood and followed by anyone. The text is often injected with humour and some accounts of my own experiences are given to illustrate certain points. I have done the 'assault course' myself, and crawled through the 'minefield', managing to hobble back with my dignity intact! I was inspired to write what follows so that others could start off their journey knowing exactly where they were going, and having a much better awareness of the obstacles they are likely to encounter when dealing with the ruthless commercial world!

All innovators, whatever their nationality, will have one common denominator in that they will have to tread the same path, experiencing the same anxieties along the way. It is quite possible that, after you have digested the full contents of this book, you may be fired with more enthusiasm, and be far better equipped to deal with the 'obstacle course' that everyone will be subjected to. On the other hand, you may soon realize that the task ahead would be too risky. The book thus serves as a practical aid to decision-making, planning, modifying, and sometimes ultimately rejecting, your idea.

All businesses and professions are founded on the principle of trade. Therefore, before we set up in any business, we must identify with whom we are likely to trade. The inventor must adopt the same principle and identify a market for his invention well before he starts spending any time or capital in developing his concept.

It is not always the invention that will make you successful, but how you deal with others, and how well you sum up their motives. This book looks extensively at the many human aspects of business that will play an integral part in your success or failure – know them well, and you will be alert as to how best to deal with them.

About the Author

Harry Cole MBIM is a Business and Property Consultant, specializing in Commercial acquisitions and giving 'start up' advice to any budding inventor, who requires business assistance.

Returning from North Africa, where he spent two years in the British Armed Forces, Harry joined a firm of Chartered Surveyors, but after a few years of study and carrying his principal's tape-measure around all day, he yearned for more action!

At the age of 27 he had risen to a position of Senior Estates Manager for a publicly quoted building corporation in the south of England, thus acquiring managerial and business skills, leading to other executive positions in a crossed section of Industry.

Harry is not an Inventor, nor does he claim to be a Designer, but being blessed with an active mind, he feels that he fits better into a lower grade of being an IDEASMAN!

In the early 80's he started to design new board games and other gadgets, obtaining several Design Registrations. His greater interest in this specific subject came about when he endeavoured to exploit his inventive talents, both in the UK and his dealings in New York (USA), Harry quickly realised, that the 'novice' and indeed, many seasoned innovators, often left themselves 'wide-open' to being 'ripped-off', because many, (including himself at that time) simply don't have a clue as to 'where to get help' or worse, 'how to protect those ideas'.

Oddly enough, says Harry, the whole PLANET appears to be full of 'latent' or potential innovators, yet there are few practical books on this subject. The books that are available, are usually written by well qualified Patent or Trademark Agents, but, because of their professional training, many strongly emphasise the patent procedures and laws, without going into any depth on just where the innovator can get help!

After all, says Harry, it seems a pointless exercise to obtain a patent on your great idea, if you haven't a clue on 'Business Awareness' or not know how to, commercially exploit your invention to your advantage!

Typical of his nature, Harry resolved to do something about it. He researched the patent system and combined his wide business experience and wrote this book.

This well researched, easy to follow and authoritative book has taken nearly 'three' years to compile, and specially written to suit all EUROPEAN INVENTORS or DESIGNERS as well as those in the United Kingdom.

Harry now 53, lives with his wife Patricia in Jersey, where he attended one of the local colleges. He is a long time member of the British Institute of Management and available for private (or group) consultations or seminars (within Europe).

'It may be easier for a one-legged
tap-dancer to perform on the stages of
Broadway than for you to find a buyer,
willing to give you everything you think
your idea may be worth.'

HC

'Discourage litigation. Persuade your neighbours to compromise whenever you can. Point out to them how the nominal winner is often a real loser – in fees, expenses, and waste of time.
As a peace-maker, the lawyer has a superior opportunity of being a good man.
There will be business enough.'

ABRAHAM LINCOLN

CHAPTER 1

The origin of inventors

The whole world is full of 'innovators' that have existed since time immemorial. As each century passes by we witness innovators' creative ability which seems to have no limitations. In our modern times the greatest achievement must surely be the successful space mission when, on the 21 July 1969, the Apollo space craft landed men on the moon. The whole world marvelled at the technological advancements America had made when United States astronauts, Neil Armstrong and Edwin (Buzz) Aldrin, landed and walked on the moon, being the first ever humans to touch the moon dust. The other equally important achievement was their successful return to Mother Earth.

Since that achievement, perhaps the excitement is less intense when we hear that similar missions are underway to land on Mars. And maybe technology has developed so fast during this last century that we have grown accustomed to accepting technology as though it simply happened, without ever giving any thought to those who are still making it happen, 'the inventors of our generation'. They are the ones who should receive all the credit but I would guess that they took second place to the accolades that were quite rightly bestowed upon the moon astronauts. But, who provided the technology in the first place, that enabled the astronauts to become famous?

Technologists, or 'Technocrats' as they are often described, are innovative in the area in which they specialize. However, although they are innovators in the true meaning of the word, and thereby closely related to inventors, they are not regarded in the same category as inventors as we know them.

Inventors are not all blessed with having university degrees, and fortunately anyone with an active brain can become an inventor. Obviously, an inventor with an engineering or mechanical background may spend more time designing something of a mechanical nature. But anyone with imagination and knowledge of their particular field can become an inventor. It is highly possible that, say, a farm employee, with very limited academic attainment or engineering skills, could conceive of an idea that may revolutionize machinery in the farming industry, thereby earning 'royalties' on his idea, which will make him wealthy beyond his wildest dreams!

People inventing for the first time, or without prior knowledge of the practical steps which need to be taken, especially those who may consider self-manufacturing, are truly blessed with an innocent naivety. Many will simply forge ahead, totally unprepared to deal with the complexities that await them, and sadly will get lost in the 'ocean of self-destruction'. While many will make it, most will not. So, just what are the chances of success? The truthful answer may never be known, simply because failures are not in the habit of courting publicity!

However, even if we assume that 95% of inventions fail to succeed, that in itself should be no sufficient reason why you should not proceed with your own. After all, you could be in that 5% which *does* succeed and, providing you exercise extreme caution, and follow the basic guidelines, using your own better judgement on occasions, then you may well have a chance of becoming a millionaire!

'If you don't have a destination . . . you'll never get there.'

HC

CHAPTER 2

The Ideasman

Our modern world has produced a special breed of 'innovators' of both sexes that we can aptly call the 'Ideasman'. I prefer to use this title rather than 'Ideasperson' simply because the latter sounds so non-descript.

The Ideasmen are those we meet almost daily; the ones who are forever thinking up wonderful ideas – not always inventive of course, but nevertheless, demonstrating their constant creative ability. The Ideasman would usually be of above average intelligence, seldom with distinctive qualifications, and usually with no capital resources. However, he may be blessed with an over-active brain, that ticks away day and night, in search of an idea that will make him rich! How often have we encountered this type . . . and wonder if they ever get any sleep at night? Yes, they often bear a strange resemblance to us, perhaps to the point of being clones of ourselves.

The aspirations of Ideasmen will vary according to their diverse backgrounds. In the main, however, wealth is what they are after, especially when they hear of someone who has made millions from what appears to be such a *simple* idea. Yet it is afterwards (yes, always afterwards) that they mutter, *I* could have thought of something like that. But, of course, they never did, did they?

The mind of an Ideasman is forever buzzing with ideas. But it is also prone to forgetfulness. Therefore, when you come up with a good idea, grab a pencil and make a note of it even if it's four o'clock in the morning. If you don't, you may lose it forever.

The most disappointing aspect of being an Ideasman or first-time inventor is the indifference, and almost disbelief, others will show regarding your ability to conceive of a potentially saleable product. After all, all you are to them is another nutcase, full of ideas, with no proven track record, so why should they be impressed? Not many will take you seriously until the day you make it – then it will be a whole new ball game!

Initially, you may be very disheartened to learn that the whole world seems full of 'sceptics'. Even more so when you have the temerity to seek assistance. The motto of the Special Air Service (SAS) would seem to apply also to the intrepid inventor: 'Who Dares Wins'.

There may be times when you might have this inner sense that your new idea could be a winner. How often have we all felt this? But do nothing for at least a week and refrain from telling the world. Exercise some self-discipline, which will not be easy, and, if after a week you still feel ecstatic, and before you speak to any-one, make detailed notes of your idea. Take a copy, date it, and send it to yourself by recorded delivery. This will establish that the work existed at this time and is your first cautionary measure to protect your idea. When it arrives, keep the letter unopened in a safe place, either with your solicitor or bank.

After you have gone through that exercise then, if you feel that you have a chance of obtaining a patent, consult first with a patent agent – I will outline the procedures to adopt in later chapters – or take steps to file your own patent application. A great many may not wish to get involved with a patent agent, and will openly discuss their ideas with anyone willing to listen. However, once your idea becomes public knowledge, you could very well lose all rights to protection under the existing patent or copyright laws. So be warned. Before you tell the world of your great invention, tell your patent agent!

Inventors and Ideasmen are universal. All will walk that same lonely path, and many will deal with such varied species of the human race that may drive them to despair.

Good friends, and even close family, could question your wisdom. Most will assume that you are going through some form of 'menopausal syndrome', while others, with a degree of kindness, will simply ignore you! If you are able to overcome those obstacles and many more, you will then be in with a chance. From then on you will be travelling on a 'lonely ocean of unchartered waters', frequently battling against tidal waves, making headway to a destiny unknown!

It would be reasonable to surmise that, as none of us are actually born inventors, becoming one must either be a quirk of nature, or indeed, a 'happening' that could occur to any one of us, at any stage of our lives.

Many people evolve into innovators during their late thirties or early forties – perhaps this is the period when most of us are somewhat disillusioned with our lives and our career prospects are non-existent. Maybe we simply seek an escape from a boring life and convince ourselves that becoming an inventor will bring us wealth that hitherto had been denied us. Whatever the case, once you are 'hooked' on this inventive business, you'll never be able to shake it off – your mind will be on constant alert. Once you dream up your great idea that you alone believe will make your fortune, your body and soul are wholly taken over by an immutable force that will be impossible to resist.

Many people will assume that you have either lost your 'marbles' or they may even regard you as being some crazy 'kooky' living in cloud cuckoo-land! You'll never convince them that you are perfectly sane . . . so don't even try!

What kind of world would we now be living in – if the world had not developed any technology over the centuries?

The next time you use your labour saving kitchen gadget, or purchase a technologically improved 'hi-fi' stereo system, or perhaps you are receiving laser treatment to remove a cancerous growth from your body, spare a kind thought to the innovators of this world – have they not contributed towards the quality of your life?

'Believe in yourself . . . even when no one
else does.'

HC

CHAPTER 3

Basic criteria all should follow

All inventors, especially those inventing for the first time, should follow some **basic criteria** or ground rules. After all, it would be a very unwise person who would play 'roulette' for high stakes without being aware of the rules of the game. It is essential that inventors learn the fundamental principles well before spending one penny on their project. But equally important, they must observe and adhere to those principles throughout their endeavours.

Ideally, you should regard *everything* you do as being important. The moment you start getting slack or perhaps over-confident, others will step in and devour you! For many, that last statement could appear to have no significance, and you might say, 'I'm only trying to exploit my invention . . . not build a nuclear reactor!' And of course, you would be absolutely correct. You *are* only trying to exploit your invention. But, after you have digested the contents of this book, you may find it easier to build that nuclear reactor!

Before you even think of spending any money or time, or indeed exposing your concept to the world, it is important, and I repeat again IMPORTANT that you observe these generally accepted, basic criteria:

(1)   CHECK FOR 'ORIGINALITY'.
(2)   IDENTIFY A NEED.
(3)   LEARN THE PATENT SYSTEM.
(4)   DON'T OVER-DEVELOP AN EXISTING PRODUCT.
(5)   BUILD YOURSELF A 'WORKING MODEL'.
(6)   BE REALISTIC ABOUT PRODUCT DEMAND.

I will devote chapters to each subject, if only to impress upon you their importance. However, having singled out these points, I must nevertheless stress that there are many other important criteria which should not be disregarded. In fact, as you get into the swing of things, you will find that most facets of your development are inter-linked with the above list. Therefore, treat every part of your development as being important; even down to keeping a record of telephone conversations you may have with interested parties.

Although you will have a much better chance by following these guidelines, success will, of course, depend upon the **invention**, or the **product**, you have invented. Lady Luck will play the leading role in your theatre! Therefore, learn your lines well before giving your 'command performance'.

Fortunes are made out of dreams. Equally, dreams are the stimulus of our objectives. Before you embark on your journey, make quite sure of the direction in which you are heading. If you are not sure of your way, or you get lost, don't be too proud to ask for guidance.

At some stage of your journey you may be fortunate enough to encounter a company willing to take your concept on board. Should you be so lucky, do not create unnecessary obstacles when negotiating your deal. Do not be foolish enough to assume that, because others are showing a keen interest, or even wanting to conclude deals, that you have to 'screw them into the ground' and command unreasonable terms. Retain your senses and, although you are bound to have sleepless nights agonizing over what to do, keep a level head and, providing you have protected your rights, enter into the field of negotiation with confidence. After all, if you do part with your concept, for whatever price or reason, and provided you have secured a reasonable deal for yourself, do not feel dejected or let this deflate your ego. Be grateful that others have recognized your inventive talents.

It may be worth reminding yourself that, apart from relieving you of the countless risks, they are putting their capital, their time, their reputation and resources on the line. So what greater compliment could they give you! If in any doubt, think very seriously of the consequences of keeping it all to yourself, with all the problems and hassles that go with it.

Treat this book as a supportive guide only. Do not regard it as a secret formula to success. Unfortunately, I am both unwilling and unable to suggest any short-cuts to success . . . there are none! If you eventually become successful after reading this book, I will claim no credit; you will have done it all by yourself with the vital support of having invented a marketable product that the world is eager to buy!

It is often said that an inventor's greatest asset is his ability to be free of conventional wisdom. No doubt that is the case, but my interpretation would be that it is due to his undaunting capacity to hang in there, despite the odds often being stacked against him.

Despite these odds, many can still make fortunes from their inventive talents, to which the brilliant inventor, Mr Ron Hickman, would doubtless testify when he collected payment of several million from Black & Decker for the rights to his wonderful, yet simple, invention called the '**WORKMATE**'.

'Despite being able to identify a need, just how long will that need be needed by the needy?'

HC

CHAPTER 4

Identify a need

There would seem to be no purpose whatsoever in going through the usual traumas of inventing or manufacturing a product if, at the end of the day, nobody wants to buy it!

Any person with only a skin for a brain, would rightly ask just what kind of fool would go to so much trouble. You may be surprised to learn that it happens quite often, when products are made that seem to have no market potential. You are bound to ask, 'Well surely, if that is the case, the manufacturer must have had some good reason to produce his product in the first place?' Excellent question, I have no answer that may satisfy your inquisitive mind. It is possible, of course, that whoever is responsible for producing products that have no use, may have been misled or even fooled themselves into believing that the whole world would be begging for their creative idea. Who really knows? And how many care? The main point of issue here suggests a total lack of **market research**.

Market researchers, one has to admit, do play an exceedingly active role in the infrastructure of general marketing. However, to my weary mind, which is always on standby to be corrected, I have formed the impression that market research can also be a form of self-deluding, promotional fantasy. Probably originally thought up by clones and inflicted by clones upon clones; I trust this bold statement, which is only my personal opinion, will not bring forth a truck load of writs to my lawyer by disgruntled market researchers who fear their cover may yet be blown!

It can be somewhat tiresome when you are stopped in the street, always when you seem to be in a damn rush, by a market researcher who thrusts a product upon your person and announces: 'I'm a market researcher . . . have you a moment?' You almost feel like replying: 'so what . . . I've got my own problems, mate!' But of course we are rarely that unkind and invariably we try and act in a somewhat dignified manner, kidding ourselves that we must be someone special, to be singled out from the thousands of people around us. Do you ever ask yourself why they honed in on you like some demented scud-missile? Could it possibly be that when they see you purposely trying to avoid eye-contact, they say to themselves, Now there's a likely sucker!

I have no wish to give readers the impression that market research has little value, or to imply that the many market research surveys that are carried out daily are done simply to keep a group of people in employment.

The point I wish to put across is, although we may be aware that market research is carried out for specific or varied objectives, the intrepid inventor should be aware also that a successful marketing research campaign is no real guarantee that products will be sold in vast quantities or indeed, have a long shelf-life. And therefore, one should not totally rely upon the theory of market research.

Naturally, there must be thousands of times when a product will be successfully launched, after carrying out an extensive programme of market research. Equally, there may be as many product failures, even after such a campaign. It is, after all, only a method of gauging public reaction to an existing or proposed product, and sometimes what we sample in the street is not always what we purchase. It will be the **consumer** that will dictate **market forces** and the principles of market research will never change that!

It must never escape the mind of an inventor that, even if their own market research proves extremely encouraging, the next stage of the game, after production, will be **marketing and promotion**. But unfortunately, should you reach this stage without having the 'financial clout', all your successful research will amount to nothing!

We are told by experts that before we get too involved in inventing or designing, we should **identify a need**. Although this is basically sound and logical advice, there is, nevertheless, a slight flaw which the intrepid inventor should be aware of. Indeed, if it was as simple as being able just to identify a need, many inventors would become millionaires over night. The problem relates to the 'human element' that overrides the law of **supply and demand** or may be this should read '**supply by demand**'.

Let the following illustration stir in your mind, whenever you steam ahead, without due regard to the 'human element' or fickleness of the general public, in the mistaken belief that, because you have identified a need and can respond to those needs, success is bound to follow.

During the early seventies, when the video recorder invaded our homes, and Chinese take-aways were multiplying like rabbits, many of the small-town cinemas were closing down and being turned into bingo-halls or discotheques, because market trends changed. Who wants to venture out into the cold night to watch a film in a cinema, when it can be seen in the comfort of your own home while tucking into your Chinese 'sweet and sour pork balls'? Who indeed! Somewhere down in the West Country of England, a town witnessed the closure of its own cinema. Months later, the natives got restless and mounted a strong campaign to their town hall officials to provide the town with a new cinema. Their sincere action touched the heart, and no doubt wallet, of a local business entrepreneur who probably lost a lot of sleep, working out just how rich he would become if he built them a cinema. After all, he had identified a need and was prepared to meet that need. Time went by and hey presto a new Cinema appeared, much to the delight of all the locals and official dignitaries.

Guess what! The very cinema that they had fought tooth and nail for closed down some six months after opening, because hardly any of the locals bothered to go there. When asked why, the general comments were: 'We knew it was there, but it doesn't mean to say that we had to go there . . . does it!'

I will leave you to figure out the significance of that story in relation to this particular chapter in the trust that you will be more aware of human fickleness! Obviously the significance of being able to identify a need, well before you start spending any time or money, is far too important for me to be flippant about, and this chapter must only be regarded as 'scratching the surface'. If, therefore, you have a potentially new product on your drawing board use your own common sense. After all, it is *your* invention. Ask yourself why you bothered to invent it in the first place. You will surely have had a good reason for doing so and, if that is the case, you will be half-way to achieving your goals. The rest will be sheer perseverance on your part.

'Never waste time in trying to re-invent the wheel . . . unless you want to keep going round in circles!'

HC

CHAPTER 5

Check for originality

Regardless of what idea you have conceived, if you are proposing to spend any time or money, **check first for originality**!

It is surprising the number of inventors who believe they have a brilliant idea, which would earn them fame or fortune, only to find later on that their 'brilliant idea' already exists. How sad, and very frustrating, for them! It must be said that, any person who forges ahead without first checking for originality can only be a victim of their own foolishness. *Question*: 'So what's the big deal about checking for originality?' *Answer*: 'Everything.' If it has been thought of before, or if a product exists, then simply in the eyes of the law, it is not original. Therefore, regardless of how clever you have been in conceiving someone else's 'brilliant idea' your efforts will be rendered less than worthless if others have already beaten you to it. Your only saving grace in this respect could be that you may have learned your lesson the hard way, and will be more aware the next time you have another display of brilliance.

Can you imagine the disappointment when we find out that our idea is not original? Apart from our own ego being deflated, it could cause other complications. For example, some years ago I was having a rare, intellectual discussion with my brother, Richard. At times he can be very inspiring and has been known to come up with some great ideas. But sadly the world will have to continue to wait until he is ready to grant us the favour of his wisdom.

Our discussion took place well before I became aware that one should never divulge ideas to anyone, save for one's patent agent or lawyer. To be honest, I thought the idea I was discussing was just great. At the time I had these grandiose visions of owning yachts and villas throughout the Continent. It just goes to show how our own mind can play cruel tricks on us. Perhaps when we surpass the barrier of reality, it also acts as a stabilizing factor to bring us back down to earth! However, this particular idea centred around a pocket-sized object, similar in shape to a standard calculator. Instead of dealing with numbers or fractions, it would contain letters of the alphabet and, when pressed, each sentence would be translated into a foreign language. Of course, I had absolutely no idea what was to follow. It was a lesson in checking for originality I shall never forget.

I recall going into every little detail, even to the point of mentioning that it could be developed by microchip – a subject I know nothing about – and, by the expression on my brother's face, I felt sure he was convinced that I was some kind of genius. Richard listened intently to my every word. Not seeking to interrupt me, he permitted me to continue until I was forced to pause for breath. By this time, his facial expression had changed to one of disbelief. He also positioned himself like a fox, ready to spring upon a defenceless prey. I had obviously misjudged his initial facial expression, as I was immediately subjected to a barrage of Anglo-Saxon abuse. It transpired that, what I had diligently described with great pride was, in fact, my brother's own idea which he had told me about some three months earlier. Both our feathers were displayed, and we were ready to commence immediate verbal attack against one another.

Neither of us would accept that the idea was conceived by anyone other than ourselves. Anyone witnessing our uncultured display may have assumed that violence could erupt at any moment. Fortunately, we both cooled down and laughed our heads off at the way we could have easily started World War Three – perhaps a better remedy than knocking each other's heads off.

It may amuse you to learn that neither my brother nor myself could have claimed any right to that particular idea. A short time later, we realised that our so-called 'brilliant idea', was the concept of others and, indeed, had already been manufactured. I can only assume that, either my brother read an article about it and told me, or I did likewise. It is now history. The important point is that neither of us bothered to **check for originality**. Had we done so, we may have been spared the indignity of making utter fools of ourselves.

Therefore, before you start getting ambitious, or indeed discussing your inventive ideas with your family, make quite certain that you have checked for originality. Perhaps the best, and only, way of obtaining details on this subject would be to carry out a 'search' with the official Patent Office, or indeed, employ the services of a patent agent.

'Possessing great knowledge is no substitute
for being outwitted.'

HC

CHAPTER 6

Learn the patent system

We often hear the words **PATENTS, REGISTERED DESIGNS, REGISTERED TRADE AND SERVICE MARKS**, and **COPYRIGHTS.** But what do we know about them or, indeed, what are their benefits? They all come under the same banner, more often known as **Intellectual Property Rights**.

How to protect your Intellectual Property Rights

I would recommend that any reader who wishes to proceed beyond the information that is given in this chapter, or indeed anyone who needs to have a greater in-depth knowledge of any related specific laws, would be well advised to see their lawyer or indeed, contact a chartered patent agent, or similar bodies who are the specialists on this subject.

I propose therefore, simply to outline the basic principles that should be adopted, whenever you seek to protect your Intellectual Property Rights.

Since researching this particular subject, I have discovered that there are many would-be inventors who are not fully aware of the various services provided by the **Patent Office.** I will endeavour to outline most of the services they offer and would suggest that any reader wishing to know more on this subject should contact the Marketing and Information Services of the Patent Office (see Appendix for full address). From my own experience of dealing with this department, I have formed the opinion that, if all other governmental departments were to be as efficient and helpful, many of us could get things done faster, and not get so frustrated! The intrepid inventor will not have too much difficulty whenever he seeks their advice or guidance.

This is, perhaps, the right moment for me to acknowledge my grateful thanks to the Patent Office, whose approval I sought, enabling me to use extracts from their own publications. I have, therefore, taken full advantage of their generosity in order to pass on this information to my readers, so that they can also share in the benefits and knowledge that I, personally, have gained after reading their well-prepared, easy to comprehend, and highly informative literature which is available to any person wishing to broaden their knowledge on these subjects.

The creation and development of new technologies and industries, and the encouragement of growth of commerce, is essential to the well-being of any country. To achieve advances in these areas depends, not only on the **ingenuity** of innovators, but also on having the **capital** to develop such new ideas. Equally important, those with the enterprise to develop their ideas must have their rights protected.

Let us now examine the various methods of obtaining protections which would cover your Intellectual Property Rights, dealing with each subject on an individual basis.

Patenting your idea under Patents Act 1977

What is a patent?

It is a document issued by the Patent Office granting the proprietor monopoly rights to the exclusive use of an invention. Those rights would last for a period of twenty years. A patent is a property, therefore it may be bought, sold, hired or licensed.

Are all inventions patentable?

No, they are not! To be patentable, an invention must be concerned with the composition, construction or manufacture of a substance, article or apparatus, as distinct from artistic creations, mathematical methods, business schemes or purely mental acts.

The basic criteria for obtaining a patent are

- Your invention must be **new**. (Therefore, check first for originality.)
- Your invention must be **inventive**. (Therefore, no new wheels, please!)
- It must be capable of **industrial application** (i.e. in the form of a machine, a process or product, although ruling out devices that allege to operate against the laws of physics, such as perpetual motion machines).
- Patents **cannot** be obtained on a discovery, on a theory, on an artistic creation, on medical treatments or, indeed, on computer programs.

How do I apply for a patent?

First you have to get a form 1/77 from the Patent Office and complete and submit this form to them. On submitting your application, you will have to pay a fee of £15.

- Note: I would recommend that any person who isn't familiar with documentation, or is unsure of the procedure, either obtain information from the Patent Office, or perhaps you may find it prudent to consult a patent agent who will guide you throughout, and treat your application in strictest confidence. Naturally, you will have to pay for their services but, quite often, they are well worth paying for, if indeed you achieve peace of mind, knowing that your application will be dealt with by professionals.

Could my application be refused?

Of course, your submitted application is no guarantee that your invention will be granted a patent. The main reason for refusal would normally be because your invention is not new, and this will be determined whenever the Patent Office carries out a **search** which you will have to pay for. There are several other reasons, such as failure to pay their fees or to comply with certain rules, which the Patent Office would inform you about. Some of those rules will be mentioned in this chapter. Obviously, you have to consider that some applications they receive are simply not patentable.

Can I tell anyone about my invention? Important warning!

The short answer is **NO!** Apart from your lawyer or patent agent, or any other person who may be advising you under the code of confidentiality, you must not publicly disclose your invention, before you have filed your application. However, even when you have filed your application and received a **priority date** (although this protects you to a certain extent) it would be wise not to discuss the finer details of your invention, as you can never be sure of the outcome of your particular application, and it is quite possible that someone else with the same invention, but a later priority date than your own may capitalize on any information that you impart which could be beneficial to them in the event of your application failing for any reason.

Assuming I get a patent, how long will it last for?

Patents last for **twenty years** from the filing date, or the priority date. During this period you will have to pay **renewal fees**, which we will look at later on in this chapter. Patent grants can be revoked by the Patent Office should you, at any time, fail to pay any of the renewal fees. It would be recommended that if you obtain a patent and you are the kind of person to change addresses frequently, or indeed leave the country, always to notify the Patent Office of your proposed forwarding address. The Patent Office is not in business to track you down. Therefore, if they send you out a reminder for renewal fees, and if that reminder is not acknowledged due to your having left your address, then the Patent Office would be justified in revoking your patent. So, if you are planning a change of address, and assuming you have not assigned your patent over to another, then notify the Patent Office.

- Note: Ignorance of the Patent Office's rules or regulations would be no defence in law!

What are the benefits of obtaining a patent?

The obvious benefit must surely be your twenty-year right to produce or exploit your invention without someone else cutting-in on your action. However, others may still cut-in on your action if, for instance, your patent grants you protection only in the country in which it was obtained.

Remember that, although the Patent Office grants you this monopoly for twenty years, it is entirely up to you to safeguard your rights from being infringed. In other words, the Patent Office will not become party to any litigation you may become involved with, nor will the Patent Office seek to protect your interest or become a party to your dispute.

Nevertheless, a patent *does* give you the right to take legal action against anyone infringing your inventive rights, and to claim damages through the courts, whereas these rights are not available to any person without a patent. Also, the mere existence of a patent is often a deterrent against potential infringers.

The other obvious benefit would be the commercial aspects. Should you have invented, for example, a kitchen gadget that would require substantial development capital, not many industrialists, manufacturers or, indeed, venture capitalists would become enthusiastic if you did not have a patent, or a patent pending.

Let us assume also that you have this great invention and sufficient capital to get it into production, but you don't have the time to bother with all this patent business. As far as you are aware, nothing exists on the market – you know this because you have carried out extensive searches. So your plan is to get started right away . . . And apply for your patent later. Do so and you would be entering into danger zones. Firstly you would never be able to obtain a patent on your product once you have started manufacture. Secondly without a patent grant, you limit your protection rights, and others may try to copy your product, with impunity, save for perhaps, breaches of your copyrights.

Furthermore, your product may have international marketing potential and therefore, why take the risk!

Is the timing of an application important?

YES! the earlier you file for your patent grant, the sooner you can establish your priority rights over anyone else who may subsequently file an application for the same invention (which frequently happens).

However, before you actually submit your application form 1/77, make quite sure that you have 'double-checked' to see whether the information that you give fully complies with the application form. And don't forget to send the fee of £15 at the same time!

Although in many cases it is advisable to forward an early application, this procedure may be more applicable to the 'individual' inventor. But if you were in the field of 'high' technology or research, you may wish to delay your application, for purely commercial reasons, especially if your research and development is likely to take longer than the period it takes for the Patent Office to go public.

Does a patent give me protection abroad?

NO! If you have obtained a patent only in the UK then you are only protected in the UK. However, most countries also have their own patent systems; therefore, if you need protection in other countries, you will need to file further applications to each country in which you seek protection. Your priority date obtained in the UK can usually be effective in other countries subject to your application(s) being filed within a year of your first application (see Chapter 7).

Can I exploit my invention before I receive a patent grant?

<u>Yes</u>, you can! Let us assume that you are quite satisfied that you have filed an acceptable application, and have received back from the Patent Office a priority date.

Once you are in receipt of your priority date, you can feel free to discuss the prospects of marketing your invention, or discussing its further development. Exercise caution, though, in revealing too much information. Remember that unscrupulous persons, or companies, could use such information for their own benefit. In other words, they could still rip you off. But, should this happen, you will, at least, have established the fact that those who ripped you off did so after you had filed your patent application. This would increase your chances of obtaining legal redress should your rights be infringed.

Therefore, although you may well have established a priority date, this does not mean that you can 'drop your guard'. You will naturally want to approach companies, or individuals, regarding the exploitation of your invention; but do so with extreme caution. For example, don't invite future problems whenever you correspond with anyone. Still make mention in your letter that you are doing so under the code of **Non-Disclosure of Confidential Infor-mation**. (I shall be dealing with this issue later on in Chapter 16.)

Meanwhile, post all letters by recorded delivery and keep a record of all telephone conversations that are connected with your invention. Open up a **file** with those you deal with. After business meetings, even if they come to nothing, write a thank you letter, keeping all copies. All this documentation may, one day, come in useful, especially if you may have to engage in litigation.

Whenever you approach companies, make it known from the beginning that you have filed your application for a patent grant. This may reduce any evil thoughts they may have harboured on taking you to the cleaners. You will find, however, that most of the established companies that you deal with will play fair but, none the less, do not give them any opportunity to change the rules to suit their game!

How real are the advantages of obtaining a patent?

I should emphasize that you are under no legal obligation to file an application for your invention. If you have an invention, there is nothing to prevent you from manufacturing your concept at any time you wish to do so. However, before you go this far, make quite certain that you will not be in breach of copyright.

There are, however, many commercial benefits when getting a patent grant.

- Firstly, a patent would give you a **monopoly** to produce your goods which would last for a period of twenty years. That alone would give you a **trading advantage** over your competitors.

- Secondly, the possession of a patent is sufficient a deterrent to ward off predators from infringing your Intellectual Property Rights. They may still try, however, but a patent would hold you in good stead in a court of law (unless your patent is successfully challenged).

- Thirdly, a patent is a tradable asset, not only beneficial to the acquiring manufacturer, but it would increase the value of your concept whenever it is sold on, or licensed out.

- Fourthly, if you do not have a patent, the chances are that the field would be wide open for any other manufacturer to produce the same goods or, in fact, modify your concept with legal impunity, whereas a patent would give you protection against such infringements (but you may still have to defend your rights in a court of law).

It's worth stressing that, in normal circumstances, being granted a patent on your invention will greatly enhance your chances of obtaining more benefits, both in the **value** of your invention and the **protection** of your invention. However, the mere fact that you have received a patent on your invention, does not imply that your invention would necessarily have any commercial benefits. Indeed, you may have invented something that simply has no commercial aspects whatsoever. Or your invention may be far too expensive to manufacture on a volume basis, therefore being of no interest to a manufacturer. However, there may still be a market in the cottage industry, but make sure you have weighed up the actual cost of obtaining a patent against the risks of not being able to exploit your invention commercially.

The Patent Office is not interested in the 'commercialization' of your invention, and will only take into account the basic criteria, as outlined. Therefore, before you put money into the patent system, or keep patent agents in luxury lifestyles, check all your facts first!

How to file a UK patent application (under Patents Act 1977)

United Kingdom patents

There are three main stages involved in filing and obtaining a UK patent.

Stage one

The Patents Act requires an application to be made in a particular way, using the official form 1/77. Patent Office will, on request, send you the necessary forms. Your application must contain at least four main points:

(1)   A request for a patent;

(2)   Identification of the applicant (i.e. your full name and address);

(3)   A description of the invention;

(4)   The filing fee (£15).

Your *application* cannot be given a filing date until **all four** of the items have been received by the Patent Office. If you are proposing to send your application by post you would be well advised to send this documentation by recorded delivery and remember to keep your receipt.

Once your application has been correctly filed, you will have **twelve months** in which to decide what to do next. During this period, you can, for example, explore the commercial value of your invention or seek finance for eventual development or develop it further without the fear of losing your priority right. If by the end of this twelve-month period, you have not taken further steps towards obtaining a patent, your application lapses and you cannot revive it, but would have to start afresh. Should this apply to you, you would no longer have a priority right and, therefore, any person who may have applied for a patent, on the same invention, but just after your application, may now be entitled to the priority right.

What is a 'priority right'?

Once you have completed your form 1/77 and posted it off with your fee of £15 you will receive a receipt issued by the Patent Office indicating the date upon which you filed your application, which further means that you have established your right to that invention as of that date. However, the mere fact that you have received a priority date back from the Patent Office does not indicate or even suggest, that you will be granted a patent. It establishes the fact that you filed an application on a particular date, which may be useful in later dealings. Any disclosure of such (before applying for your application) whether, for example, by word of mouth, demonstration of a model, an article in a journal, or an advertisement of any kind, could prevent you from getting a patent, or indeed, would be a sufficient reason for having your patent revoked, if you did get one.

Incidentally, just because you have received a priority date back from the Patent Office, this does not imply that others have not already submitted an application for the same invention. Should that be the case, then, the person with the date earlier than your own will simply have the priority date over your own.

My application is in: how long before I get my patent?

Assuming you will be granted a patent, the whole process will usually take **four years**, providing there are no official objections: I repeat, **FOUR YEARS**! The search report will take about three months; publication a further eighteen months after filing; and First Examination approximately eighteen months after publication.

If, however, you have developed your invention further, and wish to continue with your application, you are not allowed to add any of this extra matter to your original application but, instead, you would have to file a fresh application. Provided you do this *before* the end of the twelve-month period, you can claim priority from your first application.

Therefore, the filing date for your **first** application will become the priority date of the **new** application. However you should note that this priority only applies to the matter in your new application, which was also contained in the old. The old application can afterwards be allowed to lapse. If you have already paid a fee for further processing, you can **withdraw** the old application and request a **refund** of any fee for work which has not been carried out on the old application.

Stage two: Search and early publication

Before the application can proceed to this next stage, one or more claims and an abstract of the invention must be filed, as must the form requesting a search accompanied by the search fee. These must all be filed within the prescribed period (usually twelve months) from the priority date. However, all these applications can be filed when you file your first application.

The purpose of a claim is to define, in words, the invention which the patent, if granted, will protect. This determines the extent of the monopoly that you will be able to enforce. Therefore, it is of the utmost importance that you describe your claim in **full detail**, and with clarity. (See Chapter 8 before you attempt to draft your own specification).

The search is made by a Patent Office examiner, through previously published documents, mainly patent specifications, in order to find any which appear to show that the invention claimed in your patent specification is, either not new, or is obvious. A **search report** is issued containing a list of relevant documents that have been found, so that you can compare these with your invention and therefore are better equipped to assess your chances of successfully pursuing your application further. Obviously, should that search reveal that a very similar invention exists, or is being filed, then you may have to consider the possibility of abandoning your application forthwith.

However, after receiving the search report, you can file **amendments** to your description or claims, if you so wish. These will not be considered until the next stage of processing, or the **substantive examination** takes place. But, any amended claims will be published, along with the original claims, if they are received by the Patent Office before the preparations for publishing your application are completed.

After the search report has been issued and, provided you do not withdraw your application before the Patent Office is ready to publish, **it will be published exactly as you have written it**, together with the search report, and before any further examination takes place. Copies of the published patent specification will be made available to anyone who cares to purchase them, as well as being sent to certain libraries. The specification consists of the description and claims (that you have drafted and made), together with any drawings, and is accompanied by the abstract.

This early publication is an important landmark in the procedure for two reasons. Firstly, the contents of the patent specification are no longer **confidential**, therefore anyone can read them and find out about your invention. So the published patent specification may now be used to show that the invention claimed in a later application (whether filed by yourself or someone else) is either not new or is obvious. One consequence of this stage is that, if your application were to be refused at the examination stage (perhaps because of a serious defect when you drafted it), you will not be able merely to abandon it and get a patent by subsequently filing another fresh application for exactly the same invention as was described in your earlier published one, because the invention detailed in your new application will then not be new!

The second important factor is that, provided a patent is eventually granted, any claim in the specification of the granted patent carries its own protection against an **infringer** back to the date of early publication. Although you cannot take advantage of this until *after* the patent is granted, it can be important in deterring anyone from copying your invention, and in determining the amount of damages to be obtained from a successful infringement action.

- Note: The mere fact that an application reaches early publication, does *not* necessarily mean that a patent will be granted on it. Nor does it give the applicant any rights which are enforceable at this stage.

Stage three (final stage): Substantive examination

This is the final stage before grant. For this you will have to file another form and pay the examination fee within **six months** of early publication. If this is *not* done, the application will lapse.

The patent specification is now examined to see that it meets all relevant requirements of the Patents Act. These requirements include, that the description must be sufficiently clear and complete, and that the invention claimed must be a patentable invention as previously explained. The claims must also be supported by the description, and they must not cover more than **one** invention or inventive idea. The search previously done is updated by the examiner and, in the light of all search results, he will determine whether the invention is new, and also not obvious. Usually the patent specification will require amendment at this stage to avoid objections raised by the examiner.

It will often be necessary to restrict the scope of the claims so that they no longer include what is already known. It may take more than one attempt at amendment before all requirements are met. Once these have been met, the patent is granted. If the specification is not amended in a satisfactory manner, and within specified time limits, then the application may be refused. If a patent is granted, the monopoly which it gives is defined by the claims in the patent specification in their finally accepted form.

Note!

Validity of a patent

It is not possible to guarantee that a patent, once granted, is valid. Anyone – for example, a defendant in an infringement action – can apply to the court or to the Patent Office for revocation of a patent on certain grounds which are laid down in the Patents Act. The most common ground for such action is either that the invention has been published or documents not found in the Patent Office search such as technical journals or foreign patents have been publicly used, before the priority date of the invention, or that it is obvious as a consequence of the information made available by such previous disclosure.

SO BE WARNED!

I have a patent . . . what next?

There is no legal obligation for you to do anything once you have obtained your patent. However, it would be very unusual to go through the motions and expense, then do nothing! You have the right either to **assign** your monopoly over to anyone willing to negotiate for it, or, alternatively, you could find a company that would be willing to manufacture your invention (product) under **licence** and pay you **royalties**. However, do not assume that, just because you have obtained a patent on whatever you may have invented, this will be your easy way to riches: it is quite possible that what you have invented, despite passing all the prerequisites as laid down by the Patent Office, may have little or no commercial value whatsoever. Perhaps you may have **identified a need** and even **checked for originality**, but during those four years of waiting for your patent the **need** no longer exists!

What can I do if manufacturers are not interested?

Assuming you have no desire to manufacture yourself or, indeed you are unable to raise the necessary capital, then you have several options.

(1) You can sell your patent to anyone who is interested.

(2) You may be able to **exchange** it for whatever it's worth. For example, assume you have a patent on a new kind of tin opener and you are unable to exploit it commercially. Suppose you meet a person who has a classic car, and you agree to take his car in exchange for the rights to your invention. In such cases, you would need to engage the services of a lawyer to draft a short **agreement**, assigning those patent rights over to another. And, you should notify the Patent Office of your transaction.

(3) You can keep paying the fees for a couple more years in the hope that your invention may find a buyer or commercial use; as, indeed, market trends do change rapidly.

(4) After, say, four years, if you have not had any interest at all then you must seriously consider the possibility of surrendering gracefully. Write to the Patent Office stating that you will no longer be continuing your patent registration. Upon receipt of your letter, the Patent Office will **revoke** your patent, and you will be released from making further annual fees. However, only do this when you have exhausted every other possible avenue. **(Never have your registration revoked if you are able to maintain the registration fees. If you can manage to pay the fees, certainly do so, as you never know what may come along next week.)** Yes, I'm also a great optimist!

(5) **LAST ALTERNATIVE:** Before you get too downhearted and do something drastic (like reaching for the cyanide capsules), total up all the costs incurred in obtaining your patent (you will have to exclude your own time). Let us assume you have shelled out £5,000 in fees and incidentals. Why not try to sell off 50% of your inventive rights for, say, £2,500 (or for

whatever you think it is worth). It is highly possible that by placing a small advertisement in one of the nationals, journals or trade magazines, you may get some response. Obviously, they would be buying a 50% stake in your patent rights for, say, £2,500. However, if you have not been able to do anything with your patent beforehand, then half a cake must surely be better than none! Furthermore, your partner (for want of a better expression) would also have to pay half of the annual patent fees.

The real benefit, however, of selling off 50% would mean that someone else would now have a financial interest in your invention; therefore he/she would naturally want to protect their own capital investment, and would inject renewed enthusiasm. They would, most probably, be able to look at your invention in a different light, and would, no doubt, have their own ideas as to how to market, promote or sell it. Therefore, if your luck has run out, do not always blame your invention; there could be a thousand underlying reasons why you have not met with success. Your partner may be more persuasive, or have more business acumen and enthusiasm to attract interested parties. Therefore, never give up once you have obtained your patent! **You have twenty years to convince others why you became an inventor – so, if you can't do that within twenty years, then perhaps you *do* have a problem!**

CAUTION

Although I have mentioned that you do not need to do anything, once you have obtained your patent grant, I must emphasize that your monopoly right must be utilized and must not remain dormant. If, therefore, you elect to do nothing with your grant, the Patent Office can grant a 'compulsory licence' to a 'third' party should one be applied for (you will still be entitled to royalty fees). But if no licences are forthcoming after a period of years, the Patent Office have the authority to 'cancel' your monopoly right.

But before I conclude this particular chapter, there are a few details worthy of mentioning.

People often ask 'Who is the owner of an invention?'

Answer:

As a general rule, the Intellectual Property Rights belong to the person who had 'mentally' conceived the original idea or concept. Therefore, a co-inventor, is not necessarily the co-owner.

Perhaps this can appear to be a little confusing, so I'll dig deeper!

Firstly: assume that you managed to develop your invention, without the assistance of others. You, therefore, claim all ownership rights. But those rights can of course be assigned over to a company for a 'one-off' fee in which case you have no further say in whatever happens to your invention.

Secondly: let us assume that you 'mentally' conceived an invention, but you do not possess the technical ability either to process or develop your 'idea' into a concept (which is often the case) – then you will need to call in a co-inventor, thereby having to share in your Intellectual Property Rights (if they came up with the technical answers to make your 'idea' work) or the very least, you will have to share in any commercial or monetary benefits, received from the exploitation of the invention. The proportion of sharing will depend upon just 'who did what' and it could be say 60–40%. But all parties will have to bear in mind that, until someone has conceived a brilliant idea – 'who has the ability to start offering technical assistance?'

However, for legal reasons, there can only be one owner. Perhaps the best way of determining the proportion of ownership can easily be established by close examination of the 'scope of the claims' that may reveal the real in-put by one co-inventor, over the other. But to save losing face with a co-inventor, or face possible litigation, I would advise that the originator of any idea or invention, should decide just how much he is prepared to share, well before he instructs a co-inventor for assistance. The simplest way is to say 'Look here old buddy! I've got this great idea which I believe will make us both small fortunes – I know you are technically brilliant – what would you say if I offered you 30/40% share in my invention for your assistance in solving all problems necessary to get this invention of mine to work?' If he says 'OK lets give it a whirl' – then go straight to your lawyer and get an agreement drawn up. Obviously the pair of you will have to share in the cost of any development – but if you have been greedy enough to want say 60% of the lion's share, then you will have to fund 60% of all costs involved. Unless, of course, you are successful in arranging a deal with a company, on the basis that they pay for all development.

Employees' inventions

There are exceptions to the above paragraph when I stated that 'ownership' belongs to the person who 'mentally' conceived the invention. If you are engaged in research, thereby being paid by your company to produce results, all rights to your inventive achievements legally belong to your company.

However, there some exceptions to that general rule. For example, if you are employed by a company, and come up with an idea that may either benefit your company, or your company could develop the idea themselves and make a profit, providing you aren't specifically paid to invent or work in an area that is not in the scope of your employment, then it's your good fortune, and you claim title to that invention.

Many companies have a 'suggestion' box – never be anxious to feed that suggestion box with ideas that may make fortunes for your company, who may pay you only a pittance. Therefore, if you are an employee, and providing the terms of your employment contract do not imply or state that all inventions belong to your company, go along and see a patent agent, and upon receiving a priority date approach your company with your 'idea' – they may even offer you a position of Management or even a Directorship. Whatever higher status they offer, take everything they offer, but don't assign the rights of your invention over to them; grant them a LICENCE in return for royalties, mindful that, any high powered position they offer you may not last longer than the time it takes for the ink to dry on your contract!

Whenever you are dealing with your patent agent, you will often hear them utter words such as:

CLAIMS, SCOPE OF CLAIMS, LIMITED BY SCOPE, MONOPOLY, NOVELTY, PRIOR ART, INVENTIVE STEP, OBVIOUSNESS, PLURALITY, INDUSTRIAL APPLICATION, PATENT SPECIFICATION, FAMILY OF PATENTS, COGNA-TION, LACK OF UNITY, KNOW-HOW.

And probably a lot more they will throw in for good measure!

They are 'terminology' or 'jargon' most commonly used by patent agents or trade mark agents who often believe that we know just what they are talking about – of course to impress them, we say nothing, but nod our head in total agreement. The following short descriptions should help.

- CLAIMS: Refers to the monopoly rights for which you seek protection, whenever drafting your patent specification.

- SCOPE OF CLAIMS: Refers to the actual 'broadness' of your claims, i.e. if you claim too much, you may be in danger of covering what is obvious, or technically known as 'prior art'.

- LIMITED BY SCOPE: Refers to the monopoly protection that you seek, may open the doors to others trying to break your monopoly, or indeed, others may see an opportunity of getting a patent (on your invention) either by skilled modifications or fresh technology. That is why it is important to use the skills of a registered patent agent to draft out your specifications.

- MONOPOLY: This is a patent right to exploit your invention for twenty years (those rights can still be challenged) and will depend upon how well you or your patent agent have drafted your claims.

- NOVELTY: Every new patent must have a 'novelty' aspect to it. Therefore, whenever an examiner carries out his search, he will check through older patents or literature. If what you claim in your specification is already established in other patents, then your claims would prove defective and it's unlikely you will get your patent, because your invention is not novel or has no new features, sufficient to warrant a patent grant. However, you have the right to appeal to the examiner's better nature, by proving to him that your invention is novel, and not based on claims of another invention.

- PRIOR ART: This terminology is closely linked with the claims made in your specification – it basically refers to subject matters that are known already.

- INVENTIVE STEP: Before you can obtain a patent grant, you must establish that your invention is in fact new and not obvious. You must be able to convince the patent examiner that your invention may resemble another product but your changes are non-obvious, with perhaps technologically improved method of use.

- OBVIOUSNESS: Implies that your invention is 'obvious' with no new features sufficient to obtain a monopoly right.

- INDUSTRIAL APPLICATION: Basically this characteristic part of obtaining a patent grant implies what it says. Whatever you have invented must be related to being manufactured or produced in some way, as opposed to say a 'discovery' or 'mathematical formula' etc. (You can of course have claims to pharmaceutical compositions).

- PATENT SPECIFICATION: This terminology applies to

the drafting out of your claims – it is a definition of your monopoly rights.

- LACK OF UNITY
- PLURALITY
- COGNATION

The above three are interrelated and will be dealt with as such.

Your patent agent may tell you that your application lacks any unity, and he may suggest that you file further applications to cover your modification (to the same invention) that is to say your application defines more than one invention or plurality! In short, this means that you have a good opportunity of getting several patents for the same invention but obviously with modifications to each application. This is referred to as a 'cognate' application, or cognation! (or known as a 'family of patents').

There are many benefits to a cognation: firstly, you increase your asset value of your patent; secondly, it would be more difficult for anyone to challenge; thirdly, you re-inforce your chances against infringement; and fourthly, you may prevent others from coming up with new modifications to your invention, that may give them a monopoly right.

- KNOW-HOW cannot be patented but nevertheless a person with 'know-how' can often sell his knowledge, under a licence, or act as a 'consultant' to any company wishing to engage his/her services because of their experience. Know-how knowledge, is often used when a company has acquired rights to an invention, but haven't a clue on how to develop it. Therefore, if a person holds the 'key' to their success, this is worth much money in acting as their consultant, or simply trading your knowledge for a 'royalty' payment!

Incidentally, even though you may be fortunate enough to obtain a patent which will offer a measure of protection, it would also be wise to re-inforce that protection by applying for a design registration, which will give you further protection, but you can add to this by applying also for a trade mark. Obviously, you will need to choose a good name for your invention or products, before you apply for a trade mark. Obtaining all three registrations will enhance your 'asset' value and give greater protection all round (it will also increase your 'royalty' prospects).

If you decide that you only want a patent that will have effect in the UK, then it is much simpler and cheaper to file and prosecute a national UK patent application under the British Patents Act 1977.

However, should you consider that your proposed product should be commercially exploited in several countries, then the alternatives outlined in Chapter 7 may suit you best.

Symbols and their meanings

- ©   copyright
- ®   registered design
- ™   trade mark not yet registered
- (RD)

  REG. D.

  DES   article is protected by design registration
- NOTE: Although it is permissible to stamp your products with 'patent pending', it is not permissible to stamp them with 'patented' or 'patented grant'.

'You can often achieve more . . . by doing less.'
HC

CHAPTER 7

How to file a European and International Patent

The European Patent Convention (EPC)

The main advantage and purpose of the EPC is that it allows you to obtain patent rights in any one or more of the European countries. By filing and prosecuting a single **European patent application,** it may be cheaper than filing separate applications to each individual country. You have to **designate** those countries in which you want the patent to take effect, and pay a fee for **each** country.

If you reside in the UK then you should file a European patent application at the Patent Office. However, you may instead file with the European Patent Office at Munich or at the Hague, provided you have complied with either of the requirements that would come under **national security**.

Warning on national security

- If the Patent Office considers that an application contains information, the publication of which might be prejudicial to the defence of the realm or the safety of the public, it may prohibit or restrict its publication or communication.

- Any person resident in the UK and wishing to apply abroad for a patent, must first obtain permission from the UK Patent Office, unless they have already applied for a patent for the same invention in the UK. In the latter case, no application abroad should be made until at least **six weeks** after the UK filing.

The general pattern of procedure to obtain European patent rights is basically similar to that under the UK Patents Act. Up to the stage of early publication the application will be handled by the Search Branch in the Hague which carries out a search through a multi-national collection of patent specifications (including those from the USA, the UK and most European countries) and certain other technical literature.

If, after receiving the search report, you file a request for a substantive examination, then this is undertaken at the European Patent Office headquarters in Munich. When granted, a European patent has the effect of a bundle of separate national patents, one for each country that you have designated in the application. So if you have designated the UK as one of those countries, you will obtain patents rights in the UK which will be subject to UK law in the same way as a patent obtained by a national application.

Countries that subscribe, or are party to, the European Patent Convention (EPC) are:

Austria
Belgium
France
Germany
Greece
Italy
Liechtenstein
Luxembourg
Netherlands
Spain
Sweden
Switzerland
UK

- Note: Further countries may have joined this convention after the publication of this book.

- Note: Application forms can be obtained free from the UK Patent Office in Gwent (see Appendix for full address).

If you wish to apply direct to obtain a European Patent (EPC) you can purchase a booklet titled *How to get a European Patent* from:

The European Patent Office
Erhardtstrasse 27
D 8000 Munchen 2.

- Note: You can file for a European Patent from the Patent Office in London.

The Patent Cooperation Treaty (PCT)

To simply filing your patent application on an international scale, to which the UK is a party, you may prefer to consider filing through the **Patent Cooperation Treaty (PCT)** and, at present, there are thirty-nine other states each subscribing to this Treaty. Provided you are a national of, or resident in, one of the **PCT contracting states**, you may take advantage of this Treaty to simplify the process.

A single international application in one language, and in accordance with one set of rules relating to formal requirements and content, is filed at a single Receiving Office. For UK residents this will generally be the Patent Office. In this international application (and similar to the EPC) you designate those contracting states in which you eventually wish to be granted a patent.

The single application is sent to an **International Searching Authority**, where a search on it is carried out. The branch of the European Patent Convention at the Hague is one such Authority. Thereafter, the application and the search report are published as soon as possible after the expiry of **eighteen months** from the priority date, by the International Bureau of the **World Intellectual Property Organization** in Geneva. The Bureau will send copies to you and to each of the National Offices of the contracting states that you have designated and which require it.

To proceed further, you will have to make filings in the countries you have designated, normally before the expiry of **twenty months** from the priority date. You will have to supply as necessary, in accordance with the requirements of different contracting states, fees, translations and a copy of the application itself to the designated states so that they will treat the application as a national one and process it further.

This is termed entering the **'national phase'**. You can also have your application for a European patent if you have made the appropriate designation, and it will then be processed in accordance with the European Patent Convention.

Countries that subscribe, or are party to, the Patent Cooperation Treaty are:

In Africa: Benin; Cameroon; Central African Republic; Chad; Congo; Gabon; Madagascar; Malawi; Mali; Mauritania; Senegal; Sudan; Togpo.

In the Americas: Barbados; Brazil; United States.

In Asia and the Pacific: Australia; Democratic Peoples Republic of Korea; Japan; Republic of Korea; Sri Lanka.

In Europe: Austria; Belgium; Bulgaria; Denmark; Finland; France; Germany; Hungary; Italy; Liechtenstein; Luxembourg; Monaco; Netherlands; Norway; Romania; Soviet Union; Sweden; Switzerland; United Kingdom.

- Note: Application to the PCT can be filed direct through the Patent Office.

Alternatively you can purchase a **PCT Applicants Guide** direct from:

The World Intellectual Property Organization
34 Chemin des Colombettes
1211 Geneva 20.

Or both **EPC** *and* **PCT** booklets can be consulted in the:

Science Reference and Information Services
25 Southampton Buildings
Chancery Lane
London WC2 1AY

Can I obtain a world patent?

There is no such thing as a world patent. To obtain patent rights in other countries, you will have to file and prosecute a patent application under the **national patent laws** of **each** country, unless you use the options offered by the EPC or PCT.

However, it must be emphasized that patenting an invention in several countries is very expensive, and even more so if indeed you propose to use professional representation, which in the case of international or European application, would be advisable.

Comparing the patent alternatives

If you decide that you only wish to exploit your invention in the **UK** the Patents Act would be sufficient to service your needs. Applying for a patent in just one country will obviously keep the cost down to that country. However, if you are confident that what you have invented could have, say, European sales potential, then it would be wise to consider paying the extra cost of patenting in those countries for the purpose of being able to exploit a wider territory, should you decide to **'license'** your patent rights. You could then be expected to recover all your patent costs, and make a profit.

Each separate national application would cost you the official fees of that country, the fees of a professional representative (if used) and possible translation costs.

Using the EPC, you will have to pay its fees, the fees of patent agent (if you use one), but no translation fees at the initial stages, provided that the language in which you file your application is either in **English, French** or **German**. However, this initial saving is reduced in due course because claims in English, French and German have to be provided before a European patent is granted.

Most of the European countries require claims to be translated into their own languages at the stage of early publication before conferring the right to bring an infringement action against anyone infringing the granted patent specification prior to the grant of a European patent becoming effective in that country.

You will need to do a similar calculation to decide whether to use the PCT, taking into account that the costs during the 'national phase' of the application include for each designated country national fees. For example, the examination fee, according to that country's scale, and probably professional representation fees and translation costs.

- Note: The search fee for EPC and PCT is payable upon filing.

The document collection through which the UK search is made, is not as large or comprehensive as that available for the search under either the EPC or PCT. So a search made under the UK Patents Act might not reveal a previously published document, especially a foreign specification, which could be used in a 'revocation' action to show that your invention is not new and is obvious. But it's possible that this relevant document might have been found, had a search been made under the EPC or the PCT. There is, therefore, a rather greater possibility of the validity of a patent being challenged in this way, if it was filed under the UK Patents Act rather than under the European Patent Convention, or the Patent Cooperation Treaty.

Word of caution

Whichever route you adopt it is worth remembering that, if you file a national application under the Patents Act (UK) it can be used as a basis for claiming **priority** for an application filed in most other countries, or for an application filed under the EPC or the PCT, provided that the fresh application is filed within **twelve months** of the date of filing your earliest national application for the same invention.

- Note: Priority rights thus obtained, of course, apply only to the matter which was contained in the earlier national application.

Another benefit which can be obtained by filing a national application first is that you can use the UK search report to make an initial assessment of your invention, before embarking on the costly process of acquiring protection abroad. To obtain this report you would have to file an application for a UK patent, taking care to include both file and search fees; this is to ensure that your description of your invention was complete, and that carefully drafted claims were included either at the filing date, or very soon afterwards. Bear in mind that the search report is based upon the invention claimed.

Provided you did this satisfactorily, so that the processing of your application was not unduly delayed, and so long as your national application was not itself claiming an earlier priority, then you could expect to get the search report before the end of the crucial twelve-month period.

Could I handle the application myself?

Filing for a patent or prosecuting the application is no task for the inexperienced and should be left to the professionals.

Readers who consider that they *do* have the ability to prosecute their own patent applications, should exercise great caution. I cannot over-emphasize the importance of giving care and attention to every little detail, whenever they draft their specification. A well-moulded and precise definition will be paramount when staking your claim to the invention.

There is no doubt that the prospects of saving on professional fees is tempting to most of us. But in this instance, is it really worth the gamble when so much is at stake?

Those who think it may be a 'piece of cake' should look closely at the next chapter – before they start slicing away!

MORE CAUTIONARY WORDS:

Whether or not a 'patent right' can be challenged or even revoked will largely depend upon the scope of your claim – that is to say, if you claim too much, you may soon discover that others are trying to break your monopoly right on the grounds that your claim is 'prior art', i.e. it's known already and therefore is not new (or indeed combinations are not workable). But of course, you may claim too little and find yourself in trouble with infringers who may see a legal loop-hole in your patent. There are lots of other combinations so that others may successfully challenge your grant and therefore it would be unwise not to use the skills of a qualified patent agent. I do have to mention that because of the legal complexities involved here, even your agent may not be able to defend your rights from a successful challenger!

'Two slabs of wood, some tin, and two screws: Was it brilliant . . . or obvious! Which do you choose?'

RON HICKMAN

CHAPTER 8

Drafting your claims and specifications for your patent

Any person contemplating doing-it-themselves should closely observe the complexities involved in the actual submission process. The following material is an exact copy of the specification and claims made by Mr Ron Hickman in respect of his now internationally famous invention of the 'WORKMATE'. Mr Hickman first filed for a patent protection in March 1968. This document may give the reader a better awareness of what is involved and the depth of information required. This submission of his specification amounts to a legal document, which is written in such precise terms that leaves little doubt as to the interpretation of the full claim to his invention. In my considered opinion, this document should not be attempted by any person without full legal training, and should therefore, be left in the hands of your patent agent or lawyer.

The following specification is reproduced by kind permission of the Controller of Her Majesty's Stationery Office:

PATENT SPECIFICATION

(11) **1 267 032**

DRAWINGS ATTACHED

1267 032

(21) Application No. 10484/68   (22) Filed 4 March 1968

(23) Complete Specification filed 3 March 1969

(45) Complete Specification published 15 March 1972

(51) International Classification B 25 b 1/10

(52) Index at acceptance
    B4X   1A   1B
    B3B   7B2F   7B4D3   7B4D5   7B6B   7B6F3   7B6L2

(54) A WORKBENCH

(71)   I, Ronald Price Hickman, a British subject, of "Badgers", Middle Street, Nazeing, Waltham Abbey, Essex do hereby declare the invention for which I pray that a patent may be granted to me, and the method by which it is to be performed, to be particularly described in and by the following statement: —

This invention relates to workbenches. With many applications it is desirable to be able to clamp up an elongated timber or other workpiece but prior proposals have not enabled this to be done in a satisfactory manner. Specifically it has not been possible readily to clamp up a tapered workpiece.

According to one aspect of the present invention a workbench includes a pair of elongate vice members disposed in side by side relationship and having their upper surfaces lying in substantially the same horizontal plane to form a working surface, the members being supported from below by a supporting structure and means being provided to prevent movement of each member upwardly away from the supporting structure, at least one of the vice members being capable of movement towards and away from the other vice member, the said movement being caused by actuation of either one or both of a pair of spaced, independently operable, vice operating devices which are operatively coupled to at least one of the members by means which enables the gap between the vice members at one end thereof to be greater than the gap at the other end thereof.

Specifically one of the vice members may be secured in a stationary manner to the supporting structure and the other vice member be movable. The supporting structure may incorporate a pair of horizontal supports extending beneath the vice members and affording horizontal slide surfaces upon which the movable vice member bears. The vice operating devices preferably each comprise a screw threaded rod extending substantially at right angles to the length of the stationary vice member, and each screw threaded rod may be axially fixed at its end adjacent the stationary vice member and extend through a nut secured

to the movable vice member. Location means may be included which limits lateral movement of the moveable vice member relatively to the horizontal supports, and this location means may comprise horizontal vertical faces one on each of the horizontal supports and against each of which an abutment, carried on the underside of the moveable member, is arranged to engage. The nuts may partially provide the means to prevent upward movement of the moveable member away from the supporting structure, and the horizontal supports may each include a horizontal web under which the nut at least partially lies to prevent upward movement of the nut.

Specifically the horizontal supports may each include a horizontal web beneath which one of the screw threaded rods extends, with the location portion of the association nut extending upwards within a guide slot in the web, and each guide slot may be laterally wider than its associated location portion to permit limited lateral movement of the location portion and hence the nut during independent operation of the screw threaded rods. This will permit angular movement of an end (or both ends) of the moveable vice member. It will be appreciated that the same effect can be obtained in other ways, e.g. by relative movement between the associated location means and means by which it is secured to the vice member. Alternatively the relative movement could occur between the said securing means and the vice member itself. A further possibility of allowing for the arcuate movement would be to permit the screw thread devices to move translationally at their ends opposite to the ends which cooperate with the nuts. Each nut may be secured to the moveable vice member by a single vertical connection which permits arcuate movement of the moveable vice member about the axes of the vertical connections during independent operation of the screw threaded rods.

According to one particularly convenient arrangement the pair of vice members between them afford the complete working surface of the bench.

– WORK BENCH –   Patent specification

The workbench may include a base structure for resting on a floor, and an intermediate collapsible structure which interconnects the base structure and the supporting structure and
5 which is capable of assuming either an erected position in which the vice members together afford the working surface spaced from the base structure, or a collapsed storage position in which the intermediate and supporting
10 structures lie in close juxtaposition to the base structure. The base structure preferably has a larger plan area than the plan area encompassing the vice members when fully spaced apart at each end and constitutes a load-bearing
15 platform upon which a person can stand beside the vice members.

According to another aspect of the present invention a workbench comprises a pair of elongate vice members disposed in side by side
20 relationship and having their upper surfaces lying in substantially the same horizontal plane to form a working surface, the vice members being supported from below by a supporting structure comprising a pair of spaced supports
25 extending substantially at right angles to the length of the vice members, and means being provided to prevent movement of each vice member upwardly away from the spaced supports, at least one of the vice members being
30 capable of movement towards and away from the other vice member, the said movement being caused by actuation of either one or both of a pair of spaced, independently operable vice operating devices which are positioned one
35 adjacent each of the spaced supports and which are operatively coupled to at least one of the vice members by means which enables the gap between the vice members at one end thereof to be greater than the gap at the other
40 end thereof.

According to yet another aspect of the present invention a workbench comprises a pair of elongate vice members disposed in side by side relationship and having their upper
45 surfaces lying in substantially the same horizontal plane to form a working surface the vice members being supported from below by a supporting structure and means being provided to prevent
50 movement of each vice member upwardly away from the supporting structure, one of the vice members being capable of movement towards and away from the other vice member, the said movement being caused by actuation
55 of either one or both of a pair of spaced independently operable vice operating screw threads each of which is operatively coupled to a nut connected to the moveable vice member by a vertical pivotal connection which
60 enables the gap between the vice members at one end thereof to be greater than the gap at the other end thereof.

The screw threaded rods are conveniently actuated by crank handles which each may be
65 formed in two hinged sections to allow the crank to be folded for storage.

The disclosure of this application corresponds to the disclosure of Application Nos. 50755/71, (Serial No. 1,267,033), 50756/71,
70 (Serial No. 1,267,034) and 50757/71. (Serial No. 1,267,035).

The invention may be carried into practice in a number of ways but one specific embodiment will now be described by way of example
75 with reference to the accompanying drawings in which: —

Figure 1 is a perspective view of one form of collapsible workbench constructed in accordance with the present invention;

80 Figure 2 is an end elevation, partly in section, of the upper end of the workbench showing the manner in which the top members act as a vice;

Figure 3 is a front part-sectional elevation
85 of the workbench of Figures 1 and 2;

Figure 4 is a plan view of a slideway incorporated in the workbench;

Figure 5 is a cross-section of the slideway on the line T—T of Figure 4;

90 Figure 6 shows certain parts of the workbench in plan with the pair of top members of the bench in parallel spaced relationship, and

Figure 7 is a plan view showing one end
95 of the workbench with one of the top members drawn into contact with the other top member at one end only.

Figure 1 shows the general construction of a workbench having a base structure incor-
100 porating a base board 7 mounted in a rectangular framework which is supported by adjustable feet 1 and provided at each end with a vertical web 2 by which a pair of generally 'H' shaped frames 3 and 4 are located and
105 pivotally mounted at 5 and 6 respectively for movement in the manner of a parallelogram between the working position of Figure 1 and a collapsed storage position in which the top members are in close juxtaposition to the base
110 board. As shown in Figure 1 the pivotal connections of the rear frame 4 to the web 2 and a further web 13, to be described, are higher than the corresponding connections of the frame 3, so that in the collapsed position the
115 rear frame 4 partially overlies the front frame 3. It will also be noted from Figure 1 that the plan area encompassing the top members when fully spaced apart is less than that of the base, and since the pivotal points 5 are
120 situated approximately midway along the length of the webs 2, there is a forward portion on the base board 7 which provides a load-bearing platform upon which a person can stand beside the vice, and thereby provide
125 added stability to the bench as a whole.

The upper ends of the frames 3 and 4 each afford a pair of spaced limbs which are pivoted at 10 to a vertical web 13 of horizontal support formed by a generally 'U' shaped in-
130 verted channel 14 the detailed form of which

is shown in Figures 2 and 3. Thus, referring to Figure 3 the channel 14 also includes a second vertical web 15, the two webs 13 and 15 being interconnected by a further horizontal web 17. The diagonal bars 9 are secured to the webs 15 at pivot points 18 at their upper ends and at their lower ends cooperate with slots 20 to allow for collapsing of the workbench.

The work surface of the workbench is afforded by a pair of spaced elongate rectangular-section timber beams 21 and 22 having their horizontal surfaces aligned in the same plane. The beams also have opposed vertical surfaces 23 and 24 respectively which as will be described, can be drawn towards one another from their spaced apart positions of Figures 1, 2 and 6. At each end the front beam 21 is rigidly connected to the horizontal web 17 of the respective channel by means of a pair of screws 25 as shown in Figure 2, the front screw having a spacer washer 26 surrounding it between the beam and the web 17, and the rear screw 25 passing through a hole 27 in a slideway 28 formed for example of nylon or metal strip provided with a PTFE upper surface. The form of slideway is shown in detail in Figures 4 and 5. Apart from the hole 27 for the rear screw 25, it has a longitudinal slot 30 for a purpose to be described, and at its rear end is provided with a poppet stud 32 which, as shown in Figure 2, is received in an aperture 33 in the horizontal web 17 of the channel 14.

The horizontal web 17 is provided with a longitudinal slot 33 of a shape corresponding to the slot 30 in the slideway and the two slots 30 and 35 have extending upwardly through them a projecting portion 40 formed on a slide member 41 shown in Figures 2 and 3. The portions 40 provide location means which, with the vertical side edges of the slots 30 limit lateral movement of the beam 22. The upper surface of the projection 40 abuts the underside of an end of the rear beam 22 and the slider member 41 is secured to the beam 22 by a single screw 45, for which purpose the underside of the slider member 41 is provided with an open recess 46, as shown in Figure 3.

As shown in Figure 3 the slider member 41, below the web 17, is substantially wider than the width of the slots 30 and 35 so that the rear beam 22 whilst it can ride freely in a horizontal manner along the slideway, is prevented from moving bodily upward or of tilting upwards, e.g. adjacent its front edge. It is to be noted from Figure 3 that the width of the projection 40 of the slider member 41 is less than the width of the slots 30 and 35 to allow for lateral movement of the slider member in a manner to be described. For this purpose also the width of the lower, wider part of the slider member 41 is less than the width of the space between the webs of the channel 14.

As shown in Figure 2, on each side of the recess 46 the slider member 41 has a screw threaded bore 50 which co-operates with an externally screw threaded rod 51, the outer end of which, to the left in Figure 2, carries a crank handle 52 provided with a hinged end section 53 which can be maintained either in the position shown in Figure 2 for operating purposes or hinged downwards to the dotted line positiion 54 against the action of a spring biassed plunger 55 when not in use. In order to support the end of the rod 51 adjacent its handle 52 the webs 13 and 15 of the channel 14 are interconnected at the front by a vertical transverse wall 58 through which the rod 51 passes, washers being provided on each side of the wall 58 and the rod being held in position by means of a circlip.

Accordingly, rotation of the rod 51 by means of its cranked handled 52 will cause horizontal movement of the slider member 41 towards or away from the front beam 21. The extent of movement of the slider member 41 is determined in one direction by abutment of the beams 21 and 22 against one another or in the case of rearward movement of the beam 22 by abutment of the projection 40 of the slider member 41 against the rear end of the slots 30 and 35. As shown in Figure 1 the beams 21 and 22 can be drawn together or moved apart by simultaneous or independent operation of identical screw threaded rods at each end by means of a pair of crank handles 52. In this way, therefore, the beams 21 and 22 apart from providing substantially horizontal surfaces, which together provide a working top surface upon which many operations can be carried out, also act in the manner of a vice between which lengths of timber or other material can be clamped.

Assuming that the beams 21 and 22 are initially in spaced parallel relationship as shown for example in Figure 1 equal rotation of the crank handles at each end will cause the beams to be maintained in parallel relationship but it is a particular feature of this workbench that one or other of the handles 52 can be operated quite independently of the other to the maximum limits allowed by movement of the respective slider members 41. In other words one end of the rear beam 22 may be fully separated from the front beam 21 and remain so whilst the other end of the rear beam 22 is drawn up fully into contact with the front beam 21. This extreme position is shown in Figure 7. It will be appreciated that during such independent movement of only one end of the beam 22, the beam will pivot at each end about the screws 45 by which it is secured to the two slider members 41. Assuming the extreme example mentioned above where one of the ends of the beam remains stationary, full clamping up for example of the right-hand

– WORK BENCH –

end of the beam 22, with no movement of the left-hand end, in the manner shown in Figure 7, will of necessity require the slider member 41 on the right to move to the left due to the arcuate movement of the right-hand end of the rear beam 22. Such sideways movement of the slider member 41 is accommodated by the excess width of the slots 30 and 35 in relation to the width of the projection 40 of the slider member 41 as shown and described with respect to Figure 3. Figures 6 and 7 demonstrate this lateral movement of the slider member 41 between its extreme positions. Thus in Figure 6 the outline of the projection 40 of the slider member 41 is shown as engaging the right-hand face of the elongated slot 30 in the slideway 28. After full clamping up to the position shown in Figure 7 the projection 40 of the slider member 41 moves laterally to engage the left-handside of the slot 30. Of necessity in this arrangement the slider member 41 has to tilt slightly with respect to the longitudinal axis of the slot 30 in the clamped up position of Figure 7. This will cause slight lateral movement of the rear end of the screw threaded rod 51 as shown in Figure 7 but this can be readily accommodated by means of the tolerances in the manner of mounting of the rod 51 at its front end.

It will be appreciated that the relative dispositions of the parts in Figures 6 and 7 show an extreme condition in which a full movement of the rear beam has occurred at one end. In most instances such an extreme condition will not be required and there will usually be some clamping up at both ends either to the same or a different extent. The manner in which the slider members 41 are mounted to permit this independent movement avoids any difficulty of seizure of one or other of the screw threaded rods during clamping up or release as would normally be expected to occur with spaced screw threaded members of this type. Normally with spaced screw threaded members it is necessary to maintain substantially equal rotation of each in order to prevent seizure. The use of a pair of spaced screw threads of which one can be in tension thus applying a compressional load on a part clamped between the vertical faces, and the other can, if desired, take a reaction load in compression, is particularly useful for the clamping up of short parts. This is especially so where the point of grip of the part is outboard of one of the screw threads.

Accordingly, the workbench according to the invention enables a part to be clamped up within the space between the two beams irrespective of whether its sides faces are parallel or inclined to one another.

Whilst with the embodiment of Figures 1 to 7 the screw threaded rods 51 are used in tension for clamping up, this is not essential and compression screws could be used.

Whilst the twin screws have been described as being entirely independently operable it is envisaged that it may be possible to provide an optional link between them when it is desired that they should maintain the pair of top members in constant alignment. Equally it is envisaged that each screw may be provided with a quick release in order that the members can be drawn together or moved apart separately for course adjustment prior to clamping up.

WHAT I CLAIM IS:—

1. A workbench including a pair of elongate vice members disposed in side by side relationship and having their upper surfaces lying in substantially the same horizontal plane to form a working surface, the members being supported from below by a supporting structure and means being provided to prevent movement of each member upwardly away from the supporting structure, at least one of the vice members being capable of movement towards and away from the other vice member, the said movement being caused by actuation of either one or both of a pair of spaced, independently operable, vice operating devices which are operatively coupled to at least one of the members by means which enables the gap between the vice members at one end thereof to be greater than the gap at the other end thereof.

2. A workbench as claimed in Claim 1 in which one of the vice members is secured in a stationary manner to the supporting structure and the other vice member is movable.

3. A workbench as claimed in Claim 2 in which the supporting structure incorporates a pair of horizontal supports extending beneath the vice members and affording horizontal slide surfaces upon which the movable vice member bears.

4. A workbench as claimed in Claim 2 or Claim 3 in which the vice operating devices each comprise a screw threaded rod extending substantially at right angles to the length of the stationary vice member.

5. A workbench as claimed in Claim 4 in which each screw threaded rod is axially fixed at its end adjacent the stationary vice member and extends through a nut secured to the movable vice member.

6. A workbench as claimed in any one Claims 3 to 5 including location means which limits lateral movement of the movable vice member relatively to the horizontal supports.

7. A workbench as claimed in Claim 6 in which the location means comprises horizontally extending vertical faces one on each of the horizontal supports and against each of which an abutment, carried on the underside of the movable member, is arranged to engage.

8. A workbench as claimed in Claim 5, or as claimed in Claim 6 when appendant to Claim 5, in which the nuts partially provide the means to prevent upward movement of the movable member away from the supporting structure.

5   1,267,032   5

9. A workbench as claimed in Claim 3 and as claimed in Claim 8 in which the horizontal supports each include a horizontal web under which the nut at least partially lies to prevent
5 upward movement of the nut.

10. A workbench as claimed in Claim 9 in which the screwthreaded rods are axially fixed to vertical walls of the horizontal supports.

11. A workbench as claimed in Claim 5 and
10 as claimed in Claim 7 in which the abutments are formed by location portions one on each nut.

12. A workbench as claimed in Claim 11 in which the horizontal supports each include
15 a horizontal web beneath which one of the screw threaded rods extends, with the location portion of the associated nut extending upwards within a guide slot in the web.

13. A workbench as claimed in Claim 12
20 in which each guide slot is laterally wider than its associated location portion to permit limited lateral movement of the location portion and hence the nut during independent operation of the screw threaded rods.

25 14. A workbench as claimed in Claim 5 or as Claimed in any of Claims 8 to 13 wherein each nut is secured to the movable vice member by a single vertical connection which permits arcuate movement of the movable vice
30 member about the axes of the vertical connections during independent opertion of the screw threaded rods.

15. A workbench as claimed in any one of the preceding claims in which the pair of vice
35 members between them afford the complete working surface of the bench.

16. A workbench as claimed in any one of the preceding claims in which the vice members are each formed of wood.

40 17. A workbench as claimed in Claim 16 in which each vice member is of substantially rectangular cross section.

18. A workbench as claimed in any one of the preceding claims including a base structure
45 for resting on a floor, and an intermediate collapsible structure which interconnects the base structure and the supporting structure and which is capable of assuming either an erected position in which the vice members together
50 afford the working surface spaced from the base structure, or a collapsed storage position in which the intermediate and supporting structures lie in close juxtaposition to the base structure.

55 19. A workbench as claimed in Claim 18 in which the intermediate structure is hingedly connected to the supporting structure and to the base structure.

20. A workbench as claimed in Claim 19
60 in which the intermediate structure includes a pair of frames.

21. A workbench as claimed in Claim 20 in which each frame is of generally H configuration.

65 22. A workbench as claimed in Claim 20 or

Claim 21 in which the intermediate structure additionally includes at least one brace which, in the erected position, extends between the supporting structure and the base structure, at an inclination to the vertical. 70

23. A workbench as claimed in any one of Claims 18 to 21 wherein the base structure includes a horizontal platform.

24. A workbench as claimed in any one of Claims 18 to 22 in which the base structure 75 has a larger plan area than the plan area encompassing the vice members when fully spaced apart at each end and constitutes a load-bearing platform upon which a person can stand beside the vice-members. 80

25. A workbench as claimed in any one of Claims 18 to 24 in which the base structure includes a substantially rectangular framework and the intermediate structure is connected to opposed sides of the framework. 85

26. A workbench as claimed in Claim 21 in which each frame is hingedly connected at two pivotal points to each of the supporting and base structures.

27. A workbench as claimed in Claim 25 90 and as claimed in Claim 26 wherein the two pivotal points between one frame and the base structure are positioned adjacent two corners of the framework and the two pivotal points between the other frame and the base structure 95 are positioned substantially midway along the opposed sides of the framework.

28. A workbench as claimed in Claim 26 or Claim 27 in which each of the supporting and base structures affords a pair of substan- 100 tially vertical parallel webs and the frames at their upper and lower ends are respectively located against the opposed faces of the pairs of webs.

29. A workbench as claimed in any one of 105 Claims 21, 26 or 27 in which the H frames are hingeably mounted to the supporting structure and the base structure in the manner of a parallelogram.

30. A workbench as claimed in Claim 29 110 in which the hinge connections of one frame to each of the supporting and base structures are higher than the respective hinge connections of the other frame.

31. A workbench as claimed in Claim 30 115 in which the frame having the higher hinge connections is capable of partially overlying the other frame in the collapsed storage position.

32. A workbench comprising a pair of elon- 120 gate vice members disposed in side by side relationship and having their upper surfaces lying in substantially the same horizontal plane to form a working surface- the vice members being supported from below by a supporting 125 structure comprising a pair of spaced supports extending substantially at right angles to the length of the vice members, and means being provided to prevent movement of each vice member upwardly away from the spaced sup- 130

6 1,267,032 6

ports, at least one of the vice members being capable of movement towards and away from the other vice member. the said movement being caused by actuation of either one or both of a pair of spaced, independently operable, vice operating devices which are positioned one adjacent each of the spaced supports and which are operatively coupled to at least one of the vice members by means which enables the gap between the vice members at one end thereof to be greater than the gap at the other end thereof.

33. A workbench as claimed in Claim 32 in which one vice member is secured in a stationary manner to the spaced supports and the other vice member is movable, the said other vice member being connected to each of the vice operating devices by a single vertical connection which permits arcuate movement of the movable member about the axes of the vertical connections during independent operation of the vice operating devices

34. A workbench comprising a pair of elongate vice members disposed in side by side relationship and having their upper surfaces lying in substantially the same horizontal plane to form a working surface, the vice members being supported from below by a supporting structure and means being provided to prevent movement of each vice member upwardly away from the supporting structure, one of the vice members being capable of movement towards and away from the other vice member, the said movement being caused by actuation of either one or both of a pair of spaced independently operable vice operating screw threads each of which is operatively coupled to a nut connected to the movable vice member by a vertical pivotal connection which enables the gap between the vice members at one end thereof to be greater than the gap at the other end thereof.

35. A workbench as claimed in Claim 34 in which each nut is slidingly located with respect to the supporting structure to permit movement of the nut towards and away from the said other vice member and also to permit limited lateral movement of the nut during operation of the screw threads to vary the angular disposition of the movable vice member with respect to the other vice member.

36. A workbench substantially as described herein with reference to the accompanying drawings.

KILBURN & STRODE
Chartered Patent Agents.
Agents for the Applicants.

Printed for Her Majesty's Stationery Office by the Courier Press, Leamington Spa, 1972. Published by the Patent Office, 25 Southampton Buildings, London, WC2A 1AY, from which copies may be obtained.

– WORK BENCH –

Patent specification

1267032   COMPLETE SPECIFICATION

3 SHEETS *This drawing is a reproduction of the Original on a reduced scale*
Sheet 1

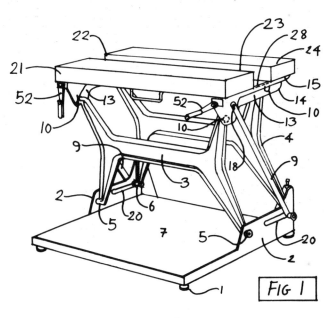

FIG 1

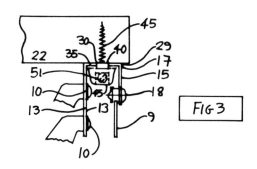

FIG 3

1267032   COMPLETE SPECIFICATION
3 SHEETS   This drawing is a reproduction of
the Original on a reduced scale
Sheet 2

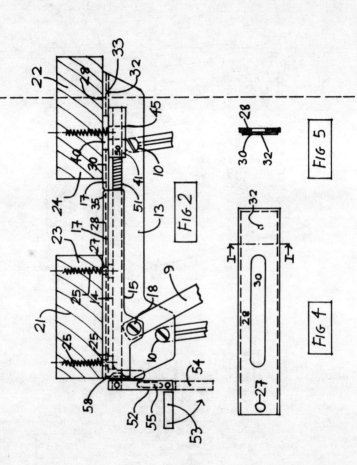

– WORK BENCH –

1267032   COMPLETE SPECIFICATION

3 SHEETS   *This drawing is a reproduction of the Original on a reduced scale*

Sheet 3

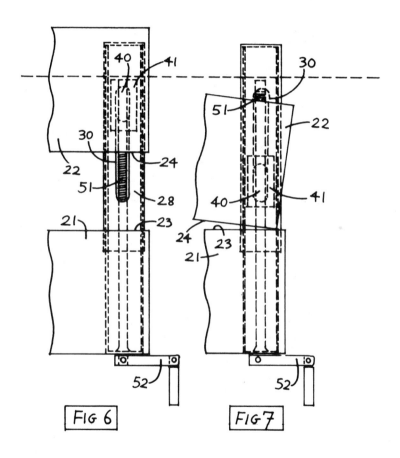

FIG 6

FIG 7

'You'll always get the goods news, but it's
how quickly you get the bad news that
counts!'

HARVEY MACKAY

'For the first few years, an inventor will be
tottering between bankruptcy or
insanity! . . . If you're really unlucky, it
could be both!'

HC

CHAPTER 9

Fees and costs for obtaining patents

Fees and charges will, naturally, vary from country to country. Therefore these figures are only meant as a rough guide. Persons wishing to apply for a patent in any country should first check on that country's costs, to ascertain the up-to-date charges.

In the UK

Fees are not all payable immediately when you apply for a patent, and the following figures may serve to act as a guide. Under the UK Patents Act the fees, as revised in June 1988, indicate that, from application to grant of a patent, costs would be around £240 (UK patent only).

However, any person who wishes to file an application simply to obtain a priority date will pay a fee of £15 upon the submission of their application. You will have up to twelve months to decide whether to proceed or not. Should you decide to proceed with your application before the twelve months have expired, you will have to pay a preliminary examination and search fee of about **£105**. This search fee could have been paid at the same time as you paid for the file fee, the benefits of which would mean that the Patent Office may have completed the preliminary examination and search during the first twelve months of filing your application.

You must not get confused between the actual fees it would cost you to obtain your patent, and the fees that you would be charged by a patent agent should, indeed, you use their services. Patent agent fees will vary according to what kind of service you seek of them. For example, if you need a patent agent to guide you through the UK patent system and process your application then their costs would be more than the fees payable to the UK Patent Office. Obviously, you will have to pay for the time that you spend with the patent agent but, basically, you are paying for their professional skills, as indeed you would expect to pay, should you engage the services of, say, a divorce lawyer. The latter may clean you out but the patent agent may be instrumental in helping you to make your fortune. Whatever you decide, *always* ask your patent agent to outline his costs *before* your proceed.

In Europe

The cost of filing European patent applications will, of course, vary according to the number of countries that you designate. As a guide, the fee for filing a European application would be about **£220**, with the search fees being about **£650** and the substantive examination a further **£775** approximately. Therefore, with additional associated fees, and perhaps patent agent fees on top, this would prove a costly exercise should, at the end of the day, you fail to get your patents. Furthermore, even if you do get your foreign grants, you would have to renew those patents each year by payment on **each individual country** that you designated in your application. Therefore, before you get carried away with seeking international protection, make sure your product is commercially viable and well worth protecting.

List of fees payable under the patents rules 1982

This list, provided by kind permission of Her Majesty's Stationery Office was revised in **September 1990** – use it as a general guide only.

Number of corresponding patents form	Item	Amount £
1/77	On request for the grant of a patent (the filing fee)	15
2/77	On reference under section 8(1), 12(1) or 37(1)32	32
3/77	On application under section 8(5) or 37(3) for authorization by comptroller	32
4/77	On request for directions under section 10 or 12(4)	32
5/77	On reference under section 11(5) or 38(5) to determine the question of a licence	32
6/77	On application to comptroller under section 13(1) and/or 13/3	24
7/77	Statement of inventorship and of right to the grant of a patent	—

Number of corresponding patents form	Item	Amount £
8/77	On request for comptroller's certificate authorising the release of a sample from a culture collection	11
9/77	On request for preliminary examination and search or request for further search	105
10/77	On request for substantive examination	120
11/77	On request to amend application before grant	27
12/77	On payment of renewal fee: Before the expiration of the 4th year from the date of filing of the application for the patent or, in the case of an existing patent the date of the patent and in respect of the 5th year	94
	Before the expiration of the 5th year from the date of filing of the application for the patent or, in the case of an existing patent, the date of the patent and in respect of the 6th year	100
	Before the expiration of the 6th year from the date of filing of the application for the patent or, in the case of an existing patent, the date of the patent and in respect of the 7th year	108
	Before the expiration of the 7th year from the date of filing of the application for the patent or, in the case of an existing patent the date of the patent and in respect of the 8th year	120
	Before the expiration of the 8th year from the date of filing of the application for the patent or, in the case of an existing patent,	

Number of corresponding patents form	Item	Amount £
12/77 (cont).	the date of the patent and in respect of the 9th year	130
	Before the expiration of the 9th year from the date of filing of the application for the patent or, in the case of an existing patent, the date of the patent and in respect of the 10th year	142
	Before the expiration of the 10th year from the date of filing of the application for the patent or, in the case of an existing patent the date of the patent and in respect of the 11th year	158
	Before the expiration of the 11th year from the date of filing of the application for the patent or, in the case of an existing patent, the date of the patent and in respect of the 12th year	172
	Before the expiration of the 12th year from the date of filing of the application for the patent or, in the case of an existing patent, the date of the patent and in respect of the 13th year	194
	Before the expiration of the 13th year from the date of filing of the application for the patent or, in the case of an existing patent the date of the patent and in respect of the 14th year	214
	Before the expiration of the 14th year from the date of filing of the application for the patent or, in the case of an existing patent, the date of the patent and in respect of the 15th year	238

Number of corresponding patents form	Item	Amount £
12/77 (cont).	Before the expiration of the 15th year from the date of filing of the application for the patent or, in the case of an existing patent, the date of the patent and in respect of the 16th year	262
	Before the expiration of the 16th year from the date of filing of the application for the patent or, in the case of an existing patent the date of the patent and in respect of the 17th year	286
	Before the expiration of the 17th year from the date of filing of the application for the patent or, in the case of an existing patent, the date of the patent and in respect of the 18th year	308
	Before the expiration of the 18th year from the date of filing of the application for the patent or, in the case of an existing patent, the date of the patent and in respect of the 19th year	342
	Before the expiration of the 19th year from the date of filing of the application for the patent or, in the case of an existing patent, the date of the patent and in respect of the 20th year	378
13/77	On extension of the period for payment of a renewal fee under section 25(4):	
	Not exceeding one month	20
	Each succeeding month	20
	(but not exceeding six months)	
14/77	On application to amend specification after grant	56

Number of corresponding patents form	Item	Amount £
15/77	On notice of opposition to amendment of specification after grant	24
16/77	On application for the restoration of a patent	114
17/77	Additional fee on the application for restoration of a patent	114
18/77	On offer to surrender a patent	—
19/77	On notice of opposition to offer to surrender a patent	24
20/77	On request for alteration of name, address or address for service in the register, for each patent or application	3
21/77	On application to register or to give notice of a transaction, instrument or event affecting the rights in a patent or application for a patent	24
	On each application covering more than one patent or application for a patent, the devolution of title being the same as in the first patent or application for a patent. For each additional request	3
22/77	On request for the correction of an error in the register or in any connected document	17
23/77	On request for the furnishing of or access to miscellaneous information (each)	3
24/77	On request for certificate of the comptroller	
	(a) by impressed stamp	3
	(b) sealed and attached to documents	12
25/77	On application for entry of order of court in the register	—

Number of corresponding patents form	Item	Amount £
26/77	On application for compensation by employee	32
27/77	On application under section 41(8) in connection with an order made under section 40(1) or 40(2)	32
28/77	On application by proprietor for entry to be made in the register to the effect that licenses under the patent are to be available as of right	13
29/77	On application for settlement of terms of licence of right	56
30/77	On application by proprietor under section 47(1) for cancellation of entry in the register	24
31/77	On application under section 47(3) by person interested for cancellation of entry in the register	24
32/77	On notice of opposition to an application under section 47(1) or 47(3) for cancellation of entry in the register	24
33/77	On application under section 48(1) for a compulsory licence or entry in the register	56
34/77	On application by Crown in case of monopoly or merger	56
35/77	On notice of opposition to application made under section 48 or 51	24
36/77	On reference to the comptroller of a dispute as to infringement	56
37/77	On application for declaration of non-infringement	56

Number of corresponding patents form	Item	Amount £
38/77	On application for the revocation of a patent	24
39/77	On application to register copy of entry made in European Register of Patents	10
40/77	On payment of filing fee upon conversion of European patent application to an application under the Act	15
41/77	On request for conversion of European patent application	15
43/77	On payment of prescribed fee and request for publication of translation	10
44/77	On application to the comptroller for an international application to be treated as an application under the Act	15
45/77	On application for order for evidence to be obtained in the United Kingdom	32
46/77	On notice that hearing before the comptroller will be attended	—
47/77	On request for the correction of an error of translation or transcription, clerical error or mistake	34
48/77	On notice of opposition to the correction of an error, clerical error or mistake	24
49/77	On request for information relating to a patent or application for a patent	8
50/77	On request for extension of time or period under Rule 110 (3) (each)	114
51/77	On declaration of authorization where agent appointed during progress of application or in substitution for another	—
52/77	On request for extension of time or period under rule 110 (3A)	114

Number of corresponding patents form	Item	Amount £
53/77	Additional fee for extension of time or period under Rule 110(3C)	114
54/77	On filing of translation of European Patent (UK) under Section 77(6)(a)	28
55/77	On filing of translation of amendment of European Patent (UK) under Section 77(6)(b)	28
56/77	On request for publication of translation of claims of application for European Patent (UK) filed under Section 78(7)	28
57/77	On request for publication of a corrected translation filed under Section 80(3)	28
—	National Fee (Rule 85(1))	15

As a general guide – if you use the services of a patent agent in filing for a British patent the combined fees would be about £1,250/1,500 plus VAT.

Obviously: If your patent agent is dealing with a 'family' of applications, applicable to the same invention, then his fees will vary according to the amount of work involved.

Note!

If you are thinking about filing a European or international patent application – the cost is going to be in several thousands (much would depend upon the number of countries that you seek protection). As a rough guide, filing in, say, ten countries using a patent agent is likely to set you back £4/5,000 (excluding your annuity fees).

'Copyright means nothing, until some
"evil bastard" infringes your own . . . then
it means everything!'

HC

CHAPTER 10

What is a copyright?

Copyrights give rights to the creators of certain kinds of material, so that they can control the various ways in which their material may be exploited. The rights broadly cover copying, adapting, issuing copies to the public, public performance and broadcasting material. In many cases, the author will have the right to be identified on his work and to object to distortions and mutilations of his work. Moreover, a rental right is given to owners of copyright in sound recordings, films and computer programs and, therefore, the exploitation of such works by renting them to the public requires a **licence** or the authority of the copyright owner.

Copyrights are often abused, and are not easy to protect; they are fraught with legal problems in that having to prove in the courts that someone has breached, stolen or indeed used your work can be a tricky business. The assertion of a copyright may be emphasized by the phrase 'All rights reserved' or simply the symbol © followed by the name of the copyright owner, and date of the first claim to originality.

Can I register my copyright?

NO! Copyright in this country is automatic and there is no registration system; there are no forms to fill in or fees payable.

How long does UK copyright last?

Copyright in a literary, dramatic, musical or artistic work including a photograph, last until **fifty years** after the death of the author. Films, sound recordings and broadcasts are protected for fifty years; but published editions are protected for only **twenty-five years.**

Can copyright protect industrial articles?

NO! Copyright may protect the drawing from which an article is made, but it cannot be used to prevent the manufacture of articles. For information on the protection of industrial articles see the section on Registered Designs.

Do I always need approval to exploit copyright material?

NO! There are certain exceptions to the rights given to the creator of material. For example, limited use of works is allowed for research and private study, criticism or review, reporting current events, judicial proceedings and teaching in schools.

How do I get approval to exploit copyright material?

Usually by approaching the copyright owner, but there are several organizations which act collectively for groups of copyright owners in respect of particular rights: they may offer blanket licences to users.

Are ideas protected by copyright?

NO! Although the work itself may be protected, the *idea* behind it is not. However, once you develop your idea into a **product,** then you may be able to get a patent. Alternatively, if your idea is in a **design** form, then you may apply under the Copyright, Designs and Patents Act 1988 for protection of your designs, which evolved through your ideas (see Chapter 11).

How can I prove originality in my work?

Whenever you have created something original, like a poem, for example, or even something as diverse as a set of rules and regulations to your new boardgame invention, you could make do by lodging a copy with your bank or lawyer. Alternatively, you may wish to put the documents in an envelope and register that envelope to yourself, but do not open the letter when it arrives. (This will establish that the work existed at this time.) Ultimately, it would be for the courts to decide on the originality of any claimed copyrights.

Who owns copyright?

The general rule is that the **author** is the first owner of copyright in a literary, dramatic, musical or artistic work or design creation. However, the main exception is where such work is made in the course of employment, in which case the **employer** owns the copyright, unless, of course, you have made agreement with your employer that certain works, not created in his time, will remain in your ownership. Obviously, if you were to create work that would normally be protected by copyright, and assign your work over to another (for example, films, sound recordings, broadcasts and published editions) then the copyright belongs to the person or company you assigned your rights over to.

Are names protected by copyright?

NO! There is no copyright in a name or a title.

Will my copyright be protected abroad?

Usually, but not invariably. The UK is a member of several international conventions in this field, notably the Berne Convention for the protection of Literary and Artistic Works and the Universal Copyright Convention (UCC). Copyright material created by UK nationals or residents is protected in each member country of the convention by the national law of that country. Most countries belong to at least one of the conventions including all of the Western European countries, the USA and USSR.

Can I protect my computer programs?

YES! Computer programs are protected on the same literary works basis. Conversion of a program into or between computer language and codes corresponds to adapting a work, while storing any work in a computer amounts to copying the work! Furthermore, running a computer program or displaying a work on a VDU will usually involve copying and thus will require the consent of the copyright owner.

General comments

Copyright is a creature of statute. There has been a series of Copyright Acts over the years. On the 1 August 1988, the Copyright Act 1956 was replaced by the **Copyright, Designs and Patents Act 1988.**

The Act sets out to restate the law of copyright, especially in so far as it relates to the essentials of what may be a copyright work, and how it may be protected, under the new Act.

What is infringement?

Copyright is infringed by doing any of a number of specified acts in relation to the copyright work, without the authority of the owner. The form of infringement common to all forms of copyright works, is that of copying, or reproducing the work in any **material** form. In the case of a two-dimensional artistic work, reproduction can mean making a copy in three-dimensional form, and vice versa, although there is an important limitation on this general rule that is dealt with in Section 51 of the Act, which provides that in the case of a design document or model, that would be defined as a record of a design of any aspect of the shape or configuration, internal or external, of the whole or part of an article, other than surface decoration for something which is not itself an artistic work, according to the definition given above, it shall be no infringement to make an article to that design.

For example, it would be an infringement to make an article from a design drawing for say, a sculpture, but it would not be an infringement to make a handbag from a copy of the design drawing of that particular sculpture, or indeed from a handbag that was purchased. In order to protect such designs, one would have to rely upon obtaining protection under the Copyright, Designs and Patents Act 1988.

Exceptions to infringement

The Copyright, Designs and Patents Act 1988 does, however, provide for a large number of exceptions to the general rule of infringement, and shall permit what is usually termed fair dealings more so on literary, dramatic, musical or artistic works for the purpose of research or private study. The fair dealing rule would also apply to works that are reviewed or for the purpose of criticism, such as literary works, articles, artistic works, sound recordings, films and general broadcasting or public recitation if accompanied by a sufficient acknowledgement to the copyright owner.

Perhaps the Act is very wise to make such provisions, otherwise the courts would be jammed packed with alleged infringers, especially when it comes to the photocopying of someone else's work. No doubt also there would be an abundance of authors who would be unable to complete certain books, unless they used large extracts of others' copyrights for the purpose of research (say no more).

'It's not how much you think your invention
is worth . . . but how much your buyer
thinks it's worth!'

HC

CHAPTER 11

Registered designs and design rights

I shall now deal with the next stage of Intellectual Property Rights that would best serve the interest of the **designer,** and his or her protective rights. The procedures are very similar to that of applying for a patent, and therefore, I shall cover only the points that would be considered necessary.

Protection for most designs can be obtained by filing an application to the Patent Office, in accordance with the guideline rule of the **Registered Design Act 1949** (now revised as the Copyright, Designs and Patents Act 1988).

What is a registered design?

It is a **monopoly right** for the outward appearance of an article or a set of articles of manufacture to which the design is applied.

How long is the right for?

It lasts for **five years** and may be extended in four- to five- year terms up to a maximum of **twenty-five years**. It is additional to any design right or copyright protection which may exist automatically in the design. A registered design is a property which may be bought, sold, hired or licensed, like any other business commodity.

Are all designs registrable?

NO! Where the **aesthetic** appearance of an article is not significant, or where there is no design freedom because the design of the part is determined by the shape of the whole, then the design is not registrable.

Designs must be specific in their purpose

Purely **functional** designs are not eligible for registration because their aesthetic appearance is not important, nor can designs such as car body panels be registered because their shape and configuration are determined by the overall design of the car. In other words, registered design protection will only be available for truly aesthetic, stand-alone designs where competitors do not need to be able to copy such designs in order to compete.

There are also other specific exclusions for certain types of designs and these include works of sculpture, medals and printed matter of a literary or artistic nature, such as bookjackets and calendars. In general, copyright protection is afforded to these excluded designs.

What other conditions must be satisfied?

A design has to be new, and must not have been publicly disclosed in the UK before the application for registrations is made, nor registered on an earlier design application. It must be materially different from any other published design for the same or any other type of article.

The difference between a patent and a registered design

A registered design applies to the **outward appearance** of an article, i.e. its eye-appeal whereas a patent is concerned with the **function, operation, manufacture** or **material of construction** of an article.

Benefits of having a registered design

Obtaining a registered design, will give you the exclusive right in the UK and the Isle of Man, to make, import, sell or hire out any article to which the design has applied. It also gives you the right to let others use the design under terms agreed with you as the registered owner and to take legal action against any infringer and claim damages. The very fact that you may have obtained registration of your designs, may be sufficient to deter a would-be infringer.

How is a design registered in the UK?

The owner of the design must apply to the Designs Registry at the Patent Office, providing representations of the design, an application form and filing fee. The Registry makes a search, mainly through previously registered designs, to determine if the particular design is new. If it is and formal requirements are also met, a Certificate of Registration is issued. Otherwise registration is refused, against which there is right of appeal.

Can modifications be registered?

YES! Further application may be made either to register a modified version of a previously registered design, or to obtain further registration of a previously registered design so as to apply it to a different type of article from that covered by the original registration.

How long does registration take?

Registration should normally be completed within six months, although a total of **twelve months** (extendable to **fifteen**) is allowed for an application to be put in order.

What will the Patent Office charge me?

The Patent Office charges fees for processing applications and in most cases this need only be the filing fee. If you wish to keep the registration in force after the initial five-year registration period, fees have to be paid for each succeeding five-year term.

Is timing of an application important?

YES! But as with the patents there are no hard and fast rules. Early filing of an application establishes your priority over others, but it may be commercially desirable to delay your application.

Does a UK registration give protection abroad?

NO! A UK registered design is effective only in the UK and the Isle of Man. However, some countries accept registration of a design in the UK as equivalent to an independent registration in the countries concerned. Otherwise the UK application can be used to establish a priority date for a separate application made in a foreign country.

Does the Designs Registry provide any other services?

YES! The Registry will conduct a search (on payment of a fee) to determine whether a design resembles a registered design. This is distinct from the search conducted as part of the processing of a registered design application.

- Note: Any person not familiar with the procedure of submitting an application, can obtain further information by contacting the Patent Office, or engage the services of a chartered patent agent.

What is a design right?

Design right is a new Intellectual Property Right which applies to original, non-commonplace designs of the shape or configuration of articles. Design right is not a monopoly right, but a right to prevent copying, and lasts until **ten years** after the first marketing articles made to the design, subject to an overall limit of **fifteen years** from creation of the design. A design right is a property which, like any other business commodity, may be bought, sold or licensed.

Do all designs qualify for design right?

NO! The design must be of the shape or configuration of an article; in other words, two-dimensional designs, such as textile or wallpaper designs, will not qualify, although these qualify for copyright and possibly registered design protection. In addition, the design must not be commonplace; in other words, well-known, mundane, routine designs will *not* acquire design right.

Who can obtain protection through the design right?

In general, design right protects designs created by nationals, residents or companies of the European Community, and designs created by nationals of New Zealand and the UK colonies.

Do I have to apply for design right?

NO! Design right is like copyright in that the protection arises automatically when the design is created. However, it may be wise to keep a note of when the design was first recorded in material form and when articles made to the design are first made available for sale or hire. This information may be useful if someone challenges your rights in the design or if you believe someone is infringing your rights and you wish to take the alleged infringer to court.

What protection does design right give?

Design right is an **exclusive right** for **five years** after first marketing and then becomes subject to licences of right for the remaining five years of its term. This means that, in general, during the first five years, design right is infringed by any unauthorized making of articles copying the design and by unauthorized trading in such articles. The design right owner has the right to take civil action in the courts seeking damages, an injunction or any other relief available to plaintiffs for the infringement of a property right. During the final five years, **anyone** will be entitled to a licence to make and sell articles copying the design. However, the rights owner will not be obliged to make design drawings or know-how available to the copier.

Are there any exceptions to design right?

YES! Design features enabling one article to be functionally fitted or aesthetically matched to another article get no protection. These so-called must fit and must match exceptions have been provided to ensure that competing designs for spare parts cannot be kept out of the market. These exceptions mean that competitors cannot be prevented from copying any features of a protected design which enable their own design to be connected to, or matched with, existing equipment designed by someone else. However, competitors will infringe design right if they copy features of a protected design where there is no need to do so.

What about semiconductor chips?

Designs of semiconductor chips will get design right protection. But in order to comply with a European Community Directive, the exclusive rights in semiconductor chip designs will last for the full ten years in the market. In other words, licence to copy will not be available during the last five years of the term.

Does the design right give protection abroad?

NO! Design right is effective *only* in the UK. Protection *may* be available in other countries under, say, a petty patent or registered design system, but usually any protection will not be given automatically and must be applied for.

Are there any other forms or protection for designs?

YES! If the design is technically inventive it may well qualify for up to **twenty years monopoly protection** under the patent system. Or if the design has eye-appeal it may be eligible for up to **twenty-five years monopoly protection** under the registered design system. Design drawings and graphic designs may get copyright protection.

'Making your "Mark" will depend upon the quality of "Service" that you give!'

HC

CHAPTER 12

Registered trade and service marks

What is a trade mark?

It is an identification symbol which is used in the course of trade to enable the purchasing public to distinguish one trader's goods from the similar goods of other traders.

What is a service mark?

It is the same sort of mark as a trade mark, but applies to services rather than goods.

Are all trade marks and service marks registrable?

NO! It is not possible to register a trade mark or service mark which consists of, or is confusable with, words and/or other symbols which other traders may reasonably want to use in the course of their business. Nor can you register a trade mark or service mark which would be likely to confuse or deceive the public about the nature of the goods or services.

Do any further conditions have to be satisfied?

YES! The trade mark or service mark must not conflict with a trade mark or service mark already registered in respect of similar goods or services.

What rights do registered trade marks and registered service marks bring?

The exclusive right to use the trade mark or service mark in relation to the goods or services for which it is registered and the right to take legal action against others who might be infringing the registration by using the same trade mark or service mark or one nearly resembling it in relation to the goods or services.

How is registration in the UK obtained?

First, the application for registration is filed at the Trade Marks Registry, a branch of the Patent Office. The application is then examined to ensure that the trade mark or service mark is distinctive, not deceptive and does not conflict with existing registered trade marks or registered service marks.

If an examiner raises objection to the trade mark or service mark, then the applicant may argue his case in writing or at an oral hearing before a senior official of the Trade Marks Registry. If the trade mark or service mark is accepted for registration, it is advertised in the *Trade Marks Journal* to allow others to oppose registration – if there is no opposition, the trade mark or service mark is entered on the Register.

Does a trade mark or service mark have to be in use before it is registered?

NO! Whilst trade marks and service marks which are already in use can be registered, it is also possible to register trade marks and service marks which you intend to put into use.

Can a mark be removed from the register because it is not in use?

YES! If registration of the trade mark or service mark affects another trader, that trader can apply to have it removed from the Register if the trade mark or service mark has not been in use for a period of **five years** during which it has been registered. Another option is **part-cancellation** where the monopoly is restricted by the trade mark or service mark remains on the Register.

Does UK registration give protection abroad?

NO! If protection of a trade mark or service mark is required in other countries, it will be necessary to apply for registration separately in each of those countries.

Can the Patent Office help exploit a registered trade mark or a registered service mark?

NO! The Patent Office cannot provide any financial or other support since this would directly conflict with the Trade Marks Registry's role as an impartial body for the registration of trade marks and service marks.

Are users of trade marks or service marks required to register them?

NO! Registration is *not* compulsory but, without registration, an owner of a trade mark or service mark cannot bring an action for infringement to protect the mark. Suing for infringement of a registered mark is much simpler than launching a common law action for passing off to protect an unregistered mark.

Why are infringement proceedings simpler than passing off proceedings?

In infringement proceedings, trade mark or service mark users can base their case simply upon their certificate of registration. In passing off proceedings, owners can only succeed if they can demonstrate to the court that they have established a reputation in their mark, and that the use complained of a passing off would be likely to confuse or deceive the public. Traders are therefore advised to register their trade marks or service marks where possible.

What uses can registered trade mark or registered service mark be put to?

Apart from distinguishing your goods or services from those of other businesses, a trade mark or service mark is probably the singlemost valuable marketing tool that most companies can have. This and other matters relating to the exploitation of registered trade marks, registered service marks and inventions are dealt with in more detail in the Patent Office booklet 'Exploiting an invention'.

Time and costs involved

On average, a successful application for registration of a trade mark or service mark will result in those marks being entered on the Register at about two years from the date of filing your application (earlier in some cases).

An initial application fee of **£160** to file for your registration. The full service fees under the provisions of the Trade Marks statutory Instrument are listed hereunder and were subject to revision on 1 October 1990. However, all fees appertaining to any registration document should be checked out beforehand.

Form number	Title of form	Fee £
TM No 1	Authorization of Agent subsequent to an application or on request by the Registrar	—
TM No 3	Application to register a trade mark, a service mark or a series of trade marks or service marks	160
TM No 4	Additional representation of trade mark or service mark	—
TM No 5	Request for statement of grounds of decision	100
TM No 6	Application to register a certification trade mark under section 37	160
TM No 7	Notice of opposition before the Registrar to application for registration of a trade mark or service mark	31
TM No 8	Counter-statement in proceedings before the Registrar	20
TM No 9	Notice to the Registrar of attendance of a Hearing	—
TM No 10	For Registration of a trade mark (including a certification or defensive trade mark), a service mark or a series of trade marks	

Form number	Title of form	Fee £
TM No 10 (cont).	or service marks IN RESPECT OF AN APPLICATION TO REGISTER FILED BEFORE 1 OCTOBER 1990	95
TM No 10a	For registration of a trade mark (including a certification or defensive trade mark), a service mark or a series of trade marks or service marks IN RESPECT OF AN APPLICATION TO REGISTER FILED ON OR AFTER 1 OCTOBER 1990	—
TM No 11	Renewal of registration of a trade mark, a service mark or a series of trade marks or service marks	230
	Additional fee under Rule 67	31
TM No 13	Restoration of a trade mark, service mark or a series of trade marks or service marks removed for non-payment of renewal fee – to accompany Form TM No 11	83
TM No 16	Request to register a subsequent proprietor of a trade mark or service mark	
	For the first mark	20
	For every additional mark	5
TM No 18	Request for alteration of trade or business address in the Register	—

Form number	Title of form	Fee
		£
TM No 19	Application to dissolve the association between registered trade marks, registered service marks or both registered trade marks and registered service marks	17
TM No 20	Request for correction of clerical error or amendment of application details	—
TM No 21	Request to enter a change of name or description in the Register	—
TM No 22	Application by the proprietor to cancel an entry in the Register	—
TM No 23	Application by the proprietor to strike out goods or services for which a trade mark or service mark is registered	7
TM No 24	Request to enter disclaimer or memorandum in the Register	13
TM No 25	Application to add to or alter a registered trade mark or service mark for the first mark for every additional mark	35 20
TM No 26	Application for rectification of the Register or removal of a trade mark or service mark	35

Form number	Title of form	Fee
		£
TM No 27	Application for leave to intervene in rectification or removal proceedings	28
TM No 30	Appeal from the Registrar to the Board of Trade	31
TM No 31	Request for General Certificate	11
TM No 32	Application to register a defensive trade mark under section 27	160
TM No 33	Request relating to the entry of an address for service in the Register	—
TM No 43	Application for directions by the Registrar for advertisement of assignment of trade marks or service marks without goodwill For the first mark For every additional mark	20 6
TM No 45	Application for the conversion of the specification of goods of a registered trade mark	8
TM No 50	Application for registration of a registered user of a registered trade mark or registered service mark For the first mark For every additional mark	50 6

Other fees

The office of Patents and Trade Marks Integrated Computer System (OPTICS) on-line word search is available for public use, charge at a rate determined by the length and complexity of the search.

Representations of trade marks and service marks in the form of a classified index of devices is maintained and may be inspected free of charge.

How long does a registration last for?

Indefinitely! But renewal fees have to be paid at regular intervals. Registration lasts initially for **seven years** and renewal fees are payable for a subsequent period of **fourteen years.** On 1 October 1990, the renewal fee was set at **£230**, but it would be wise to check first for any subsequent increases.

Are there any other costs involved?

NO! But you are strongly advised to obtain the services of a professional trade mark agent or chartered patent agent whose names and addresses can usually be found in the yellow pages or you can write to their respective professional bodies who will gladly send you a list of their members of which some may be close to your area. Naturally, if you engage their services, you will pay them in accordance with the services they provide. Always ask them to give you an estimate, but better still, ask them for a quotation. Names of those professional bodies can be found in the Appendix at the back of this book.

While on the subject of trade and service marks, I recall having some pleasant dealings with George Myrants of Trade Mark Consultants Co. (address listed in the Appendix). I found George very helpful and responsive to my needs at that time. George is a specialist in this area and has written books on the subject. If you happen to be reading this particular book George, don't be too hard on me – I've done my best!

A closer look at trade and service marks

A service mark is primarily a means of **identification.** It is a symbol which a person or company uses in the course of business in order that his services may be readily distinguished by the general public from similar services provided by others.

To achieve this object it is clear that a service mark must be **distinctive,** that is to say different from anything that others may wish, and indeed should be free, to use in the normal course of their business in relation to the same service. The more descriptive a service mark is of the service for which it is used, or the more the matter within the mark is in common use by businesses providing a service, the less does it tend to be distinctive in the relation to that service. Registration of a mark confers a statutory monopoly in the use of that mark in relation to the service for which it is registered, and the owner has the right to sue in courts for infringement of the mark.

Subject to the requirements regarding distinctiveness, a mark will be registrable as a service mark if it is used in a business to identify a service provided to the public by a particular supplier. The business must be for reward and not merely an adjunct to the trading in goods as, for example, the giving of advice in the normal course of the business of selling goods. Services are internationally classified into eight classes, the class headings of which are as follows:

- Class 35 Advertising and Business
- Class 36 Insurance and Financial
- Class 37 Construction and Repair
- Class 38 Communication
- Class 39 Transport and Storage
- Class 40 Material Treatment
- Class 41 Education and Entertainment
- Class 42 Miscellaneous

Each of these classes covers a wide range of services and it is unlikely any one applicant will provide all the services included in one of the classes. It is apparently well established in trade mark law that an applicant must be trading in, or has a real intention to trade in, the goods covered in a trade mark application. An application for a service mark in respect of a wide range of diverse services in one class will therefore be queried by the Registry.

Some services provided by the applicant may well fall into more than one class and, where this is the case, a separate application must be made in respect of the service in each class.

If the application is made in the name of a firm or company, the application form should be signed by a partner(s) or company secretary or director or another authorized officer. The designation or title of the person signing, should always be stated on the application forms.

Applications may be made either by the owners of the marks or by their appointed agents, which in most cases would be their trade mark agent or patent agent. The servicing of the application must be conducted from an address in the UK.

Where a mark consists of or includes characters other than roman, these should be endorsed upon each of the forms and signed by the applicant or his agent a transliterate of such characters, stating the language to which they belong and their meaning.

What may be registered?

Every application will be examined under three general headings: (a) distinctiveness, (b) deceptiveness, and (c) confusion with other marks (already on the Register or for which application for registration has been made). There are two parts to the Register – Part A and Part B. If a mark is registrable, the degree of distinctiveness in that mark will determine whether it should be registered in Part A or Part B. The protection given by a Part B registration is less extensive than that given by a Part A registration.

Distinctiveness

A mark must not consist of matter which others may legitimately wish to use in relation to their services. The following are not distinctive and thus are not registrable in Part A of the Register - names of individuals, companies or firms (unless these are represented in a highly stylized form); surnames (unless very rare); nearly all geographical names; words which are descriptive of the character or quality of the service and any other matter which should be free for all to use in the normal conduct of their business, such as letters of the alphabet, laudatory words and devices (pictorial marks) which represent a feature of the service or are commonly used in relation to the service.

The standards of distinctiveness for registration in Part B are less rigorous. Marks are registrable in Part B of the Register if, for example, they consist of one of the following:

(i) Names of small geographic locations in the UK except for services which are essentially local in nature, such as plumbing, shoe repairing, taxis, etc. For the local type of service, the names of small locations in the UK will be registrable only if the service is to be provided in an area well isolated from the named location.

(ii) Foreign place names, except such place names will not be registrable in respect of services which are of an international nature, such as banking, import export agencies, transport, etc., unless the named place is of little significance.

(iii) Personal names or surnames, if the surname in both cases appears not more than fifteen times in the London telephone directory or thirty times in a relevant foreign telephone directory. If the service in relation to which the mark is to be used is essentially local in character, as in (i) above, personal names or surnames if the surname in both cases is a foreign one or appears not more than fifteen times in the London telephone directory.

(iv) Words which according to their dictionary listings are descriptive of the nature of the relevant service but nevertheless are not the most apt words to use to describe this nature, or words which resemble descriptive or non-distinctive words but are sufficiently removed from these not to hinder the use of the descriptive or non-distinctive words by others.

(v) Any non-distinctive matter, such as letters of the alphabet, devices, etc., which is represented in a novel manner.

Deceptiveness

If a mark contains matter which, would lead the public to expect the service in relation to which it is used to be a particular kind of service, the mark would clearly be deceptive if used in relation to services other than the kind indicated by the mark. To overcome a deceptiveness objection it is necessary to restrict the services to those indicated within the mark.

Confusion with other marks

Marks are prohibited from registration if they are identical to, or nearly resemble, marks on the Register in respect of the same service, services of the same description or goods associated with the service. Furthermore, where another application has been made in respect of the identical mark or nearly resembling mark for services or goods as above, priority will be given to the applicant with the earliest application date unless the later applicant can establish he has used his mark from a date earlier than the date of the prior application. If both applicants have used their marks before filing their applications, the applicant with the earliest use will be given priority unless both marks have been used for a considerable period of time (normally seven years or more) in which case both applications may be registered so long as the applications are not in respect of the identical mark for the identical service provided in the same area.

Application may be refused in cases where the following appear upon marks

- The royal arms, crests or armorial bearings.
- The British royal crown, British royal or national flags.
- The anchor devices shown on the admiralty seal and the admiralty flag.
- The wings and anchor device distinguishing the fleet air arm and air branch of the royal navy.
- The eagle device and wings device shown on the Royal Air Force badges.
- Representations of the Geneva and other crosses in red or of the Swiss Federal Cross in white on a red ground or silver on a red ground, or such representations in a similar colour of colours.
- Devices or insignia which may be confused with any of the above.
- Anzac, or any words or letters used in such a manner as to be likely to lead persons to think that the applicant either has or recently has had royal patronage or government authorization.
- The word patent, patented, registered, registered design, copyright, entered at Stationers' Hall, to counterfeit this is a forgery (or words to like effect), Red Cross, or Geneva Cross.
- Representations of Her Majesty or any members of the Royal Family, or any colourable imitations thereof.
- In cases where representations of the armorial bearings, insignia, orders of chivalry, emblems, decorations or flags of any state, or any city, borough, town, place, society, body corporate, institution or person appear on a mark the registrar may require justification for their use, or the consent to their registration and use of persons entitled to give it.

- Where the names or representations of living persons or persons recently deceased appear on a mark the registrar may require the consent of such living persons or of the legal representatives of such deceased persons.

Personal search for conflicting marks

On payment of the prescribed fee anyone may search among the classified representations and indexes of trade marks for goods in all classes at the Trade Marks Branch of the Patent Office. The indexes include a classified index of devices, and alphabetical indexes of words occurring as trade marks or parts of trade marks arranged according to their beginnings and endings. The indexes include pending applications as well as those marks already protected by registration. **No indexes of service marks will be available until after the acceptance of service mark application.**

Applications which encounter official objections

If the examiner raises objection to a mark, for whatever reason, the applicant may put forward arguments in support of the mark in writing or apply for an oral hearing before a senior officer of the Registry. If there has been significant use of the mark prior to the date of application, this may be of assistance in establishing distinctiveness and evidence of this use may be submitted for consideration. Otherwise, in some cases, an objection may be overcome by a slight amendment of a mark or of the services claimed in an application. If objections are maintained a written statement of the reasons for refusal of an application may be sought by filing a fee-stamped Form TM No 5.

If the applicant is so minded, he can appeal to the Court or the Secretary of State once he has received the written statement of grounds.

Advertisement of applications

All applications which pass the examination tests must be advertised in the weekly *Trade Marks Journal*. The purpose of this is to enable anybody with a just cause to oppose the registration of any application. One month is allowed from the date of advertisement within which opposition may be lodged. A camera ready copy of the mark must be provided by the applicant (when requested by the Registry) for advertisement purposes except where the mark consists only of a word or words in plain type.

Opposition to registration

Any person who wishes to oppose the registration of a mark must give notice of his intention to do so by filing Form TM No 7 within one month from the date of advertisement of the mark in the *Trade Marks Journal*, or such further time as the Registrar may, on application, allow. The notice must state the grounds of opposition, and the opponent's address for service in Great Britain or Northern Ireland, and must be accompanied by an unstamped duplicate, which will be transmitted to the applicant by the Registrar.

Formal opposition should not be lodged until after notice has been given by letter to the applicant for registration so as to afford him an opportunity of withdrawing his application before the expense of preparing the notice opposition is incurred. Failure to give such notice will be taken into account in considering any application by an opponent for an order for costs if the opposition is not contested by the applicant.

Registration

When an application has been advertised in the Trade Marks Journal, and either the prescribed or extended period has elapsed without opposition being entered, or such an opposition has proved unsuccessful, and when all the conditions precedent to registration have been complied with, the mark will be entered on the Register on payment of the registration fee. Certificate of registration will be issued to the applicant without request. The effective date of registration is the date of receipt of the application.

'Information is only as good as your ability
to use it wisely.'

HC

CHAPTER 13

The Patent Office Search and Advisory Service

It is only natural and quite common for any person, be they experienced or otherwise to forge ahead with their brilliant idea, whilst fired with enthusiasm, without firstly checking for **originality.**

Obviously, the many who do not bother to check for originality when setting out will usually achieve nothing more than problems. Those problems will often lead to depression, especially whenever they realize that they have wasted considerable time and other financial resources.

However, much will depend upon the concept that you're developing, and I advocate that everyone should closely examine the commercial aspects, *before* spending hundreds in obtaining searches from the Patent Office. Try to discover whether or not your idea or concept is worth exploiting in any commercial sense: after all, why go to all the bother and expense of carrying out searches if, in the cold light of day, your concept would not be worth more than a row of beans? It may well transpire that no one else has bothered to obtain a patent on your idea before, simply because they have identified that either no market exists for such a product, or perhaps the development and production costs would far outweigh any financial returns. In other words, you may have something that is original but far too costly to exploit commercially.

Therefore, before you start getting excited spending hundreds on searches, try to analyse your concept in a **business sense**. Even if you fool yourself into believing your concept is worth exploiting, you may not be able to fool others, especially if you have to rely upon their capital and other resources to make your dream come true! So, first of all, be honest with yourself, and, if **you** are having trouble wondering how your venture could earn you any money, then it may be worth thinking again and directing your energies elsewhere – your next 'brilliant idea' or invention, for example!

Let's assume that you *have* convinced yourself that whatever you have conceived would have a ready market and you have **identified** that market which has inspired you to proceed a stage further. The obvious next step would be to contact the **Search and Advisory Service** of the Patent Office. You can do this either by direct approach to the Patent Office, or alternatively you could commission a registered patent agent to carry out the necessary searches through the Patent Office system, on your behalf.

Whichever course of action you take, the Patent Office Search and Advisory Service, can provide the information that you require, and assist you in a similar professional manner that you would expect from a patent agent. Today, the Patent Office has over 300 highly qualified staff, each a specialist in a particular area of technology, and each having a wide experience in both searching and in general patent matters.

The Patent Office has a database of about four million documents, with some fifty qualified examiners with experience in search and evaluating the results obtained from manual and on-line trade and service mark databases.

Your search would be carried out by an experienced Patent Officer, specifically trained in this field of knowledge. So, whatever your problems, the Patent Office will have the experienced staff available to deal with your queries, either by post, or invariably on a one-to-one basis. Naturally, the professional code of conduct will prevail at all times; therefore, your details will be treated in confidence.

The search results can be evaluated by an examiner, and copies of relevant patent documents supplied. This service is completely independent of the filing of an application for patent protection.

The costs

The precise cost of carrying out your search will depend upon several factors, mainly the **time** it takes to scan databases and other reference libraries, also the **number** of databases you wish to scan (in other words, how extensive is the scope of your search; is it just UK or international?)

In order to save on costs, I would strongly recommend that any person wishing to avail themselves of the Patent Search and Advisory department, should make their minds up on the scope of the search required. But more importantly, you must be able to explain in simple terms exactly what information you require, which obviously must be well supported by the nature of your inventive endeavours. In other words, it's no use telling the researcher minor snippets of your dream - how the hell are they going to start scanning databases for information on your dreams without having all the facts! Therefore, if you wish to keep your costs reasonable, help yourself by helping the researcher: give them all the relevant details of just what it is you have dreamt!

However, as a rough guide, searches attract a standing charge of **£20** (bibliographic search) or **£40** (subject matter search). To this are added on-line charges for each database (around £3 per minute) and, where appropriate, database print charges would be added. Full details, including costs for evaluating search results and for supplying copies of patent documentation, are available upon request, by contacting the Search and Advisory Service. Meanwhile, a straightforward UK search only would probably cost **£100** (1991) or about £1,000 for an international search.

If you are making a search direct to the Patent Office, they will need to know the following information:

- Your full name
- Your address
- Your day-time telephone number
- A fax number or telex (if any)
- Details of the search request
- Scope of search (i.e. which databases) (if you prefer, the searcher can select the databases appropriate to your requirements)
- Whether you want the results posted, telephoned or faxed, or whether you wish to collect them in person.

Time it takes

The Search and Advisory Service aims to process requests for the service within **48 hours**, but obviously this may take longer depending upon the circumstances. However, if you make a personal call to their office, they will make every endeavour to provide the results that same day. Naturally, if you are proposing to pay them a personal visit, do not call into their office at say 2 pm and expect instant action. It would be worth speaking to someone the day before you arrive, so that you and they are prepared.

Terms and conditions

The following are the Patent Office terms and conditions for
providing on-line structure search services.

All customers who commission the Patent Office to perform
one or more of these services, do so subject to these terms and
conditions, and shall be deemed by the act of commissioning,
and therefore will be contractually binding.

(1) Whilst the patent office takes every reasonable care in the
provision of its services, it does not 'guarantee' the accuracy
of its Publications, Data, Records or Advice. Nor does it
accept any responsibility for errors or omissions or their
consequences.

(2) The Patent Office makes every effort to perform its
services as advertised and within a specified period. It does
not, however, guarantee to do so in all circumstances. The
Patent Office reserves the right to amend, extend or withdraw
without notice any search or allied service not required by
statute.

(3) All copyright subsisting in the search results and all other
matter is reserved, and multiple copies may not be made
without the express written permission of the Patent Office.
Copyright in search results obtained by assessing on-line
databases remains the property of the database producer,
whose written permission *must* be obtained for multiple
copying or republication.

(4) The charges incurred will be detailed on an invoice which
must be settled before the search results can be released
(unless other arrangements have been agreed by the Patent
Office). Payment may be made in cash or by cheque, money
order or postal order made payable to 'The Patent Office' and

crossed. Deposit account debits are also acceptable.
Payments, should be sent or taken to the Cashiers Office at
the Patent Office in Gwent.

- Note: Requests for further services will not be accepted
  until outstanding invoices are paid.

Anyone who wishes to avail themselves of the Search Service or
indeed, require some assistance in this regard, should contact the
Search and Advisory Service at the Patent Office in Gwent.

'To enter into litigation you have to be
either rich or insane . . . Many times the rich
end up insane and the insane end up rich!'

HC

CHAPTER 14

Basic 'remedies' against copyright infringement

Owners of copyrights that are being infringed do have several legal remedies available to them. Those remedies are incorporated within the scope of the Copyright, Designs and Patent Act 1988.

Upon becoming aware that your rights are being infringed and, depending upon the gravity of the situation, the first step would be to consult with your lawyer. He may suggest that he, in the first instance, should write a strong letter warning off the infringer; perhaps your lawyer would imply in his letter that legal action would be taken, if the infringement persists.

While this legal tactic may work in some cases, I have my doubts as to whether it would be effective in all cases. For example, it is highly unlikely that your lawyer, or indeed yourself, would have sufficient information as to *who* is actually behind the infringement. Naturally, the source of supply or manufacture would be the first target. It is likely to take several weeks, even months, to track down the perpetrators.

Even if you do manage to locate from where the problem emanates, and your lawyer directs a stiff letter, exactly what is it likely to say that would have the *immediate* effect of putting a stop to someone who is making a fast buck at your expense? Furthermore, it is possible that your copyright could be challenged, in which case by the time your lawyer exchanges letters with the other party's lawyer more time would have been lost, thus causing more financial loss and risks to your own empire.

More often than not, you may encounter a situation whereby you get to hear that your copyrights are about to be infringed, in other words, not exploited on the market as yet, but about to be. In the first example, your lawyer would apply to the courts for an injunction to prevent further infringement. Where the infringement is only threatened, the courts will, in appropriate cases, make a *quia timet* injunction to prevent the infringement ever taking place. Another remedy offered by the courts is the interlocutory injunction which stops an infringement at an early stage, without having to await the outcome of a full trial.

Obviously, in all cases, you will have to prove conclusively to the courts that you are the owner of the copyright, or that you indeed can claim originality on whatever is being infringed. But more importantly, that you have actually taken measures to protect your Intellectual Property Rights. In most cases, you may claim for financial compensation, firstly in the form of **damages.** These will usually be calculated upon evidence of the loss caused to you. The courts are frequently basing damages upon the basis of what would have been a proper licence fee, had the infringer sought a licence for the acts complained of.

Additional, and possibly substantial, damages may be awarded in rare cases for flagrant infringements (see Chapter 24 where I make reference to court case, concerning a Professor Robert Kearns and Ford Motor Company (USA). Professor Kearns won substantial damages, for a flagrant infringement of his copyright, by Ford Motors). Apart from claiming damages, you may also apply for

seizure of all goods that have been copied or manufactured, in contravention of your protected copyrights.

I have mentioned that any infringement of your copyrights would be a **civil** and not **criminal** offence. However in a small number of areas, unauthorized imitation or reproduction of goods *may* constitute a criminal offence. These would include false trade descriptions and the sale or manufacture for sale, of unauthorized copies of books (that pleases me to know), records, films and videotapes (when the vendor or manufacturer knows that the copyright has not expired). If you suspect that a criminal offence has been committed, inform your local Weights and Measures Authority, or Trading Standards Department, or notify the police of your suspicions.

Protection overseas

The word **counterfeiting** will feature in many cases of infringement. Although we usually associate counterfeiting with forgery of currency notes or coins, or indeed other documents such as passports, it does also apply to piracy and the illegal copying of manufactured trade goods.

Counterfeiting affects a very wide range of products – everything from hand tools to talcum powder, with a good imitation of Rolex Watches, can find a way on to the market. It is an offence to import counterfeit goods; therefore, when you are next holidaying in the Philippines, don't be tempted to purchase a Rolex Watch off street traders even though it may be a tempting offer! It will almost certainly be a fake, so if you get caught while bringing it through the Customs, you may face criminal charges. At the very least, your Rolex would be confiscated by the customs officials.

Remember that if you do not protect your product abroad, you will not be able to prevent counterfeits being manufactured and sold abroad. Obviously, if you have a UK patent, or other forms of Intellectual Property protection, even though your protection may be limited to the UK you are protected against the importation of fake goods.

Taiwan has been the major source of counterfeit goods, and presents special difficulties to companies seeking to protect their products against counterfeiting. Taiwan is not a party to many international conventions for the protection of copyright and other forms of Intellectual Property. Nevertheless, it *is* possible to seek protection or redress under Taiwan's patent, copyright and trade mark laws, and where it is considered that there is a risk of counterfeiting, British firms should seek competent legal advice on how to protect their interests. However, for safe measures, and assuming that the risk would be too high for your product to be 'copied' by Taiwan, the simple answer is for you to seek protection of your goods under their own patent systems.

Therefore, designs, patents and trade marks can be registered in Taiwan with the national bureau of standards, and applications should be made through local patent or trade mark agents (not the UK Patent Office).

The UK does not have diplomatic relations with Taiwan, but in cases of difficulty, companies may wish to contact the Anglo-Taiwan Trade Committee at:

4th Floor
Minster House
272–274 Vauxhall Bridge Road
London
SW1V 1BB
Tel: 071 829 9167

If you have any problems with copying or whatever with your products, whether home or abroad, you should contact:

> The Department of Trade and Industry
> Consumer Affairs Division
> Millbank Tower
> Millbank
> London SW1P 4QU
> Tel: 071 211 3000

OR:

> (Name of country, i.e. Germany)
> Overseas Trade Division
> Department of Trade and Industry
> 1 Victoria Street
> London SW1H 0ET
> Tel: 071 215 7877

OR:

> HM Customs and Excise
> General Customs Division B
> Kent House
> Upper Ground
> London SE1 9PS
> Tel: 071 928 0533

OR:

> The Patent Office
> Concept House
> Tredegal Park
> Cardiff Road
> Newport
> Gwent NP9 1RH
> Tel: 0633 814000

Other useful sources of information

Anti-Counterfeiting Group (ACG)
c/o Quilthorn Ltd
2 Lewins Yard
Market Square
Chesham
Bucks HP5 1ES
Tel: 0494 449165

British Technology Group (BTG)
Information Division
101 Newington Causeway
London SE1 6BU
Tel: 071 403 6666

BTG, which combines the service of the National Enterprise Board and the National Research Development Corporation, can provide assistance through its patenting expertise against industrial counterfeiting. It is also currently providing financial support for development work on a wide range of inventions and is definitely worth contacting.

Assistance from British posts abroad

The commercial department of the British Embassy including the High Commissions and Consulates abroad, can often help with counterfeiting problems, and will give advice on the local legal system. However, they cannot take legal action on behalf of British companies in pursuit of counterfeiters, any more than the government can in such cases within the UK.

Legal costs

There is no special form of assistance available to assist towards the legal costs of civil action against industrial counterfeiting at home or overseas. Although legal aid is a theoretical possibility for actions within the UK, in practice few, if any, would qualify, under their financial thresholds.

Summary

Although the Copyright, Designs and Patents Act 1988 is enacted to safeguard our Intellectual Property Rights, the copyright owner must not assume that, because of these protections, they can lower their guard and go about their business without a care in the world. That would, indeed, be foolish. Most laws of the land are there to safeguard the interests of all parties, whether you be the plaintiff or defendant and you would expect fair play. You may assume, however, that your rights are well protected, simply because you have document that says so. This could cause you to become complacent which, in turn, might lull you into a false sense of security.

Any law, no matter how simple or complex, will have to be interpreted by others. Therefore, what you may assume to be a watertight case of infringement may, in the end, turn out to be a costly exercise which you may well regret.

Furthermore, legal costs in such cases of infringement can be quite substantial, so ask yourself if you could afford to fight to protect your rights. If the legal cost of litigation on home territory is likely to be beyond the reach of most pockets, imagine what the costs would be, should your rights be infringed on an international scale.

Despite all the so-called legal 'remedies' that are available, the financial implications and costs of actually having to defend one's Intellectual Property Rights in a court of law, may well prove counter-productive. Or, at the very least, they could act as a deterrent against the average innovator seeking legal remedies to protect their rights!

Personally, I believe governments who issue patent grants should become joint-litigants whenever those rights are being infringed by others. A central fund could easily be established, and perhaps administered by the Department of Trade and Industry; even the Patent Office itself could become involved in the protection of its grant certificates. To some extent, I do appreciate it may be a costly exercise for the government, which would have to be borne by the taxpayer. Nevertheless, the economic well-being of any country must surely rely heavily upon the efforts and entrepreneurial skills of the innovators, who provide the manufacturing industry with its main source of existence.

It is also possible that, a potential infringer who is made aware from the off-start that, infringing someone's Intellectual Property Rights (appertaining only to patent grants or other governmental registrations), would mean not only doing battle with the individual concerned but also with the country that issued that grant, may well have second thoughts, before ripping off the protected rights of others. Maybe, this is only wishful thinking on my part. Nevertheless, it is a subject that should be addressed, by all countries that subscribe to the protection of patent and other forms of Intellectual Property Rights.

Having said my party speech, it will be fair to say that the UK government is making some headway as the following paragraph will testify.

Patent County Courts –
special jurisdiction

In accordance with the provisions provided for in the new Copyright, Designs and Patents Act 1988, patent and design infringements can now be heard in special courts, known as Patent County Courts, which have special jurisdiction under Section 287–88 of the Act as follows:

287

(1) The Lord Chancellor may by order made by statutory instrument designate any county court as a patents county court and confer on it jurisdiction (its special jurisdiction) to hear and determine such descriptions of proceedings

(a) relating to patents or designs, or;
(b) ancillary to, or arising out of the same subject matter as proceedings relating to patents or designs, as may be specified in the order.

(2) The special jurisdiction of a patents county court is exercisable throughout England and Wales, but rules of court may provide for a matter pending in one such court to be heard and determined in another or partly in that and partly in another.

(3) A patents county court may entertain proceedings within its special jurisdiction notwithstanding that no pecuniary remedy is sought.

(4) An order under this section providing for the discontinuance of any of the special jurisdiction of a patents county court may make provision as to proceedings pending in the court when the order comes into operation

(5) Nothing in this section shall be construed as affecting the ordinary jurisdiction of a county court.

288

(1) Her Majesty may by Order in Council provide for limits of amount or value in relation to any description of proceedings within the special jurisdiction of a patents county court.

(2) If a limit is imposed on the amount of a claim of any description and the plaintiff has a cause of action for more than that amount, he may abandon the excess; in which case a patents county court shall have jurisdiction to hear and determine the action, but the plaintiff may not recover more than that amount.

(3)   Where the court has jurisdiction to hear and determine an action by virtue of subsection (2) the judgement of the court in the action is in full discharge of all demands in respect of the cause of action, and entry of the judgement shall be made accordingly.

(4)   If the parties agree, by a memorandum signed by them or by their respective solicitors or other agents, that a patents county court shall have jurisdiction in any proceedings, that court shall have jurisdiction to hear and determine the proceedings notwithstanding any limit imposed under this section.

(5)   No recommendation shall be made to Her Majesty to make an Order under this section unless a draft of the Order has been laid before and approved by a resolution of each House of Parliament.

Any person wishing to have his case heard in one of these special courts can dispense with expensive barristers to act for him, therefore, another saving on legal fees. For the first time in legal history, chartered patent attorneys have been granted the right to act for their clients (in these special courts). Obviously patent attorneys will charge for their services, but would not need the usual legal entourage that barristers enjoy but paid for by their clients. Chartered patent attorneys are in fact legally qualified and specialise in patent law, therefore, who could be more qualified to act for you in cases of infringement?

The presiding Judge will also have expertise in the patent law and the whole process has been 'streamlined' so that innovators who are having their rights infringed, can obtain swift action to prevent the infringement and for a reasonable cost of which I understand could be a fraction of High Court costs.

However, there are limitations to any one claim as section 287 and 288 of the Act sets out. But nevertheless, this legal opportunity is a great step in the right direction and no doubt, this added provision of the law will in the fullness of time, be modified or strengthened, to assist further the innovators and give them more opportunities to defend their Intellectual Property Rights.

For further advice on how to deal with cases of infringement refer to Chapters 20 and 23.

'Patent agents are the midwives of inventors.'

HC

CHAPTER 15

Are patent agents worth their salt?

To safeguard against all eventualities, I would strongly recommend that, whenever you have any doubts as to whether or not a product exists, or whether a patent has been issued, seek the advice of a patent agent. The agent will carry out a thorough search on your behalf. Alternatively, you could conduct your own search by going along to the Patent Office and paying a fee for a search. Obviously, you will have to provide the Patent Office with as much detail as possible, because it can take literally hours in scanning databases or checking through reference libraries. You may find that the fee charged by the Patent Office will be lower than that charged by a patent agent. But although you will have obtained the same information, by the time you have added the cost of travelling to the Patent Office, losing a day's pay in the process, there may be little to gain in the way of saving on fees (unless you conduct your search by post).

At the Patent Office, the staff are highly professional and skilled in providing information, and a complete novice will come away with some invaluable knowledge of the patent system. However, at the end of the day, despite the fact that the Patent Office will furnish you with all the information you need to know and, assuming you are now aware that no patent has been applied for or granted, you still have to submit your own application. Personally, therefore, I would recommend that you make an early appointment to discuss your ideas with a patent agent, whose names and addresses can be found in the appropriate section of the Yellow Pages. Or, if you live in a small community, ask your local Chamber of Commerce to recommend one to you.

Engaging the services of a patent agent will relieve you of form-filling and the anxiety of making costly errors or omissions on the application forms. Agents offer a specialist service in that they are familiar with all aspects of the patent system. Therefore, you can rest assured that your concept will be dealt with in a highly professional manner. With the added benefit of knowing that, apart from the assistance they give with regard to the protection of your rights (in so far as they can be protected), every detail that you reveal to your patent agent will be treated in complete confidence.

Do not assume, however, that, because a patent agent accepts you as a client, you are *bound* to obtain a patent or design right to your concept – this will not be the case. Each submitted application will be judged on its merit and originality by a panel of experts from the Official Patent Office, and your patent agent will have little or no say in the matter once your application leaves his office. But he *can* ensure that your application has the best possible chance of succeeding.

Patent agents will also be able to provide you with engineering or design drawings based on your own drawings that you may have neatly scribbled on the back of a cigarette packet and placed with great pride on his desk. Naturally, if you wish to avail yourself of those services, apart from being of great benefit to you when submitting your application to the Patent Office, those additional fees will have to be met by you.

The question of patent agents' fees will, naturally, feature prominently in your initial meeting. Do not be afraid to ask what it will cost. But do not expect anything other than a rough guide.

Their costs will be directly related to the nature of your particular application, and the services that you require. However, based on their experience, they should be able to indicate the likely costs, rather than looking at you and saying to themselves, 'He looks good for a grand or two'.

When you enter the offices of a patent agent for the first time, you may be over-awed by the display of modern technology. You will observe that most desks are buckling under the weight of communication wizardry that would include computers, faxes, telexes, word processors and telephones by the score, with an equal amount of personnel to operate them. One cannot fail to be impressed, especially when your patent agent receives three very important phone calls when dealing with you; one from Hong Kong, another from Turkey, and one from a chap in Skegness who wants to know if his patent has been approved yet. It's a world which may be unfamiliar – even threatening – to you. Try not to be intimidated, however. After all, everything that you see displayed before your very blood-shot eyes, has been paid for by the keen efforts of the inventor and Ideasman in the first place! To be fair, you do have options. You can either do-it-yourself and pray that you do not make a complete 'cock-up' of your application. Or you can engage the services of a professional patent agent, thereby keeping him in the lifestyle he believes he deserves, trusting that his loving care, and professional attention, will enable you also to eat on a regular basis! Should you wisely choose to use their services, apart from being able to offer you all kinds of other services, many will be able to introduce you to useful connections. And having useful connections is what your game is all about.

If you are unable to find a patent agent in your locality, then write to the Secretary of the Chartered Institute of Patent Agents, Staple Inn Buildings, London, WC1V 7PZ. The Secretary will gladly provide you with a list of their members, at no cost to yourself.

In answer to the title of this particular chapter, I would say ... **'Yes they are!'**

'Secrets are kept for no longer than it takes to hear them.'

HC

CHAPTER 16

Non-Disclosure of Confidential Information

An idea is just another idea: it has no protection under any existing laws. However, you do have certain safeguards whenever you are discussing your personal or business matters that may include your idea under the generally accepted code of **confidential information**.

Obviously, we have to define exactly what is confidential information, and what is open gossip. Much will depend upon the circumstances in which we reveal this confidential information but, more importantly, **to whom**, and **for what purpose.**

For the benefit of this chapter, your idea may not necessarily have any patent protection but, nevertheless, it may be exploitable. Secrets are kept, usually for no longer than it takes to hear them. Therefore, we need to exercise greater caution whenever we are dealing with our ideas. On the other hand, when we discuss our business affairs with, say, our lawyer or bank manager or, indeed, our health problems with our doctor, we do expect confidentiality. How can we be sure that whatever we say will be held in confidence? The fact is, we can't! We can only rely upon their integrity.

However, to gain some protection against others plagiarizing your idea, you would be advised to reveal your ideas under an agreement commonly known as **Non-Disclosure of Confidential Information.**

If you are writing to a company, always find out the name of the Managing Director, and write direct to him or her, marking the envelope 'Private and Confidential' to ensure that the correspondence is opened by the addressee and not the secretary. If you have drafted a well-composed letter, and it sounds interesting enough, you should receive a reply in due course. If you have not had a reply within three weeks – forget them!

Regardless of the person or company you write to, always enclose a stamped addressed envelope. Most will not use it, but it is courteous to enclose one, also, never write to **anyone** in connection with the exploitation of your idea without sending that letter by recorded delivery. Remember to keep all receipts for at least five years.

Should you ever receive a telephone call responding to your letter, never give too much away in your conversation. If they have bothered to telephone you, then it is because they are interested in what could be in it for them! Therefore, tell them only enough to whet their appetite until you receive their signature on your document of Non-Disclosure of Confidential Information. It makes no difference if the voice on the other line tells you he is the Chairman of ICI. Even if he is, politely point out that, until you have received the duly signed document back from his company, you cannot, or will not, reveal in depth, the precise nature of your idea.

Assume that you have overcome the ritual of obtaining signatures to a Non-Disclosure of Confidential Information document, the company concerned would certainly wish to instruct their lawyers to check out your claims to originality. You may have told them, even convinced them, that what you are offering is your idea and, despite the fact that you do not have shifty eyes, lawyers acting for the other side will carry out searches to ascertain that you are no fraud, or indeed have not copied your idea from someone else. If your idea is not original enough for them to take a commercial risk, then I am afraid there ain't going to be no deal, and you don't get to eat for a while.

However, let us look at one more angle dealing with the same issue, and the same company. OK, they write a polite letter stating that their lawyer advises against taking up your offer because, they say, it's not original, and that's the end of it. Or they may write, stating that they cannot proceed because their production costs would expose them to many financial risks, even though they imply in their letter and, indeed, have told you a dozen times at various meetings, that your idea is simply great, and they love it!

Any rejections are bound to bring a lump to your throat, but never despair, many times rejections can often turn out in your favour. For example, several months, or even years later, you are casually lounging about with both feet up on the settee, watching television, when suddenly you nearly choke on your drink. Your idea for a new game show which you had desperately tried to sell to a dozen television companies (all of whom booted you out of their office) is now displayed on your screen for the whole world to see!

So, what's your next move?

This could be your well-deserved lucky break, if you adopted the correct procedure by obtaining their signatures on your document of Non-Disclosure of Confidential Information, **BEFORE** you revealed your great idea. Subject to your claims to originality being proven by you, or acknowledged by the television company, or upheld by the courts, then adopting all these procedures may prove to be worthwhile.

Should any person or company fail to honour that agreement, and you subsequently find out that either they have breached the essence of those terms in which you revealed your confidential information, you may have a good case to sue them for damages.

Whenever you are dealing with your Intellectual Property Rights, act cautiously at all times, even if they tell you that they are a descendant of Moses, get them to sign that agreement, before you become converted.

Never go to any meeting unprepared, or reveal your 'concept' if indeed you have not worked out the final details. Many times, if an over-enthusiastic person has not got his act together, and has to rely upon others to complete the 'puzzle', he will not have sole claim to his Intellectual Property Rights.

If you don't protect your originality all you'll end up with is putting your ideas into someone else's head!

However, you will find that many companies will not sign any documents of this nature. Or, if they do, they would most certainly wish to include a disclaimer which lets them off the hook, should your idea become public knowledge. Other reasons why companies would be reluctant to sign any forms of confidentiality would be to safeguard themselves from having the same idea. For example, let us assume that the company you write to is already developing the same idea from another source of information. How would you react if, directly after your meeting with them, they reveal that your idea is not new, and they knew of it already – or were, in fact, developing it themselves! Would you believe them?

Perhaps you may be extremely lucky to pass the screen test and, of course, it is always possible to earn a fortune from an idea, despite the risks one would have to take when exposing their idea!

When you have an 'inventive idea' that you believe is original but have doubts as to whether it is patentable or even protectable, the safest way of obtaining some protection is by filing for a patent or endeavouring to get some other form or registration. So, make an early appointment to see a patent agent (before you publicly reveal the source of your idea). Patent agents would be able to assess your chances of obtaining some protection, or show you how to develop it further, so that you may be able to file for a patent.

When you are ready to write to various companies, keep your letter brief. Don't go 'singing like a canary' or divulging any technical details, otherwise, if you have told them all they need to know in your letter, you're unlikely to get any signature to your document.

When drafting out this document, or if you prefer your lawyer to do it for you, don't make it into a legal drama by 'puffing' it out in legal jargon. Such a form is likely to go straight into the bin.

In reality, one or two pages is going to be quite sufficient. All you are seeking is their undertaking that, if you tell them your secret, they will keep their trap shut. It's as simple as that. That document has no particular value, apart from the fact that you may be able to sue for damages, should they betray your trust.

In many cases some companies may turn the ball back into your court by agreeing only to sign your document if you are prepared to sign theirs. Be extremely wary on signing, without consulting with your lawyer first.

You may find that their document is legally astute, and drafted in a manner that basically gives them complete immunity from action you may take, should they breach your confidential information. Therefore, you are placing all the trust in them, and getting absolutely no protection in return. There may be a dozen good reasons why large industrial companies are reluctant to sign any documentation. Many companies simply do not like dealing with unknown individuals, probably to safeguard against the possibilities that you, yourself, could be an industrial spy, purporting to be an inventor. Therefore, many of these companies who are involved in 'high tech' or research, will only deal through credible sources, such as established licensing agents, transfer agencies or professionals such as patent agents. You may find that it would be easier to deal firstly with small to medium size companies, who themselves may structure a deal with larger companies.

Whatever the circumstances, always make every endeavour to get your document signed, but at the end of the day, it comes down to a question of trust and I'm afraid that is all you can expect!

Most Non-Disclosure of Confidential Information agreements are likely to be structured in various ways according to whoever is drafting it out. Your lawyer will obviously be the expert in such matters, but because of his legal training and over cautious nature, he/she may go over-board and draft out a 'volume' whereupon, it may prove to be counter-productive, especially if the other party is uneasy about signing such a lengthy document. The recipient may not fully understand the full implications, therefore, it either goes straight into his bin, or to his lawyer, thus creating further expenses for both of you.

The moment you reveal the final details of your brilliant ideas, is the moment when you have effectively lost control! The next phase is being fortunate enough in having revealed your ideas to those with enough integrity to respect them.

Obviously, the whole issue of dealing in a confidential nature, is fraught with difficulties, not only for the innovator, but industry also.

However, for the moment, and until someone can come up with a better alternative (which is not impossible, if a lot of legal thought went into it) the document of **Non-Disclosure of Confidential Information** is all the safeguard you have, unless of course, your concept is likely to be patentable. And if it is, don't take any chances whatsoever, in revealing your Intellectual Property Rights until after you have filed for a patent grant. Even then, still act with extreme caution!

With regard to the actual document that you must get signed by the party to whom you are proposing to reveal your confidential infor-mation, I must emphasize that it can come in many shapes and forms – ask ten different lawyers to prepare such a document and you will receive ten different variations.

I have, however, prepared my own document, thus leaving out all the legal jargon and which the reader may find useful – being mindful also that despite the fact that a one page letter, signed by the other party, stating that they will not divulge your confidential information to a third party may be quite sufficient in many cases, a signed form that resembles an agreement (and in fact is an agreement) may add substance in a court of law, should the other party fail to honour their obligations of that agreement.

The following may serve as a useful guide.

This Agreement: hereafter referred to as **NON-DISCLOSURE OF CONFIDENTIAL INFORMATION.** Made and entered into by:

(state your full name or name of your company)

....

hereafter referred to as the **"OWNER"** (which expression shall, where the context so admit, include his heirs, executors, administrators or assigns) of:

(state your full address)

....

....of the one part:

AND:

(full name of person or company that you are dealing with)

....

hereafter referred to as the **"EVALUATORS"** whose registered address or main operational address are situated at:

(state full address of company)

....

.... of the other part:

WHEREAS

1. The OWNER has invented (or designed) state very briefly what it is you have invented without giving away too much technical detail.

2. The OWNER has/has not filed an application for a Patent or Design registration (but if you have, state date of application and number of your application).

3. The OWNER claims all Intellectual Property Rights to his invention/design as herein described or revealed under the terms of this agreement.

NOW THIS AGREEMENT WITNESSETH as follows:

(a) The OWNER will divulge the confidential nature of his invention to the evaluators for the express purpose of determining further research, evaluating the general feasibility or commercialization of the said invention, or for the purpose of estimating general costs appertaining to the development, manufacture or general marketing of the said invention.

(b) The EVALUATORS undertake not to discuss or disclose to third parties details of the invention without taking every reasonable care that all disclosures will be made only under agreements of Non-Disclosure of Confidential Information.

(c) The EVALUATORS undertake not to use or make adjustments, modifications or changes to the said invention, that would either be in breach of the owner's Intellectual Property Rights or exclude him from monetary or royalty benefits.

(d) To deliver to the OWNER immediately on the OWNER'S

request all documents and any other material in the possession, custody or control of the evaluators that relate to the invention or concept.

(e) Nothing contained in this present agreement shall be construed as an offer or agreement by the OWNER to grant to the EVALUATORS any rights in the said invention or concept.

(f) The EVALUATORS undertake to take such steps as may be reasonable to enforce such obligations.

TERMINATION: The OWNER reserves the right to terminate this agreement by giving ONE month's written notice of his intention – but if the OWNER has not excercised his right, this agreement shall subsist for a period of FIVE years from the date of signing hereof. Thereafter, all parties to this agreement will be relieved of all obligation, save for any blatant breaches of copyright, perpetrated by the evaluators or their assigns.

This present agreement shall be interpreted in accordance with English Law (or Scottish Law if appropriate).

IN WITNESS whereof the parties hereto have signed (and sealed) this present Agreement this _____ day of _____ in the year One Thousand Nine Hundred and (whatever) in the presence of the undersigned witnesses.

Signed by the said:

B. A. OPTIMIST   ....

in the presence of: Inventor

....
Witness

The Common Seal of:
(Name of company if any)

Was hereunto affixed in the
presence of:

....
Director/evaluators

Witnessed by:

....
Company Secretary (or another)

- Note: Despite the fact that many companies may be willing
  to sign your document, as previously mentioned, many of
  the larger industrial companies have a policy of not
  discussing anyone's invention until such times that the
  inventor has submitted a patent application, and received a
  file date. Furthermore, many companies (mainly medium to
  large) will not arrange to see individual inventors,
  irrespective as to whether they are in receipt of a file date,
  unless the initial contact is made through either:

- Your patent agent
- Your trade mark agent
- Your lawyer
- Your technology transfer agents
- Or: appropriate professional bodies.

On reflection, this is a wise policy to adopt as it not only saves
their valuable time in dealing with no hopers, having a third party
involvement may reduce the inventor's risk element!

However, regardless of whether or not you can make your own appointment, or you do this through a link, still make every endeavour to get your Non-Disclosure of Confidential Information signed before you start discussing the full aspects of your invention. Even though you may have a priority date. Some patent agents would argue that it isn't necessary to seek signatures on Non-Disclosure of Confidential Information, after you have received a priority date because that in itself is your safeguard. I maintain that it should still be obtained as it establishes a fact that discussions took place whereupon, at that meeting, you may have revealed aspects of your ideas that may benefit them, assuming they are developing similar projects to your own invention!

Insure yourself against the worst

Everything happens in our lives when we least expect it or at least prepared for it. Therefore, it would be prudent to arrange an early consultation with one of the larger insurance groups and discuss an insurance policy which would give you protection against (not an exhaustive list):

a) Infringement of your Intellectual Property Rights
b) Being sued for breach of copyright
c) The possibility of your own patent grant being
   challenged by another company
d) Your patent grant becoming 'invalid'
e) Non-payment of royalties due to company going bust
f) All other contingencies that may affect your copyrights.

Insurance is not cheap but is essential. However, your policy could be structured around your pocket, and probably the best cover would be for being involved in a litigation case which could set you back a cool £50/100,000 in legal fees. Therefore, you can take out cover against litigation which will cover all your legal fees and incidental costs.

I'm told that premiums can be quite substantial, depending upon the limitation of cover required, but because you are an innovator, you will constantly, even if unwittingly, be dealing in 'murky areas'. Therefore could you afford *not* to be insured?

'Always play fair . . . but make sure you
have the advantage.'

HC

CHAPTER 17

Become streetwise and stay in the game – where to get help

Nothing but doom and gloom!

Whenever we read in the paper that some inventor has made himself or herself a small fortune, not many of us take the trouble to find out how he or she did it, even less are we concerned about the problems the inventor had to overcome before reaching a successful stage.

I have purposely not over-stated the daunting tasks faced by innovators, because, all innovators are by nature 'individual'. Some will sail through quite comfortably, while others fall at the first fence. If the true facts are ever known and revealed to the unsuspecting world, I'm afraid, there would be no individual innovators in this world, and therefore, the world would lose out on their individual talents. However, fortunately, there are always going to be those who are prepared to take risks, mainly because they are not too familiar with what those risks are before they start off, and their enthusiasm is more than sufficient to overcome most fears. Furthermore, many hold the view that just because others are abject failures, that isn't sufficient reason why they should become one also. If you take this positive attitude, rather than concerning yourselves with the failure rate, this indicates a measure of confidence you have in your concept, and in my personal view, that is enough to move forward cautiously.

Perhaps the operative word is **CAUTIOUSLY.** No amount of advice that you can ever give anyone who is fired up and ecstatic about their 'brainwaves' is ever going to deter them from entering this 'battleground'. And we, the consumers, should be proud that, there are those who are prepared to risk all for our benefit. Therefore, far from lecturing them on the obvious dangers, we should offer them as much support as they need. Many times of course, it's not our own money they are using, so why even try and dampen their enthusiasm?

I have to say that I met with a lot of negative attitudes whenever I mentioned that I was involved in writing this book: some enquired 'have you ever written a book before?'

I usually reply, 'well Shakespeare had to start somewhere!' which is sufficient to stifle any further negative comments. Of course, a wise innovator quickly learns never to engage in conversation, or seek opinions that he simply doesn't want to hear. That's why it can be a lonely existence (similar to writers).

The following is not meant to crush your enthusiasm, but we all have to live in the real world, despite the fact that most of us spend our lives trying to escape from it!

The following pointers are not in any sequence of importance nor are they exhaustive. But despite being all negative, any inventor worth their salt should be aware of them.

- Most inventions end up on the scrap-heap.
- Most inventors start off being 'poor' and end up 'poorer'.
- About 80% are likely to lose their homes, and wife (if some get lucky). Sorry Pat!
- The most daunting task is raising capital.
- It could take up to 3/5 years before your concept gets off the
ground.
- Don't bother to become a 'part time' inventor.
- Expect to negotiate for several years with the same company, before a deal is concluded.
- Don't simply rely on anyone's integrity.
- Be prepared to be rejected several times.
- If you get an offer – don't get greedy!
- The world is full of innovators, so get your priority date – before they do!
- Remember, no one will give a 'damn' whether you are a genius.
If your concept has no commercial value, their value of you will be even less!

And this is only for starters!

Build yourself a prototype or working model

The title of this particular section may be fairly obvious and needs little explanation. Nevertheless, there could be many first-time inventors who may not realize the importance of building them-selves a **working model** that will greatly enhance their chances of selling their concepts; especially at the time of demonstrating to the world how it works.

Before I extol the virtues of building yourself a working model, it may be prudent to mention that a **prototype** is really another form of working model but, in order to avoid confusion, it may be best to explain their meaning. Although basically both serve the same purpose, and both are built with the intention of being a working model, a prototype is associated more with mechanical or electrical parts and, as development takes place, modifications can be introduced, up until the time of final test approval.

For the benefit of this section let us assume that the words 'working model' and 'prototype' mean one and the same. Both, after all, will be developed into a three-dimensional, moveable object, constructed for either further testing or, in most cases, a demonstration model built before going on to the next stage of factory production.

Whenever it is possible, and much will depend upon the concept that you seek to develop, it would be good advice to build yourself a model of your concept. It will make no difference whether you have to 'scale up' or 'scale down', the purpose of the exercise is to demonstrate, not only to yourself, but to many others, that your invention can be built, and more importantly, that it works and functions in accordance with your 'blueprint'. You will find that it gives you a great feeling of satisfaction and it is not uncommon to get emotional and want to keep on looking at your model, even to the point of getting up in the middle of the night to admire it and check that it is safe.

If you do not have the dexterity or ability to make your own model, you will need to engage the services of either a model or pattern maker, depending upon the nature of your concept. Naturally, costs will have to be discussed and agreed well before you grant them approval to proceed. In many cases you could find some retired gent living in your locality, and with the skills that you require, to make your model. This not only would be saving on costs but could make some person happy to be involved with your concept. If you are in need of assistance in this regard, place a small advertisement in your local paper. You could be surprised at how many replies you receive.

It is not unusual for an inventor or Ideasman to have the ability to invent without having the necessary skills actually to make or develop the product themselves. After all, you cannot be expected to do everything! The invention or idea is the most important issue; without those there would be no products. How many architects do you know that build the houses they design?

When you have your working model in front of you, you will doubtless feel proud of your own achievements. Others around you will begin to take your endeavours more seriously. Former sceptics will be more encouraging. But once the euphoria subsides, it is on to the next hurdle. Your model, which you have come to cherish, will now have to be subjected to intense critical scrutiny by those with the power either to dash your dreams, or indeed to make them come true!

Project a good business-like image

Regardless of whatever we do in our business or working lives, it is essential to develop and maintain a good self-image. Any image is better than none at all!

Those we deal with tend to judge us on how well, or how poorly, we conduct ourselves in their presence. Consequently, if at times we do not make a conscious effort, say to improve our attitudes, we may be on the losing end of whatever could be on offer. Whether we are applying for a job, or selling our goods, or endeavouring to exploit our invention, we unconsciously reveal much about ourselves by the way in which we conduct ourselves. Our approach will determine whether or not people will wish to deal with us. On the other hand, if we do not like their attitude towards us, we can always tell them to 'off-ski'.

The innovator possibly reveals a lot about himself by the way in which he negotiates with a potential buyer. The buyer will soon establish whether the innovator is likely to be 'an easy deal' or, in fact, 'an easy steal'! The innovator will need to take a little more care and attention in the way in which he conducts his business affairs. It should start at the point of contact, which is usually the letter stage. A tatty letter, written on cheap paper, may indicate an unbusiness-like approach. Therefore, whenever writing to a company about your invention, take the trouble to compose a good letter, on reasonable quality notepaper, drafted in a legible fashion preferably typewritten. Nobody expects anyone to have the talent and phrasing ability of Shakespeare; nevertheless a scruffy, tatty, illegible letter usually finds its way to the bin. However, there is one exception to my last comment, in that perhaps the recipient of a scruffy, tatty letter, in which the author describes in full detail his marvellous invention, may just be excited enough to prompt an immediate reply. Why? The answer is simple. The recipient of your letter may think that you could well be 'easy pickings'. Therefore, get help in composing your letter, should you feel it necessary.

Always attend interviews in a respectable manner, which means not turning up sporting a 'five o'clock shadow', or as the yuppies would say, 'designer stubble'.

I am sure you are now probably saying to yourself, 'What's it to him how I act, or how I dress?' And, 'It's none of his business how I write my letters, or what I write them on'. You will probably conclude by saying, 'I'll do as I damn well please. After all, it's a free country and, hopefully, we are still living in a democratic society'. I could not agree with you more. It is a free society and it is your choice entirely as to how you choose to conduct yourself. But, my advice remains, 'Get smart – and stay in the Game!'

Consider franchising your concept

If you have had many unsuccessful attempts of selling your idea and are getting quite exasperated, especially when you are so convinced that your concept has great marketing possibilities, then see whether you may have some chance of getting into the **franchise market**.

Many will tell you that franchising is a specialized field but, although you do need marketing skills to get started, once you have overcome the co-ordination problems, the rest is reasonably easy to handle. Naturally, you will need to have a concept that lends itself to the franchising type of business and the best possible way of finding out is to ask yourself whether or not you would be interested in taking on an area franchise if someone offered you the chance, assuming he was the inventor of your concept!

Many **Small Firm Centres** offer excellent advice and guidance in this regard, with the possibilities of assisting you with the capital that may get you started.

Obviously, my comments on this subject are very brief – designed only to 'plant' ideas into your head. There are excellent books and magazines on the specific subject of franchising and if you think that your concept may be an acceptable way of exploiting it in this manner, then get down to your local newsagents right away and seek out the magazines that deal with this subject.

There are dozens of new franchising businesses being started each week and if you look in your local or national papers, you will probably note that some company or other is advertising some franchise or other. Therefore, go along to one of their meetings in the pretence that you are interested in buying into the franchising business. I bet within half an hour of listening to all their sales chat and 'hype' you will come away with as much if not more knowledge on franchising than the sales person dealing with you. You will soon realize that everyone with products that are not even innovative are getting into the act of franchising. It is now 'big business' and perhaps franchises flourish more in recessionary times when many are laid off work and use their redundancy payments to get into anything that will make enough money to pay their rent and keep their family together.

Obviously, if you came to me for advice on 'buying' a franchise, I would have a completely different story to tell you. There are so many 'cowboys' in this growth industry and those who are seriously contemplating getting into this type of business need expert advice, well before they pay one penny! Equally, there are dozens of franchisers on the circuit that are professionally managed and organized by experts and your local bank will usually have the management expertise to guide you.

I have mentioned before, the government assisted **Small Firms Centres** are set up throughout every region in the UK. These Centres are run and operated by the **Department of Employment**. Therefore, the chances are, your local Employment Exchange or Job Centre will direct you to the nearest one where you will be given every possible assistance to set up your own business or company. All centres are staffed by business and professional personnel who are specifically trained to help you! So get along to one of those Centres and find out what they can do for you. One day, when you become successful, your country will benefit from your innovative ideas or business expansion. And everyone will have benefited!

I cannot list every Centre here; therefore, should you need their assistance, they do offer a free telephone service (for information to your nearest centre only):

Dial 100 and ask for 'Freefone Enterprise'
OR:
If you prefer to write contact:
Small Firms Division
Department of Employment
Steel House
Tothill Street
LONDON SW1H 9NF.

- Note: The Small Firms Centres also provide free business booklets as follows:

Starting and running your own business

How to start exporting

Franchising

Marketing

All booklets give you a great insight into starting and operating a business and offer excellent reading coupled with sound business advice. It would be wise to get your free copies as soon as possible!

If you need to know more about franchising there are several good magazines obtainable from your local newsagency, or you could contact the:

British Franchise Association
Franchise Chambers
75A Bell Street
Henley-on-Thames
OXON RG9 2BD
Tel: 0491 578049 or 0491 578050.

Government Innovative Centres and assistance

Raising capital or getting development assistance will prove to be the most frustrating part of an innovator's life. Many individual innovators who are involved in high technology or research will experience cash starvation, far more than the guy who has invented a new kitchen gadget.

Naturally, the high risk factor involved in projects that require years of research and development are mainly attributable to the chances of similar products being launched by other companies with the same product lines. Therefore, many worthy concepts are abandoned mid-stream rather than continually funding a project that would eventually have limited commercial existence or market impact! Perhaps the chemical and pharmaceutical industries would be good examples of duplicated lines, although they are more than likely to recover quickly their entire development costs from the development of one new 'wonder' drug that would reach world-wide markets.

However, there are many excellent schemes available that are wholly funded by the UK government which are more suited to the small company or individual innovator, and I shall outline a few of these schemes which would come under the auspices of the **Department of Trade and Industry (DTI)**. Meanwhile, it is quite evident that the British government are playing their part in giving support to the innovators of this country by setting up various **Regional Innovative Centres** and **Small Firm Centres**. These centres are operated by skilled technicians who will be able to provide further development support, as well as offering marketing skills. Some concepts also qualify for a government assisted grant but, quite naturally, those who qualify for a grant may have to demonstrate that their concept would have strong possibilities of providing employment for the manufacturing or allied industries. It should not, however, deter any sole individual from seeking their assistance, as the schemes are available to anyone with marketable ideas.

Because of varying economic climates, I would suggest that innovators keep themselves well up-to-date with what the government has on offer as it's quite possible that, by the time of the completion of this book, new schemes which may suit you better have been further introduced. Therefore, to get more information, go along to your local Job Centre or go direct to your regional **Department of Trade and Industry**.

Apart from the technical back-up these Innovative Centres will offer you, they will be able to put you in touch with manufacturers or put you in touch with companies who may be willing to 'take over' the complete development of your concept. Also, you will be among 'friends' who have the same objective as yourself, therefore these centres are well worth getting involved with.

Your local government authority

You would not be wasting your time by going to see your local authority. They would be eager to attract any kind of new business or industry into their area, and therefore, they would know of any government assisted innovative schemes. Alternatively, they would certainly point you in the right direction. So it's worth a try!

Chamber of Commerce

If you are not a member of your local Chamber of Commerce, don't let this deter you from seeking their advice. Your local Chamber will know what's going on in their territory and invariably will be able to guide you or perhaps put you in touch with some of their members who may offer financial assistance development expertise. Sometimes, it pays to keep your business 'close to home' and deal with established companies or businessmen in your immediate areas. So it's worth a try!

Small Firm Centres

There are hundreds of Small Firm Centres throughout the UK. All of these centres offer practical and business expertise. Government grants are also available from these centres to assist innovative schemes. Your local Job Centre would be your contact point. So it's worth a try.

Business and Innovative Centres (BICs)

EC inspired, about seven BICs are currently in operation. BICs are professionally managed organizations which provide comprehensive services to innovative small firms with growth potential, including premises with common services and a range of training advice on entrepreneurial skills, with access to loan financing.
For further information contact:

European Business and Innovation Centre
205 Rue Belliard
2nd Floor
B 1040 Brussels
Tel: 32 2 231 07 47
Fax: 32 2 231 10 16.

If you are in the field of technology or research, the following contacts may be useful.

MOD research

Small Firms Research Initiative (MOD) set aside a large development and research budget for small firms dealing with defence projects: application and further information contact:

MOD New Supplies Services
(Small Firms Group)
Room 318
Lacon House
Ministry of Defence
Theobalds Road
London WC1X 8RY
Tel: 071 430 5851.

The Enterprise Initiative

In addition to establishing various forms of business consultancy to help small business (and innovative schemes) the Enterprise Initiative includes a scheme of **Regional Enterprise Grants (REG)**. The scheme is open to firms which are located in Development Areas and which have fewer than twenty-five employees. For innovation projects, grants of 50% of the agreed cost (with a maximum) are available to support product and process development. The grant is awarded to a project considered as a whole, and it must be deserving on that basis. However, patent costs, including those of obtaining patent searches, are eligible for support as part of the overall package, as are the costs of registering trade or service marks or industrial designs. These grants are not automatic, but the application forms are simple and streamlined.

For details of these grants and the area they operate from, and also any other grants or business schemes available, it would be advisable to get in touch with your regional office of the **Department of Trade and Industry**.

Although most business and innovative support schemes are run by the Department of Trade and Industry there are other government sponsored schemes available together with several private support groups; so check them all out and find the best scheme or assistance that suits your circumstances.

Technology transfer agents

Regional Technology Centres form a national network of centres which assist in the transfer of new technology from the research field to manufacture. They offer industry easy access to information about the latest technology and offer a training consultancy.

For further information contact:

> The Director
> H2 Room E/601
> Training Agency
> Moorfoot
> Sheffield
> Tel: 0742 703740.

British Technology Group (BTG)

This group now licenses scientific and engineering products to industry and provides finance for the development of new technology. BTG offers finance to companies on commercial terms who wish to develop new products and process based on their own technology. Through its industrial project finance, BTG can provide up to 50% of the funds required for the development and launching of a new product, and will expect to recover its investment by means of a percentage levy on sales of the resulting product or process.

For further details contact:

> British Technology Group
> 101 Newington Causeway
> London SE1 6BU
> Tel: 071 403 6666.

British expertise in science and technology (BEST) database

This database enables companies with a technical or scientific problem to locate experts in exactly the right field to help them to find a solution. The search can be made nationwide and usually takes less than fifteen minutes. Contact the Director of Marketing and Service for costs related to services required.

For further details contact:

> Director of Marketing
> Longman Cartermill Ltd
> Technology Centre
> St Andrews
> Fife KY16 9EA
> Tel: 0334 77660.

The National Reference Book

The government's Small Firms Service provides a free information and signposting service to **anyone** starting or running a business via Freefone Enterprise. Dial: 0800 222999.

Furthermore, the need for a quick and accurate response to telephone enquiries has led to the (UK) government to develop a computerized **database** containing the information sought by business proprietors and those advising them. All information is now available on diskette which is called the **National Reference Book.**

Database contents

The National Reference Book has over a hundred subject headings. There are three main sections within each heading:

- Useful contacts;
- Information on the subject;
- Publications by the Small Firms Service and others, including leaflets, other reference sources and suggested reading and training information.

Access

Access to the information is straightforward. Each subject has its own self-contained page and can be accessed by page number, page title or keyword.

The package

The National Reference Book is available as a package comprising:

- A system disk containing software;
- 5¼ inch or 3½ inch diskettes containing the current edition of the database;
- A short user guide.

The package is for use with any **IBM or IBM compatible micro with a hard disk.**

Payment and Service

The database is offered on an annual subscription. In addition to the initial package, subscribers will receive three quarterly updates in the first year. Thereafter an annual subscription entitles the recipient to quarterly updates. There is also a central enquiry point for subscribers to contact first, if they have any queries, on the system operation of data.

- **Note:** All items are Crown copyright.

To get your information:
Telephone Freefone Enterprise on 0800 222999.

What more can your government do for you? So get on that telephone and take everything they offer!

Private innovative centres

Technology transfer agents – a word of warning

There are a number of privately operated agencies which seek to 'marry' together innovators with companies who may offer to take on licences or provide further development capital, or indeed, purchase the exclusive rights of someone's idea or concept.

Banks or large firms of accountants can often arrange deals between their clients and the innovator; therefore it costs very little to write to some accountants in your local area or ask your own bankers if they have any contacts they could put your way.

There are various companies dotted about the country that offer a full service but, because they are not government funded, they operate like any other business, and invariably they will have to charge the client for the service they provide. (The genuine companies charge only upon results!)

Because they are privately operated, the innovator must be **exceptionally cautious** and deal only with well-established companies. Furthermore, there are some operators who rip off the gullible innovator or, at the very least, charge him excessive fees for absolutely no result whatsoever.

I am afraid that the over-enthusiastic inventor, who perhaps is unaware that these sharks exist, may fall easy victim and become just another sucker for these sham organizations. As much as I would like to expose these bastards, I do have to exercise some caution for legal reasons.

However, perhaps an indication as to their honest motives could be identified whenever they ask you for a large up-front payment to cover their administration charges. Do not give them a penny until they have proved themselves by either doing some in-house development (should this be needed), or by actually introducing a buyer for your concept, and I don't mean just an introduction, but a serious offer by a willing, ready and able buyer.

Some of these 'sham' companies will give you all the 'bullshit' under the sun by telling you that they have worldwide connections who are just waiting to get hold of your invention. All they do is get you so hyped up into believing these phoney tales that you simply cannot resist writing out a fat cheque. Your cheque will soon be put to good use in paying for the rent on their prestigious city offices which, incidentally, are easily located to safeguard you becoming lost.

When you enter their offices you get the feeling that the place is 'buzzing' with action. But do not be fooled, the excitement that you sense has been well-orchestrated by them, due to having another potential victim on their premises. Do not let that victim be you!

The fees to cover 'administration' could be anything from a few hundred to perhaps a few thousand pounds. Much will depend upon their perception of you, once you are snared into their net. However, even if they only ask for a couple of hundred, sometimes this is a ploy simply to get you hooked. Once you are on their books, it may be a question of making regular payments which could quickly accumulate into the thousands, and you still may not have received anything more than hope and false promises from these merchants. Possibly, hope and false promises are all you are likely to get for your money.

From time to time you may receive a written report stressing the lengths to which they have gone, to introduce your concept to a dozen or so nameless companies, and telling you that they have some very encouraging feedbacks, again not revealing the names of those interested parties. You may regard their report as being highly encouraging, and feel they are doing a great job and that the fees you have paid them so far have been certainly well worth the money. But hold on a minute! What the hell have they actually given you, apart from a couple of encouraging reports which, incidentally, you cannot prove or disprove, simply because their company policy will not permit them to reveal the 'identity' of their clients?

You may also find that these companies are forever changing their staff. It is quite possible that this is because they do not hold themselves liable should their staff give you a load of 'waffle'. So they have a change of staff every so often to cover themselves in this way.

Furthermore, you may notice that none of their glossy brochures actually mentions any fees whatsoever. I find this highly suspicious. At least we know how much it is likely to cost us for a train journey, but it seems some of these companies can 'take us for a ride' and we won't know the full cost until we finally arrive at our senses!

You will hear them say things like, 'We think you are going to become a very rich man'. But, of course, they do not actually mention that they will be instrumental in making you rich! Then they may go on to say, 'As you know, we have worldwide connections'. It may only be hype to sustain your enthusiasm. They go on to say, 'We feel confident that we may get an offer'. But they do not mention just when this will happen. If they come back with an offer of £100, that would let them off the hook. Do not be over-eager to withdraw your cheque book but, if you do, then you will hear, 'Well, the next stage of the game is for us to get your "concept" evaluated by one of our "panel" of experts!' In fact, what this could mean is, 'We'll get our tea-lady to give it the "once over" before she goes home!'

Then they may go on to say, 'When it's evaluated by our "experts", they have to write out a "report" which is then sent over to our head office in America (or they may name some other foreign, far-away country), who will carry out further evaluations to assess the "market potential"'. What this probably means is, 'Look chum, we've got your money and, if our tea-lady says your concept is a "load of crap", then we have to abide by her judgement. And if we have to abide by her judgement, so will you!'

You might have the nerve to ask them just how long all this is likely to take. Do not expect a positive answer. 'Usually about three to six months, or possibly longer', they may reply, giving you the impression that the fee you have paid over is going to be good value, considering the long period in which they will be working on your behalf! Therefore, if you find yourself being asked to pay a hefty up-front payment, get out of their office quickly.

Let me give you another piece of advice which may be worth remembering. Let us assume that the up-front payment is either not asked for, or dispensed with after you have refused to pay. They have already told you that their head office is in America or some other far-away country. What would be the situation if you went along with a great idea (maybe you have filed for a patent in the UK but nowhere else). How do you know that, as soon as you leave their office, they will not telex all your great ideas to their head office in America or wherever? In fact, how do you know that they are not funded by their head office simply to plagiarize the best ideas for themselves? The simple truth is that you don't know, and, in fact, may never know! Therefore, you will have to trust in your own instincts.

Whenever we ask a company for the name of one of their satisfied clients, they invariably will say, 'I'm sorry, all our dealings with clients are strictly confidential', which is their way of saying, 'Get lost!' You may notice in their well-prepared brochure that they even mention a dozen or so satisfied clients who give glowing testimonials, but never state their full name, address or telephone number so that you can contact them. For example, they will print things like, 'I have nothing but praise for your company, and your staff are marvellous and have helped me in my success. I will definitely recommend you to all my other friends who have brilliant ideas. Thank you, thank you, thank you! And another thank you from my husky dog. Signed, B. F. (Alaska).'

I doubt whether any of these testimonials are genuine, and one can assume these organizations have a great scriptwriter working on their behalf.

Transfer agents are 'agents', nothing more and nothing less. If your estate agent asked you to pay him before he sold your house, what would be your reaction? If they do provide good service, or technical expertise then, certainly, they would be worth every single penny! But, before you get carried away and let them take your burden over, get the terms of your deal in writing. In other words, know exactly just what it will cost you, should they be successful in introducing a buyer for your concept. But, get in writing the cost of their 'administrative service' – that's the most important issue! Don't always expect them to perform 'miracles', they can only do their best for you. Obviously, if they are going to get paid on results, then they will put more effort into helping you.

There are probably dozens of agencies in the UK who provide a professional and genuine service to the innovator. Some may not be listed here simply because they did not respond to my questions I asked about their charges. However, they have every opportunity to be represented in the next edition of this book, should they care to send those details to my publisher.

Meanwhile, I can only warn you to be extremely cautious whenever being asked to pay sizeable up-front payments to companies who may very well appear to be genuine, or indeed, could be genuine but, because they conduct their business (or imply they do) in other countries, you have no method of checking them out, or even knowing whether they are in operation just to take your money.

Incidentally, you may be approached by an individual or company that operates under the title – 'patent brokers' or call themselves, 'innovative brokers' whatever name they choose to trade under, it is always wise to 'check' them out first – well before you commit yourself in any way. Also, you may wonder how the hell they knew of your invention! After all, all you've done (usually through your patent agent) is submit an application. Their approach may even excite you into believing that the whole world is after your invention. This is usually enough for you to lose all control over your senses: but hold on tight to your senses . . . and your cheque book!

Many of these so-called brokers are searching the various patent applications almost daily for new inventions. Naturally, none is aware of confidential information, until after your application has reached STAGE TWO (search and early publication).

Nevertheless, their approach will usually be in the form of a letter, that says very little, apart from giving you the impression that you've made it! It is always wise to ignore such letters, but if you simply cannot resist temptation, then don't make any visits to their office with your cheque book, and sign absolutely nothing on your first visit. I'll pray that you may be wise enough not to have a second visit!

Furthermore, you may of course receive approaches from genuinely interested companies, who have rummaged through the patent applications, searching for new inventions. In which case the golden rule must be − 'let them pay for all your expenses'.

Don't start taking time off − or spending your money on travelling to see them. If they are genuine, and suggest that you should go and see them − be direct, open and honest and say . . . 'Are you prepared to refund all my expenses?' If they say . . . certainly not! then you may draw some conclusion as to the kind of company you may be dealing with. If they are going to quibble over your expenses, then the chances are, they are not genuinely interested in your invention, or indeed, they may prove somewhat difficult in negotiating a fair deal with you. Most of the time, you will simply have to act upon your own better judgement, which is usually the 'wisest' of options. Making judgements is best only when you have the full facts before you − acting upon hypothetical situations propounded by so-called business experts (including authors) cannot possibly suit every occasion. In short, if I knew all the answers to every given situation, I would probably not bother to have written this book − presumably because I would be a millionaire!

If you still want to 'go private' . . .

The following companies and organizations may prove helpful to those wishing to use private services or agencies. I should mention that I have no financial interest in any of the companies listed in this book. Whether I believe them to be genuine or not does not mean that you should not make your own enquiries and judge for yourself.

International Technology and Innovation

This company is one of the leaders in its field, being a well-established and approved innovative broker and a professional Intellectual Property Rights licence negotiator.

ITI (formally known as International Licensing) offers a comprehensive service which basically means that if your concept is innovative enough and has excellent commercial and marketing attributes, ITI will take it on board and place its extensive services at your disposal. Each concept received, whether 'high tech' or 'low tech', will undergo several evaluation stages before ITI's extensive resources, which include full in-house development and research departments run by highly skilled technicians, are finally offered.

In my view, this selective process is a strong indication of the company's integrity: it is not in the business of giving any innovator false hopes or asking for up-front payments. Obviously, ITI is not a charitable organization, but structures payments with its clients, usually based upon 35% of what it can get from your invention or product. I believe those terms are extremely equitable when you consider that, from the day ITI accepts your concept, your financial burden is lifted off your shoulders.

I must emphasize a couple of points. First, ITI does not pay for any patent or other registration fees. All fees in this regard must be paid by the inventor although the company is often able to introduce your concept to industry at an early stage, thereby shifting some of this expense over to those either interested in exclusivity or licences.

Second, ITI cannot guarantee success – indeed, no one can. It will do its best, which would probably be considerably better than you endeavouring to do it all by yourself.

ITI does not differentiate between concepts it takes on, as it has an extensive register of worldwide clients who seek anything from boardgames or household gadgets to pharmaceutical or health products.

Even if you have only reached the 'visionary' stage, ITI has the in-house technology to develop your vision into a product. But, before you waste its valuable time, be reasonable and adopt a sense of business awareness, as at the end of the day, ITI will need slightly more than your vision and enthusiasm to sell to its clients.

ITI publishes its own monthly magazine aptly called *International Technology and Innovation*. This publication is purchased in over ninety countries and is crammed with information on new product inventions for which the manufacturer is seeking licences throughout the world. It also carries an excellent appointment section. The publication accepts private or company advertising, so if you wish to advertise your concept, or seek a manufacturer or licensee, then this magazine could be useful. Unfortunately, it can only be purchased by subscription (£95.00 for twelve monthly issues), but, with a readership spread throughout the industry and commerce, it may well be worth you, as the inventor, considering.

For further details contact:

Mr Nick Bartman
Managing Director
International Technology and Innovation
Technology House
Risborough Road
Stoke Mandeville
Aylesbury
Bucks
HP22 5UT
Tel: 0296 614040 (International 44 296 614040)
Fax: 0296 612174 (International 44 296 612174)

The Institute of Patentees and Inventors

The Institute offers an invaluable and comprehensive service to its members. Therefore, if you have a patent, or have filed for a patent, then contact the Secretary to find out what they can do for you. Their address is:
Suite 505A
Triumph House
189 Regent Street
London W1R 7WF
Tel: 071 242 812

Further sources of development and research universities

When ferreting around for more information to put into this book, I fortuitously came across a great guy called Peter Robson, who resides in Jersey, an Island so wealthy it can afford inventors to lounge about all day, thinking up further ways of making themselves rich!

However, Peter is an established inventor, with several successes to his credit, none least his latest brainwave called **Toúac Fastening System,** which is an innovative type of (zip) fastener, which seems to have all the ingredients of hopefully making Peter become famous. I have to admit, being in the company of this knowledge-able man was a little intimidating knowing that he obviously knew the business! After I had convinced him that I was not after his 'crown' and surreptitiously dropping a hint or two that I know a lit-tle about his craft, I sensed that he was more than willing to impart some of his knowledge my way. Now I am not the kind of guy to let good opportunities slip by. And indeed, I milked him to almost saturation point, often wondering why he had never bothered to write such a book, but cautiously, not actually mentioning any-thing, just in case I would give him the 'idea'. This may have been a selfish act on my part, but I figured that he has enough success coming with his invention of the Toúac Fastening System. Whereas, I only have this book to feed me!

However, quite apart from a number of useful pointers I picked up, Peter did mention that he was extremely surprised that I had not bothered to mention the value and benefit of innovators making more or better use of Universities.

I have shamefully, to admit that, had he not muted the thought, I could have easily overlooked this invaluable source. Most Universities have Research and Development departments, usually headed by some Professor or other with scientific or technological skills at their fingertips. Many Universities are renowned for being instrumental in innovation, development or research, and more often than not, if your concept fits in with their own development or training programme, you may find the solution to your many problems, at affordable prices. Or perhaps you may be able to structure a deal whereby the Head or Professor, would undertake the research or development work, for part of your subsequent commercial exploitation.

I am going to emphasize here that, although the University may offer their technical services, with or without a percentage of your action, and despite the fact that they may have been instrumental in solving technical problems with your invention, you still retain your Intellectual Property Rights.

No one, even University Professors, have the ability of solving problems unless they are given problems to solve in the first place. In other words, you may not have the technical ability or scientific knowledge actually to get your concept to work yourself, and the 'boffins' will come to your assistance. But, it was your 'idea' in the first place, therefore, claim the full rights to your Intellectual Property. Obviously, if you wish to share those rights with anyone willing to solve the technical problems, then this is a commercial judgement that you must consider. If you are ever faced with this daunting decision, ask yourself, if half a cake is better than nothing! Furthermore, most Universities are usually closely linked to industry: many of their students are employees of industry, sent to University to gain their degree, therefore, it's more than possible that, if your concept is considered by the University to be a worthwhile concept, chances are industry will know about it and may come with a contract in their hands. Don't be slow in approaching these Universities, just because you consider your concept to be 'low tech': a concept is a concept, if it has commercial value, then you will find that most Universities will be more than helpful. But please, if you eventually become successful after utilizing the skills of Universities, have the grace to acknowledge publicly their innovative assistance. Their government funding depends upon their success, so if you get help, tell your local MP just where that help came from!

The NSP Group

NSP is a unique multi-channel distributor of innovative products. Originally set up by Nigel Swabey in 1981 primarily as a direct marketing consultancy to advise on the creation of merchandise catalogues, it has since gone from strength to strength. In addition to direct marketing, they distribute, promote and sell merchandise through mail order, retail and the sales promotion industry. Their customer base is far-reaching and varied. Their Central Merchandise Team reviews literally hundreds of products and ideas every month through clients visiting NSP House and at national and international trade shows. Between them they attend around a hundred international trade shows every year and are constantly on the look-out for exciting and innovative products.

If your product, concept or idea is

- unique
- original
- exciting
- innovative
- offering genuine consumer benefit or advantage
- worthy of telling an interesting story
- of good quality, properly packaged

- at the edge in its category
- ideal for use in the promotion market

then contact their Central Merchandise and Product Development Team.

If, in addition, your product/concept/idea could be exclusive to NSP and respond to imaginative presentation then NSP could put at your disposal:

- exposure in over 65 million catalogues
- low cost advertising
- display and promotion in the UK's retail stores and outlets
- access to the world's mail order catalogues and upscale retail chains
- opportunities for consideration in major sales promotion campaigns in the UK
- possibilities of product development funding could be arranged for highly innovative and marketable concepts.

As you would expect, if your product/concept or idea has none of the attributes listed, you are probably wasting your own time and theirs. Therefore, please adopt a good measure of COMMERCIAL AWARENESS before you contact anyone!

Other services used by NSP clients

- Access to unique and innovative merchandise.
- Syndicated catalogues.
- Catalogues created to a brief.
- A full merchandising service.
- Complete sales coverage of retail and mail order in the UK Europe.
- Premium sourcing service.
- Incentive and motivation programmes.

- Consumer and trade promotions.

- Access to over 1.5 million mail order buyers via a wide range of demographic and lifestyle selectors.

- Comprehensive fulfilment service.

- Marketing consultancy.

- Creative consultancy, print brokerage and mail management.

- Retailing.

All these services are supplied by specialist companies with dedicated skills.

If you believe that you have a concept, product or idea that you think would fit in with this multi-organizational company then waste no more time in contacting Clive Beharrell, Judi Fox or Gary Simmonds at:

NSP Group Ltd
NSP House
211 Lower Richmond Road
Richmond
Surrey TW9 4LN
Tel: 081 878 9111
Fax: 081 878 9582

Prestigious awards

Small Firms Merit Award for Research and Technology (DTI)

Organized by the Department of Trade and Industry for firms with less than twenty-five employees and with a good business idea entailing technological innovation. It offers substantial awards up to £50,000. For further information contact your nearest DTI Regional Office.

The Prince of Wales Award for Innovation and Production

This prestigious award is open to anyone attempting to create new business based on a British invention or idea. The finalists are invited to demonstrate their product or process to HRH The Prince of Wales on a special edition of BBC Television's 'Tomorrow's World'. A special award is also to be made for a finalist with less than fifty employees if they are not the winner. Winners will be offered help in reaching production and be allowed to use the Award emblem for five years.

Even the final contestants would stand an excellent chance of inviting interest from financiers. For further information contact:

The Engineering Council
10 Maltravers Street
London WC2R 3ER
Tel: 071 240 7891

How to assess your royalty payments

Having sifted through the list of chapter contents, I bet the reader of this book turns to this section on royalties first. Perhaps it may be the most valuable piece of information you need to know whenever you find yourself around that negotiating table.

I will outline in brief the generally accepted method of negotiating royalty payments. But remember that the system of payment can widely vary according to individual circumstances.

What are royalty payments?

They are another form of payment made to the inventor by the manufacturer or licensee for the right either to manufacture or to exploit commercially your idea or concept.

Why agree royalty payments?

The answer is quite simple. Many inventors usually have a high-valued perception of their concept and quite naturally, they seek the best price obtainable. In many cases, the innovator is quite justified in expecting high financial rewards for his inventive ability and more often than not, those in industry can quickly assess the sales potential, but may not have the capital resources to buy the invention for a 'one off' payment, which could cost them tens of thousands, plus an equal amount to prepare for manufacture and establish the marketing and promotion network.

Unlike the intrepid inventor, the industry has to show a profit and service the needs of their shareholders. Therefore, as much as they would like to give you a bundle of notes and send you on your way, the commercial risk factor will dominate all dealings, regardless of the enthusiasm they may show for your concept.

The industry will be looking more at the high risk factor in relation to the production line, the sales potential, the expectations on sales potential, whether or not they could sub-license out your idea in other countries, the assessed shelf-life of the product – for example, will it have a shelf-life longer than a supermarket tomato?

All these factors and many more, will have to be closely evaluated and assessed by industry, because together they represent a **capital risk**. Many inventors are totally oblivious to the financial risks and huge funding it takes by industry to introduce new products into the marketing system, and invariably they feel somewhat cheated or rejected whenever industry offers them a low royalty percentage.

Likewise many inventors, who are new to the game, wrongly assume that they are the ones who can dictate terms, and soon discover, to their disappointment, that that is not the case. Those negotiating royalty payments with you will have weighed up the 'risk factors' and will endeavour to play fair, perhaps more so if they can quickly identify a possible market sales phenomenon. But I'm afraid this seldom happens and future success will be based upon nothing more than talented guesswork.

Let us assume that you have been offered say 5% when you hoped for at least 10% or more. What would be your reaction if the potential buyer says, 'Look here, the only possible way we could increase your percentage would be if you shared some of our production costs'. If you knew those costs would be excessive or well beyond your financial resources, how would you deal with that likely situation? If you are wise, take what's on offer, unless you have received better offers, otherwise you could probably end up with nothing! Even if you have only been offered say 5% on the manufacturer's sale price, you could still make a fortune if the company that has taken a licence off you, is efficient, financially well-structured and perhaps have worldwide distribution networks.

Many times, royalties, spread over a number of years, can achieve far greater wealth for the inventor than a deal that has limited product exposure. After all, you have this monopoly right for **twenty**

years, therefore, try to place your concept with a company that is geared to long-term expectations, rather than dealing with one that may not be around long enough to honour their obligation to you.

Calculating a royalty percentage

Oddly enough, there are many innovators who are quite confused on the actual percentage they should aim for, and many have been all the more confused when they read misleading articles in the national papers claiming that some inventor has become a millionaire overnight.

I am sorry to say this is a gross distortion of the true facts and I have yet to establish how such good fortunes could ever happen to anyone in the field of innovative technology. As I have already outlined, the industry will act cautiously to all new innovations. Regardless of how brilliant an invention may be, it still has to be manufactured, promoted, distributed, and finally sold in the shops. That takes much longer than it takes to read one of these articles: many months of preparation, even years before we witness the launch of a new product. Even then, assume you are on say a 5% royalty, which returns you twenty pence on each unit sold, you would need to sell five million units of your product in order to make your one million.

Now I am not implying that is impossible, but not many manufacturers would be able to gear up to this high volume stage, by the time the journalist had finished his glass of sherry in Fleet Street. I suppose it makes great headlines, and certainly opens the bank vaults to that inventor. But in reality, miracles do take that much longer.

The royalty payment is usually based upon a percentage of the company's selling price 'not the retail selling price'.

However, it can get confusing (unless your contract specifically states otherwise). Often a company will be in a high volume business; therefore, his buyer will be looking for large discounts which invariably have a reducing effect upon profit margins. So make sure that your agreement states quite clearly and in simple terms that your royalties are based upon either the **manufactured units**, or, if you are not dealing directly with a manufacturer, but another party such as a distributor, then it's going to be based upon a percentage of their sales. However, all companies like to keep agreements straightforward and simple and I would advise that you don't get too clever, whenever you are negotiating your deal.

Once you have successfully thrashed out an equitable royalty payment, you will like to know how quickly you can start getting some payments. Sometimes, you may be lucky enough to negotiate what is generally called, 'pre-production payment', which is a fancy name for an advance. Advances are based on the expectations of the future sales; therefore, you will not come away with a large fist full of cash until those sales are generating, and the company that you are dealing with can see a steady return on their investment capital. However, in most cases, you will be able to get an advance, especially if you have a potentially saleable product and, in many cases, this may be arranged in the form of regular monthly payments, which would obviously constitute advanced royalties, at least until the sales income gains momentum.

Remember that, whenever you are negotiating your deal which involves the payment of royalties, make absolutely sure that you have a clause in your contract, stating the specific date for that company to start production. One hears of dreadful tales about inventors who, in their eagerness to tie up a quick deal, forget to ask or insist upon the date of production. More often than not, if it's not specified, the company that you negotiated with may not wish to start manufacturing your idea for several years.

Furthermore, the inventor must always be alert and make sure that he is dealing with a company who can weather the recessionary storms. In such cases, it's wise to take out some insurance against the company that you deal with becoming another victim of hard times. Better still, always try to get an advanced payment on royalties and, indeed, endeavour to get regular monthly payments, rather than the usual twice-a-year payments, so that if the company does go down the pan, you would have been paid *something*. I would emphasize again, that in this eventuality, the invention still belongs to you, unless of course you have sold the exclusive rights. And if you have, this chapter would become irrelevant.

It is somewhat difficult to be more specific when it comes down to what percentage of royalty you should aim for. As a general guideline, if you have invented a product such as a vehicle component which is likely to be licensed out to many car manufacturers, thereby selling millions, the rule of thumb may be between 2 and 3% or even lower. Other percentages may increase to, say, between 7 and 10%, but it's highly unlikely a deal would be safe, should someone offer you above 10%. Anyhow, it's not the percentage that really counts, but the yield of that percentage. So if a company offer you only 2% don't be offended 2% may work out far more than someone else offering you 15%. There are naturally going to be many imponderables whenever you are negotiating royalties and it would be wise to get professional help or at least have a good knowledge of the industry that you are dealing with. But above all, know the sales potential of your product! As a general rule, any individual who has only a 'patent pending' to negotiate royalties with, should expect to receive payment of only 'half' the agreed royalties, with full amount, starting as from receipt of patent grant.

Notice

- If there are more technology transfer agencies (government or private) or indeed any other established organization that can provide services to the innovator and who wish to be included in the next edition, please send your full details and costs or terms of those services provided to the publisher. (The publisher offers no guarantee of publication.)

- If there are any readers who have been ripped off after dealing with any transfer agency, or who paid up-front payments and received no service whatsoever (and can prove that they received no service) then write to the author (via the publisher enclosing SAE.) The author will give no guarantee that he will be able to do anything about your treatment, other than perhaps indicate strong cautions to alert others from dealing with those companies. Naturally, the author does not want to hear 'gripes' if genuine companies acted in good faith, but your concept let you down. Or you were unsuccessful due to circumstances beyond the reasonable control of those who were acting on your behalf. (Please keep all correspondence reasonably brief!)

Lawyers, lawyers, lawyers . . .

It seems that we have no way of escaping their presence.

I mention in Chapter 20 that, although most law firms will be able to advise on all matters relating to the Copyright, Designs and Patents Act 1988, it is perhaps slightly unusual to come across a law firm that does little else but specialize and practise in this specific area of Intellectual Property Rights.

It is pleasing, therefore, to be able to mention one such new firm that offers a comprehensive service to its innovative clients. Georgina Richards LLM, BSc specialized in Intellectual Property law during her studies at the University of London, and was formally a research scientist working in industry. She is therefore aware of the complexities of product protection and deals with the full range of related issues including licences, assignments and infringements of Intellectual Property Rights.

If you need a specialist lawyer to guide you, contact:

Georgina Richards & Co.
Solicitors
Premier House
8–10 Portland Terrace
Southampton
Hampshire
SO1 0EG
Tel: 0703 211600
Fax: 0703 236437

• Note: There are probably dozens more law firms that specialize in this related field and I would be delighted to add their details to my list in future editions upon receiving their information.

'Never place all your trust in an expert's opinion!'

HC

CHAPTER 18

What is someone else's 'opinion' worth?

Indeed, just what are opinions worth and should we readily accept them or reject them? Both questions could be answered quite succinctly; simply because an expressed opinion, whether we have asked for it or not, will either be 'worthwhile' or 'worthless'. The value of someone else's opinion will never be known until we have either accepted or rejected that opinion and, even then, we can never be absolutely sure that whichever option we took regarding an opinion, we have taken the right course of action.

In many ways most of us are guilty of 'being opinionated'. We express opinions on almost every topic, even more so when our opinion has not been called for. How often do we hear ourselves say, 'I don't think much of that', or 'That will never take off'. Both sentiments are usually expressed when we are evaluating someone else's product or idea. In essence, all we are doing is expressing our own thoughts which are usually based on nothing more than our own egotistical notion that our opinion must be right! If, however, our opinion proves to be wrong, we simply shrug our shoulders and say, 'Well it's only an opinion after all', which implies that we are not infallible nor are we to be held responsible for expressing our opinions – it is our easy way out!

The consequences of accepting or rejecting someone else's opinion may drastically alter your circumstances. You may go along with it and still come a 'cropper'. So how are we to assess the value of an opinion? This is not easy because opinions are usually sound judgement and judgement can often be equated with someone's professional, business or life's experiences.

An opinion is not founded on certainty or proof and we can therefore assume that by accepting an opinion we are demonstrating our confidence in the person giving that opinion. Conversely, when we don't accept others' opinions, it is a polite way of telling them that we have no confidence in what they have to say on that particular issue.

In almost every case fate will determine the outcome of an expressed opinion, and opinions should only be regarded as being some form of invited encouragement or discouragement as the case may be. We humans are strange creatures! We almost beg for someone's opinion yet, when it is offered, we rarely take any notice. Even less if that opinion is not what we want to hear or does not accord with our own opinion. Yet we are mortally wounded, and deeply offended, when our own opinion is disregarded. Also, have you noticed that on rare occasions when we offer the 'right opinion' to our family or work colleagues, we never let them forget just how clever we are.

To value an opinion we must firstly value the person giving it, but how do we know that opinion will be well-founded and right for us? The simplistic answer is we don't! But we do have a choice. We can either take it at face value – in other words we can act upon it – or we can take no notice of it. Oddly enough both choices are a kind of positive action.

Opinions are valid only for the time it takes to express them. In short, this means that opinions do have a kind of time factor attached to them.

Let us now look at an example with which most of us will be able to identify. It may serve the purpose of finally exposing the true worth of an opinion and perhaps we may discover that the word 'opinion' was originally created by lawyers to protect themselves against the client for whom they are acting.

Let us assume that your neighbour has built a wall within your boundary and without your permission. Naturally, the first step you take is to try to resolve the problem before going to your lawyer. After hearing all the facts (only yours at this stage), and probably inspecting a plan of the property deeds, he gives you an opinion based on his professional experience. In his letter it probably states that, 'In my considered opinion . . .' etc., etc., and he may indicate that the best way of resolving this matter would be through the courts. You accept your lawyer's opinion and advice to proceed with litigation simply because you trust your lawyer's judgement. After all, he has been trained in the law and obviously knows best – at least better than you do.

The big day arrives and you find yourself in court. Your lawyer seems to give a very good account of the position and you sit back with confidence, occasionally glancing over at your neighbour who is looking distinctly tense – you take this to be a sign that his case is weak. Some time later you think you hear the judge say that he finds for the defendant and awards costs against the plaintiff. You immediately descend upon your lawyer who is sitting close by and say, 'What's going on?' He replies, 'I'm sorry to say we lost the case'. 'We indeed', you murmur! Outside the court you ask your lawyer what went wrong. 'Sorry old chap, it's just one of those things. The other side won on a pure technicality', he proclaims. 'But I based this action on your opinion,' you protest. 'Of course you did, but it was, after all, only my opinion' he says with dignified pride.

You might rightly ask what are opinions to do with your inventive endeavours – in a word, **EVERYTHING!** You have conceived of an invention and, quite naturally, you are proud of your achievement and seek encouraging support from others by inviting their opinions. You must, however, keep an open mind because the feedback from those opinions will be so diverse, simply because each person you ask will invariably view your concept from a different angle. But let us be fair. If we placed too much credence in others' opinions wouldn't life be complicated! Do not, however, waste valuable time in seeking out the opinion of those close to your concept. Members of our family and close friends are far too kind to hurt our feelings by telling us what they really think. Nevertheless, we all need our egos nurtured from time to time and there is no reason why we should not feast on a little adulation occasionally.

Finally, when you are down (and nearly out!), give a thought to Mr Ron Hickman, the inventor of the **'WORKMATE'**. The story goes that Mr Hickman offered his invention to Stanley Tools, a well-established tool company, rich in worldwide products. Presumably one would have assumed that they would have had the foresight to see a worldwide sales potential in the **'WORKMATE'**, but, of course, how many of us could claim to be possessed of such foresight? However, we now know that the Stanley Tool Company rejected Mr Hickman's invention, presumably because they could not perceive the **'WORKMATE'**'s sales potential which now sells universally. Was a decision to reject the **'WORKMATE'** based on someone's opinion? My guess is that it was!

Fortunately Mr Hickman had every confidence in his invention. Being an engineer he must have had a 'gut' feeling that his invention would sell in thousands to those gifted with a trade, and also appeal to the DIY enthusiast. The rest is history. He eventually sold his exclusive rights to Black & Decker, and that one invention made Mr Ron Hickman a multi-millionaire.

I often reflect upon Mr Hickman's good fortune and wonder just what his situation may have been if he had acted upon the advice of those so-called experts. Perhaps you may care to give that some thought also when your 'chips are down', and everyone is expressing opinions that you simply do not want to hear. However, the illustration of Mr Hickman and his good fortune will show that, on many occasions, those we get opinions from are not always correct. Perhaps Stanley Tools may have identified the potential of Mr Hickman's invention but, at the time, had their hands full with other equally important projects. Whatever the case, if you have been turned down a dozen times there is always the possibility that your next attempt may prove successful. It is wise, therefore, to exercise extreme caution before you either forge ahead or abandon your project. But bear in mind this is only *my* opinion – and what's that worth!

'If you ever want to experience levitation
ask your accountant to advise on your
business expansion.'

HC

CHAPTER 19

Get yourself an accountant

This heading may be obvious, but it is surprising how many of us wrongly assume we can muddle through without one.

Have you noticed that the world seems to be full of accountants? If you have, that's a good sign. You, too, have the power of good observation. Most of these accountants are 'nice guys' (their description, not mine), and they do provide a worthy service for the intrepid business person.

Why you should employ an accountant

The advantage of employing an accountant, before you set up in business, should be obvious, but usually isn't.

An eager entrepreneur, fired with enthusiasm and ready to pursue his dream, is often negligent with regard to tax planning and simple accounting methods until it is too late, when he may come up against problems of his own making due to placing too little regard upon detail. It's no use, at some later stage in the game, to realise suddenly that, by adopting a different strategy, tax or VAT could have been avoided, or payment of tax deferred, quite legitimately, if only certain steps had been taken first. It is equally frustrating if business opportunities are lost due to inadequate accounting methods, and haphazard filing systems not providing the information required at the time. Keeping your notes on the back of an envelope is no substitute for personal organization!

How to avoid this state of affairs is relatively simple. Before you go ahead with your business plan, employ a good accountant. Explain your plan to him, including how you intend to finance it, and invite his comments. Merely discussing it with a knowledgeable, uninterested party can often highlight flaws in your plan, that you may otherwise have never considered.

You must, of course, be prepared to pay for his time, so do not waste it. Go to the meeting with all the facts at your finger-tips, taking with you all relevant documents you intend to discuss, including a copy of your business plan, so that your accountant can retain it, and comment upon it, at your next meeting. You must arrange the time of the next meeting at the end of the first meeting so as to provide a deadline for you both to aim for. At that second meeting you will be listening to the advice you are paying for, so take it on board; it is costing you money but it should be money well spent and could well repay itself many times over.

Depending upon your business plan, your accountant may advise the formation of a limited liability company in which to channel that business. Alternatively, he may advise you to operate as a sole trader for the moment. He may also advise you on the possibility of operating a franchise, or even suggest one to acquire. He could suggest various ways in which tax may be minimized, if the business is successful, provided you follow certain paths which he will outline to you. It is also possible that he will suggest how you should maintain your accounting records, and advise on the introduction of a simple accounting system so that, right from the start, you are in command of the mechanics of the business, and are aware of how it operates.

Your accountant should be one of your business friends and confidantes to whom you should turn to ask for advice of a business nature. It may be that he has contacts he could put your way or has experienced similar problems to your own, which he has overcome. His experience is at your disposal, and is cheap at the price – especially when compared with the cost of 'going it alone' without his assistance, with the resultant muddle, confusion, lost opportunity and heartburn that this can often bring.

How to choose a good accountant

First, make enquiries to see whether any of your business colleagues can recommend their own accountant, and check whether he is suitably qualified, i.e. in the UK, either a chartered accountant or a certified accountant. Ask your bank manager or your solicitor for the name or names of a reputable firm of accountants, and go to see them before making your decision, to find out whether you are 'compatible'.

Do not pick a firm at random from the Yellow Pages of a telephone directory, or just walk into the first accountants' office you come across in the high street. You may be lucky and come across a first-rate firm that will suit you well, but luck should not be allowed to figure in your decision here. You must make rational choices based upon experienced recommendation.

When compiling this chapter, I asked my friend and chartered accountant, Eddie Winter, why it is we need accountants so much. Apart from giving me some useful tips, which I have incorporated into the chapter, Eddie's immortal words were, 'Try running a successful business without us!' I believe Eddie sums up this chapter quite succinctly . . . don't you?.

'The first thing we do, let's kill
all the lawyers.'
WILLIAM SHAKESPEARE

CHAPTER 20

Get yourself a lawyer

That sounds simple enough, and no one should have any difficulty in engaging their services. Lawyers appear to be propagating, even more so than accountants who, themselves, seem to be lurking in every corner of the office block throughout the globe.

So just why are there so many lawyers to choose from? A well-posed question, and one which has baffled science for decades. I do believe that I have found the answer, and will reveal my scientific reasonings later on in this chapter. However, a recent study was carried out by a group of anthropologists from the University of California. They discovered, purely by chance, that lawyers, or attorneys as they are better known in America, and accountants are, indeed, closely related and both have many similarities, strongly indicating that both species are in fact 'human' despite the lack of 'human' expression and distinct silence that come over them whenever they are being asked to give an 'opinion'.

Although scientists now know for certain that they are of human extraction, their origin remains a mystery. Some say that they originated from a remote area of Transylvania, which may account for their wearing of 'cloaks' and their liking for 'blood'!

Some lawyers evolve into barristers, and many end up as judges, the hierarchy of their particular clan. The judges can often be seen wearing strange dress-like robes and long flowing wigs. The barristers tend to favour wigs reminiscent of two 'shredded wheats' sewn together. They are permitted to wear this strange apparel with legal impunity. Yet, an ordinary citizen seen walking the streets of London in this attire, would soon find themselves under lock and key, accused of being some weird 'transvestite'.

On rare occasions, when the judges have had a bad day (or been harassed by their wives), they don the 'black' skull cap, thus indicating their dislike for the person that has been brought before them. In the main, however, lawyers have integrated well into our modern society. You can either like or dislike them, but you simply cannot ignore them! They are professionals trained in the law, and it seems we now find ourselves having to consult them throughout our entire lives.

Oddly enough, it was not that long ago that lawyers were more aloof, and the public had very little contact with them. Perhaps only on such occasions as when our Aunt Aggie passed away and the lawyer was instructed by Aunt Aggie (well before her demise) to administer her will or estate. It is usually at such occasions that we pray that our name will be on the lawyer's lips.

There are now many specialist lawyers. It is common practice to find lawyers grouping themselves into a partnership wherein each partner deals with his own speciality. For example, one partner may deal in corporate law, another in property and conveyancing, while others are happy dealing in criminal or tax laws. Some lawyers will, however, simply be content to be in general practice, dealing with the 'trials and tribulations' of Mr and Mrs Average.

There are also lawyers whose speciality lies in patent and copyright laws, but they are not usually found in the everyday legal practice. Your lawyer should, however, be experienced enough to deal with most of your demands. Nevertheless, should you be unfortunate in having to ward off predators, for example, should someone be in breach of your copyrights, your lawyer would deal with this in his own way. He would do this, firstly by either writing a warning letter or, if that fails, by taking out an injunction against those who seek to impinge unlawfully upon your protected rights. Obviously, should this lead to a situation whereby the other party challenges your legal rights, and it proceeds to litigation, your lawyer may call upon the assistance of those other lawyers who specialize in this specific area of the law.

Assuming that you already have a lawyer and, providing you get on well together, it would be pointless to seek another. Your present lawyer will be familiar with your background, whereas another lawyer, upon meeting you for the first time, may be suspicious of your approach, and may ask for a large up-front payment – and you don't want that happening . . . do you?

Naturally, you will have to play fair with your lawyer. Never question the size of his account. Even if its £250 for an hour's consultation, you must still show him some consideration and pay up immediately. When you pay promptly, you will feel so proud of yourself, in knowing that your prompt payment of his fees will mean that his sons can enjoy a further period at Eton College. Therefore, your unselfish act, will be contributing towards the education system that will produce more lawyers. (Don't you feel a sense of pride when this happens?)

If you are one of the fortunate ones having a kind and considerate lawyer, he may suggest that because you are no longer worth a 'bean' he may be able to get you **legal aid**. Any person, receiving this offer, is bound to be full of gratitude, and I trust you will show yours by dropping to your knees with respect for a system that looks after you when you need it. However, don't be saddened when you receive his account for 'arranging' legal aid for you, after all, Eton College wants another payment for school fees, and you are not the kind of guy to deny your lawyer's sons their education rights, are you?

Pay this arrangement fee, even though some 'evil bastard' told you that the legal aid system had been introduced to keep lawyers in business, once all their clients have been 'screwed to death' by the legal system. Obviously, you don't want to hear this nonsense do you! So pay up, and be grateful that we have a legal system designed to protect us against all 'evil bastards' . . . who may rip us off.

A lawyer's indispensability

Naturally, there are many times when having a good lawyer on your side will pay dividends, and despite our reservations on the fat fees that they charge, they can play an important role in our business life. Without their expertise, many of us would be worse off! But, of course, many would claim that they would be far better off without lawyers. Regardless **DO NOT** under any circumstances attempt to draw up your own legal agreements or contracts, in the belief that you will save on legal fees. This is foolish and too risky, and must be avoided. Even if you are encouraged to do so by the 'other party' who may say, 'Yes, that will be OK by us!' Resist all temptation in this direction. Should things go wrong, and you have to fight for your rights, how many lawyers are waiting around, and are prepared to defend a client who tried to 'take the caviare from their mouths'? Obviously, you can draw up your terms and conditions of the deal, perhaps in draft form, and clearly stating 'Subject to Contract'. But let your lawyer prepare and witness the final contract.

NEVER I repeat **NEVER** sign any agreements, or indeed any form of documentation, provided by the other party, even if you feel pressurized to do so, *without consulting your own lawyer first*. Should you be far away in another part of the country, or even abroad, fax a copy to your lawyer first, seeking his legal advice.

NEVER write to any person or company without placing the words **'Subject to Contract'** on your correspondence. Obviously, if you have already done the deal and **exchanged contracts**, there would be no need to put 'Subject to Contract' on your correspondence, unless, of course, you are dealing with an entirely different issue.

The reason why you should insert the words 'Subject to Contract', is that you are still in the stages of negotiating your deal. So far, you have not reached full agreement on terms or conditions. And while you are still in the negotiating stages, you will not wish to give the impression, to those you are in correspondence with, that the contents of your letter constitutes a formal contract, or is legally binding in any way. Therefore, to safeguard against any person assuming that they have bought your rights for 'a song', put the words, 'Subject to Contract' on the first page of your letter. Continue to do this on all further correspondence, regardless of how many letters you write, until the day you exchange contracts or your deal is completed.

You may note, however, that some correspondence which you receive omits these words. In some cases you could use this to your advantage but leave this matter entirely to the judgement of your lawyer. Whether they put 'Subject to Contract' on or not, do not be lulled into a false sense of security.

Being ripped off – when to bring in your lawyer

Throughout this book, I have made several references to the remedies anyone should take whenever they find their concept or other copyrights being plagiarized or abused.

My usual reaction to such a situation, would be summed up in a few words, like for example, 'sue the bastards', whenever they violate your rights! Perhaps, the reader may feel that I could have expressed my choice of phrasing in a less distasteful manner, as my expressive words, although well meaning, do lack cultural taste. Nevertheless, any person who has been ripped off by these merchants, may not themselves be able to merit them with higher status. I offer therefore, no apologies, simply because I cannot, at this moment, find words that would come close to my true definition of those who take advantage of others in this way.

However, despite the fact that legal recourse may be your only means of redressing your problem, I do urge you to think very seriously, and endeavour to find other solutions, well before you engage in expensive litigation. Explore all the 'passive' options, well before spending one penny with your lawyer. The opportunities are there to deal with this situation, and therefore, whenever you have to fight to protect your rights, try fighting alone, without the immediate intervention of expensive lawyers.

The time to bring in lawyers, is when you have been beaten to a pulp, and not before, unless you have unlimited funds to squander. Whenever you are aware that others are abusing your copyrights try and make every effort to find out who's ripping you off and their main base of operation. When you have established this fact, and it won't be easy, go along in person, if that's possible. Take along a witness (two sets of knuckles, are better than one!). Also take all the relevant facts relating to your concept that you seek to protect.

When you track down the 'abusers of your divine rights' approach them in a civilized manner. It will pay dividends, if, for example, they may not be fully aware that they are in breach of your rights. When you are face-to-face, use this opportunity to your benefit, by being able to gauge the size of their operation. If the size of their operation looks impressive, suggest that you will not proceed with legal action if they cut you in on their action!

They may be quite willing to negotiate an agreement to pay your royalties than face the consequences of a **civil action** being instituted against them. Also, when you have confronted the situation face on this may impress them with your initiative and opportunities to do more business with them, in other countries, may be negotiated. So before you get agitated, and make rash judgements, like calling in your lawyer, try to sort it out and come to some bargaining position yourself.

Even if you have to call in your lawyer, try and get all the relevant facts to hand. Find out who is behind masterminding the operation. Find out just how many 'outlets' your goods are being sold at. Find out whether the retailers are aware that the goods that they are selling are in breach of your copyrights. Most of the retailers may not be aware, or most of them may not care less. However, tell them that they may be party to a civil action. You may get a lead to the main operator, if you pressurized the retailer first.

Give hell to everyone who's a party to ripping you off. From the retailer, from the distributor and from the main source of manufacture. Don't let these bastards off the hook, unless they are willing to cut you in on their action! Naturally, not everyone will be reasonable to deal with; therefore, you may need to show them 'proof' of the rights for which you claim protection, which may be sufficient to prevent further abuse, or indeed they may just call your bluff!

From the very first day that you instruct your lawyer to sort out your problems, his fees will be registering much faster than a parking lot meter, not in loose change, but in pounds, per minute! Therefore, consider the outcome. What happens if you lose the case, on some technicality? You will be faced with heavy legal fees that may very well include the other party's costs as well. The cost of legal fees, often amount to far more than the worth of what you are trying to protect. Even if you win a case, the judge may not award you costs. There are so many imponderables to consider. Therefore, before you rush off and buy your lawyer another new Rolls Royce, ask yourself what can he do for you, apart from just taking your money and lingering out the case, to suit his own financial benefits. Perhaps you should ask yourself just what he will do to you if, indeed, he loses the case and you can't pay his fees!

But perhaps more important, ask yourself if you have explored every possible avenue to rectify the matter yourself, without the involvement of your lawyer. Naturally, if there's nothing you can do without bringing in your lawyer, then he must become involved.

Oddly enough, all laws seem to have been created by lawyers, to enable lawyers to defeat the law! Nevertheless, whatever we may think of our lawyers, when they are not messing up one of our important deals, that took months to put together, they do provide a useful service and, to be fair, we have all benefited by their legal expertise and wisdom. Your lawyer should be your silent business partner. You both need each other. He needs your work to provide him with a living, (even if it's only sufficient to pay his fees!). However, so that you can also eat on a regular basis, make sure that *you* remain in charge of your business destiny. In other words, whenever your lawyer starts interfering to the extent that your deal is in danger of being lost, politely remind him that you need the deal much more than he needs to win every legal victory! In short, you are the client, and you make the business decision.

Why lawyers became lawyers

Many lawyers are usually 'economical' when giving the true facts, especially when it involves their method of practice. Don't even bother to ask your lawyer how much a high court case is likely to be – how long is a piece of string?, they will say. Don't even expect to get paid – even if you do win a court case – that is something else lawyers do not tell you before accepting your instructions to sue someone.

Let me give you a brief outline of what once happened to me, which made me wonder whether litigation is only for the insane!

Back in the early seventies, I agreed to purchase a house. It was a large house, set in its own grounds of approximately one acre, and which suited both myself and my fiancee (now my wife). The price was agreed at £33,000 (perhaps, at today's prices, the same house would be valued more in the region of £300,000 – if so, I may just now be able to afford the garage, given the same situation today!).

However, it was agreed that the vendor would not vacate the house until such time as he had found a suitable property to move into. We exchanged contracts, therefore, on this understanding I paid over the 10% deposit (£3,300).

Now, being mindful that we had, in effect, an open contract, he still had a hold over me by having full possession of the property, until he determined otherwise – not to mention my £3,300 deposit.

To cut a long story short, I put the wheels in motion to get the part-finance that was needed to complete the sale. However, this took much longer than anticipated, and some exchanged telephone conversation and letters played an eventful part between myself and the vendor who was, by now, getting anxious to complete, preferably immediately!

The vendor wrote me a letter indicating that, although he had received a much higher offer, he would complete with me as soon as my arranged mortgage came through.

By writing that letter, he had effectively, in law, kept the contract alive (in other words, he had not legally terminated the contract).

A month went by before I was informed that my finance was available, and I could now complete the deal. However, upon contacting my lawyer, I quickly learned that the vendor had, in fact, recently exchanged contracts with another buyer, at a much higher price. OK, sometimes you win, and sometimes you lose. I asked for my deposit back, which was refused on the grounds that I had failed to complete and was, in fact, in breach of contract.

Now that didn't make me happy one little bit. Losing the property *and* losing my deposit, was too much for me to accept. My human instinct encouraged me to seek revenge – which is not always the wisest of options!

My lawyer at that time was unenthusiastic about my chances of recovering my deposit. However, I instructed him to institute legal action; I recall having had a couple of counsel 'opinions', both varied in the extreme.

As the years went by, I hassled my lawyer to get on with it. Each time being told, let the law take its natural course. Some seven years later, I am getting quite fed up. However, a year after that I am instructed to attend the high court (in London). The hearing lasted nine days, each day becoming a new drama. Finally, the judge found in my favour, and I was awarded costs, my deposit, and the seven years' interest on my deposit.

Naturally, I was delighted, simply because it was not an easy case. There was a very strong element to suggest that, I had, indeed, failed to complete the contract on time, therefore forfeiting the right to recover my deposit. But there was one legal flaw that weighed heavily against the vendor, in that in his letter he to implied that he was willing to complete the deal, as and when I had arranged my finances. Therefore, in the eyes of the court, the contract he had with me was never legally terminated.

After the high court hearing, I discovered that the vendor was, in fact, suing his lawyers for giving him the wrong advice. In other words, his lawyers had told him that he was entitled to keep my deposit, even though he had increased the sale of his property by several thousand.

So this delay of some eight years may have been contrived by our respective lawyers in the hope that either I would get fed up and write if off, or that the vendor may return my deposit.

Now winning this important case was not the end of the matter. I say important case, as I do believe it made legal history as it created a legal precedent for such cases. However, I played little part in the court drama, other than wanting my deposit returned.

After the court hearing, when everyone, including myself, had stopped congratulating ourselves for bringing such a clever action, and after lawyers had drunk all my champagne, I timidly enquired as to when I could expect payment. The lawyers looked at me as though I had grown another head! Payment, they said, Yes, I replied, after all, I did win the case, did I not? No disputing that, old boy, said one of the barristers. My lawyer then took me to one side and said, I'll try and sort this out for you later. How much later – I have been waiting for nearly **eight** years! I replied.

Would you believe, I had to go through the hassle of taking out a judgement to recover my dues, despite the high court award, which meant a further delay. Even then, as I recall, my lawyer told me that the poor vendor was suffering from financial hardship, and would I be willing to settle for less! Yes, I replied, if you would be willing to let me have all the advance legal fees that I have given you. Suffice it to say, I got my full award in the fullness of time.

Now, the moral of this true story is to make sure you think very carefully whenever you may be contemplating legal action. Perhaps legal action should be more accurately defined as 'legal non-action!'

But, who gives a damn now! The fact is, I had the courage of my convictions to make a stand – not so much on the 'legal' issue, but more so on the moral issue at stake, which was far more foolish!

Summary

(1) **DO NOT**: Sign any agreements or documents, whether legally prepared or not, without consulting your lawyer first.

(2) **DO NOT**: Attempt to draw up your own contract no matter how clever you think you are.

(3) **DO NOT**: Enter into any negotiations without firstly inserting the words **SUBJECT TO CONTRACT**, on all correspondence.

(4) **DO NOT**: Make promises that may compromise your legal standing – or place you under any legal obligation (before contract stage).

I stated at the beginning of this chapter that I had figured out why there are so many lawyers in this world. My theory, yes it's only a theory, leads me to believe that perhaps lawyers belong to some secret organization that we are not aware of – maybe with Sicilian connections. After all, how many other professions also get well paid on a 'win' or 'lose' basis? If you refuse to pay their extortionate fees, what other lawyer is prepared to do battle against a member of his own secret society!

I will say no more on this subject, just in case I go to bed late one evening, and find a horse head on my pillow, or perhaps the next time I meet my own lawyer, who incidentally is a genuine straight guy, he may just make me an offer I can't refuse! All I will say is, **'A person who acts as his own lawyer, usually has a fool for a client!'**

I rest my case M'Lud.

'You can't solve a problem unless you first
admit you have one!'

HC

CHAPTER 21

Identify your personality change

In the main, inventive types are regarded as being rather strange creatures or 'nut cases' depending upon how closely we observe them. Many will live in their own silent world, occasionally making their presence known only when they emerge for food and water to sustain their existence.

Who can blame the general public, however, for forming the view that inventors are some kind of 'fruit cake'? How many times have we been in the company of an Ideasman or inventor who express elation over some idea or other and who are almost 'out of their minds' with excitement? Yet, when you ask them to reveal just what they have invented, they invariably adopt a vow of silence or reluctantly divulge minute snippets that would require a science degree in telepathy to understand. This symptom of over-protectiveness is quite common with the first-time inventor who may suffer a period of paranoia. Fortunately, when they realize that the world is not hanging around waiting to steal their invention, they soon recover both their dignity and sanity.

Most inventors will have an idea they think is brilliant and may be blinded by their own enthusiasm. They will defend to the bitter end any suggestions on modification and may almost get hostile towards any person being remotely critical. If you find yourself getting like this, get out quickly . . . (unless you can live alone!)

Most inventors will spend months, even years, perfecting their concept and, during that stressful period, all will go through some form of personality change or possibly mild mental disorder. Obviously none will admit to anything other than being sane, but people close to them will observe their changed attitude. Inventors are selfish by nature and usually so wrapped up in their project that they fail to recognize the symptoms of their own irrational behaviour.

The most common signs are **neglect**. They neglect themselves, their family and loved ones and many will fall into debt thereby putting their home at risk. What causes all this to happen? I will leave that question unanswered! Some day you may have to justify your own behaviour and you will know the answer.

The other common sign is **deceit**. Many inventors will not only deceive themselves, they may, without being fully aware of the consequences, deceive others who pose a threat to their endeavours. Obviously, this deceptive manner is not carried out with any criminal intent as most inventors are decent, fair-minded and law-abiding citizens. But, for some, it may be applied purely as a means of survival!

To demonstrate my point on irrational behaviour that will be tinged with deceit, you may find the following illustration has a ring of truth. You may even believe that I have found you out! If that's the case, do not despair; you are not alone!

You may be gainfully employed and may not be able to concentrate on your work – your mind will be elsewhere, mostly on your project. Your work colleagues are aware of your slack attitude and bad time-keeping, not to mention the amount of time off you are forever taking. They are a nice bunch and cover up for you as much as possible, assuming that you have some family problems. But your boss is no fool and, before long, you have some explaining to do. This happens several times and one day, without further warning, you are again summoned into the boss's office. On entering you notice that your cards and pay cheque are on his desk and your boss says, 'Well Harry, I did warn you enough times, did I not?' He hands over your dues and wishes you every future success. Your now ex-employer is somewhat mystified – months earlier you were a respected part of a successful works team, liked by all in your company and, upon dismissal, you haven't even bothered to plead for your job. However, in your confused state, you fool yourself that your ex-boss has done you a favour, you now have all the time in the world to get on with your invention – but little food in your larder!

Before you clear your personal belongings from your desk for the last time, you telephone your wife, telling her that you will be a little late getting home as you are having a few drinks with some work colleagues. Your wife says, 'Someone's celebrating darling?' to which you reply 'That's right, I'll tell you all about it later.'

You arrive home after a good skinful. Although slightly emotional, you remain composed. Your wife greets you with a kiss and, before you have time even to take your coat off, she says, 'Well, aren't you going to tell me all about it?' Christ, she knows already! What bastard has told her! But you are puzzled – your wife is still looking happy. 'Tell you about what?' you say, looking slightly concerned. 'You know . . . why you've been celebrating' she says. 'It's nothing important, I'll tell you all about it after dinner' you reply.

While enjoying your dinner, you notice a pile of letters placed neatly by your plate. On one the words 'Private and Confidential' stand out; it looks as though it has been delivered by hand as there is no stamp on the envelope. You open all the others first. Most are bills including a hefty telephone account in red print indicating that it is your final warning. The ominous letter without a stamp arouses your curiosity but you decide to leave it until later and when you are alone. Containing yourself no longer, you rip the envelope open, almost tearing the contents with it. It is from your bank manager. It appears that whilst he was having lunch he just happened to bump into your ex-employer who just happened to mention that you were no longer employed by the company. He wished to see you immediately to discuss your outstanding loan facility. You murmur under your breath, 'Uncaring bastard'. Your wife upon hearing the tale-end enquires, 'Bastard – who's a bastard?' You assure her that it is nothing for her to worry over.

When you are more relaxed and feeling more confident you tell your wife that there are some changes going on at work, saying that they are cutting down on middle management, but that they had offered you a senior post abroad, not saying where until your wife asks. Sure enough, she asks! You then tell her that it was in South Africa, knowing full well that she is anti-apartheid and dislikes hot climates. However, at this point, you decide to 'come clean' but remain economical with the true facts and you say, 'I told those sods just where to stick their job . . . and to think I have given them the best years of my working life and that's the gratitude they show me'. You then go on to say, 'Can you imagine me swanning off to Africa, leaving you and my family, despite the attractive salary?' all the while praying that your wife will not say 'Yes, I can!'

Fortunately, your good wife is now agreeing with your every word, but she shakes you rigid by saying, 'Darling, your company have treated you dreadfully – I'm going down there first thing in the morning to sort them out . . . just who the hell do they think they are?' By now the beads of sweat are forming pools in your furrowed brow, but you will yourself to remain calm, even though your phoney story will soon be exposed.

Eventually you persuade your wife to reconsider her actions by telling her that your union will be making strong representation on your behalf and any trouble she may give could affect your claim for compensation. She agrees! You heap silent praise on yourself for possessing the skill to extricate yourself from a potentially dicey situation. Your performance in front of your wife would undoubtedly have won you a scholarship to the Royal Academy of Dramatic Art (RADA).

During a peaceful interlude and, now that your wife is psychologically brain-washed into believing your phoney stories, you cunningly mention, with a hidden smirk, 'Well my love, we have adequate savings put by until I find another job; I suppose I shall just have to plod on with my invention', taking every care not to sound over-enthusiastic. However, you put your wife's mind at rest by assuring her that your job prospects are very good but, almost in the same breath, outline the advancement you have made with your invention; perhaps very subtly indicating just how wealthy you both may become once you have launched your project. Upon hearing the prospect of wealth, your good wife almost swoons with excitement – her imagination running into top gear, believing that soon her nimble fingers will be adorned with huge diamonds.

Weeks, or even months quickly go by during which time you have made excellent progress and lots of useful contacts. Your prospects are looking great; you have even managed to secure a patent on your invention and others are beginning to take a keen interest in your activities. Keep praying however, that those others do not include the administrators of your local asylum. While everything is running smoothly you have failed to notice that your financial position is deteriorating rapidly, simply because you have been so wrapped up in your project worrying over money has not entered your head. However, your good wife has, so far, been very supportive until the final demands start bombarding your letter-box almost daily. Then, without any warning, your wife's attitude changes and she tells you that you are 'A lazy good-for-nothing bastard', and injures your pride further by declaring that 'Your stupid bloody invention will never make any money'. And to add insult to injury she says 'Why can't you be like Mr Nice Guy . . . he loves his wife and family and he's never out of work'. Mr Nice Guy is your next-door neighbour with whom you have an occasional chat over the garden fence when your wife is mowing the lawn!

At this crisis point you try not to remonstrate with your wife, letting her release all her pent-up feelings. In your heart you know what she says is absolutely true and you feel a tinge of guilt, but you assure her that, if you don't 'make it' soon, you will get another job. Whether or not you ever get that other job will depend upon how self-deceptive you have been! Or, of course, just how successful you are in your inventive endeavours.

The above example may seem a little extreme but, believe me, it outlines a trap many could easily fall into if they are not in total command of their senses. Unfortunately, any person, so wrapped up in whatever they do, unwittingly becomes selfish in the eyes of those who may wish to command their attention. It is like a drug to many, especially whenever the chances of success appear within easy reach. Yet to others, success could be a long, long way away.

In general, innovators are fired by a great surge of enthusiasm. Unfortunately, this surge of enthusiasm is not shared by others, and therefore, this is bound to cause problems in family life, whenever the finances become non-existent and pressures are mounting. Many innovators, who find themselves in this position, and most do, are not able to cope very well with the constant feeling of being rejected. Many will suffer fits of depression, not only about being rejected, but also about having to fight constantly with their own conscience, whenever self-doubt looms on the horizon.

This feeling of depression or anxiety is shared also by the many who may be employed in research or other forms of technological development in industry. Although they may receive a monthly pay cheque, this does not preclude them from experiencing great stress, especially when they are not producing the desired results that their employers are expecting!

The constant decisions that the private innovator is torn between making are based on whether or not to proceed further, or to abandon his project. Obviously, the decision to 'abandon' will be the decision he will delay making the most.

It is not easy to abandon a 'once in a life time dream' but sadly, this happens to many who just simply cannot cope with the pressures that are placed on the shoulders of the innovator. However, it must be appreciated that those pressures are usually self-induced.

However, even if you have the funds available, and no pressures whatsoever, that is not enough to guarantee success. And if you do not have 'Lady Luck' on your side, then you are going to have an uphill struggle. So if 'Lady Luck' is not with you all the way, give yourself a break for a couple of months, examine what may be going wrong, and come back with renewed vigour and confidence . . . or at least with your sanity intact!

'The single most powerful tool for winning a
negotiaton is the ability to walk away from
the table without a deal!'

HC

CHAPTER 22

It's a wise negotiator who gets the best deals

Many readers may not be fully aware that, from the moment we are born until the day we die, we apply the science of negotiating, even though we may not be conscious of the fact.

From the age of two or three we are quick to learn that, if we are good little kids, our parents will lavish more affection upon us and give us sweets or other goodies. We are also aware that, whenever we misbehave, we will find ourselves at the receiving end of our parents wrath, which usually means ending up with a thick ear or, in most cases, a tanned backside.

We also follow the trend of negotiating throughout our schooling years. Perhaps, when we start out in employment, we learn the craft quicker, and become wise to the fact that, whenever we want an increase in salary, we may have to exercise a little 'blackmail' by threatening to withdraw our labour, or by using other forms of blackmail designed to bring the boss to his knees!

However, you can only suck so much juice from a lemon, and the final test of who's the best negotiator may only be known when the employee receives promotion, or finds himself out of a job due to his own greed. Those who find themselves in the latter situation were obviously not skilled enough to realize that they must not pick all the meat off their employer's bones at once! Do it gradually, and continue to get fed longer!

Attractive ladies are not immune from applying their tactical skill when it comes to negotiating. How many red-blooded men have been overpowered by the flutter of an inviting pair of eyelashes. This could be enough to throw us off our guard and reduce our resistance. Oh, what suckers we can be at times!

Whenever we enter into some kind of transaction with others, we experience all kinds of human emotion. More often than not, these emotions can affect the outcome of our dealings, or indeed, weaken our negotiating power, if displayed too forcefully.

The most common forms of human emotion that we experience whenever wrapped up in some business deal, or even purchasing goods can be:

SUSPICION
MISTRUST
FRUSTRATION
ANGER
WARMTH
CALMNESS
CONFIDENCE.

I will refer to these emotions throughout this chapter, and explain their significance to particular situations that you may identify with.

You do not have to be in a high-powered position, or have to be negotiating a million-pound deal to experience these emotions. They present themselves throughout our daily lives, as the following mundane illustration may reveal.

We fancy a pound or two of apples. We point to the fruit that we would like to buy, and the trader starts taking the apples from underneath the ones we selected. Now wouldn't you be **suspicious** of the trader's motives?

If we remonstrate with the trader, as most of us would, this could lead to us becoming **angry.** Or we may make the trader **angry** if he thinks we **mistrust** him. We could rightly assume that the trader's actions, by taking the apples from the underneath of the tray, were very **suspicious** indeed.

However, if the situation gets out of hand, and the trader tells us to 'off-ski', we may also experience feelings of **frustration,** because we are not going away with the apples we wanted, and if that is the case, we would certainly never buy from him again. We would **mistrust** him.

If, on the other hand, the trader acts with **calmness** and places those apples back, and gives us the apples we chose in the first place, then we may experience the emotion of **warmth** towards that trader.

All this for a few pounds of apples!

Whenever we are negotiating, dealing, bargaining, buying or selling, our pulse rate increases which, in turn, increases our blood pressure. This is quite common, regardless of our skills of negotiation. We all experience different emotions, whenever we become directly involved in dealing with the sale of our own property, be it our house or our car. It is quite extraordinary how oddly we behave. Apart from suffering anxiety of varying degrees, our behaviour can become unbelievably irrational and would baffle the mind of a top psychiatrist!

Let's take another example. We decide to replace our car and buy another. Instead of trading-in our old car, we advertise it in our local paper. Before we do so, most of us check to see what our car is worth. Our car is much better than most (another human misconception), and we advertise it for, say, £4,000. Everyone has told us that we may be lucky to get our asking price, so we expect to have to negotiate.

However, a guy telephones to say that the car sounds just what he is looking for. He arrives and, after a test drive around the block, he says, 'I'll take it, mate', and hands over a fist full of fivers, amounting to £4,000. You hand him the keys and other documents, and he drives away.

Now, just what do you think our first reaction would be? Most of us would consider that we would be delighted and full of admiration for the buyer. Not so, we are **suspicious** and now assume that, because he was the first caller, he must know better than we do as regards car values, and we may now believe he has 'taken us for a ride'. This, despite the fact that he gave us the £4,000 we asked for. Strange behaviour indeed!

Let us now look at another situation that would produce different emotions. We advertise our car for £4,000, and a buyer comes along and offers us £3,750. We accept his offer and feel delighted with the deal. We may even consider that we did a great deal, and express our thanks and gratitude to the buyer. Now isn't that even stranger? We took £250 less, yet, we are happier with the deal. Don't ask me why! I believe it is because we assume that it is the accepted principle to have to negotiate a deal, and that is exactly what we did. Whereas in the first illustration there was no element of negotiaton. The buyer just paid the asking price, and drove off into the sunset . . .!

Emotions also apply to the buyer but perhaps in reverse.

For example, a buyer will see our car advertised for £4,000. After kicking the f... out of our tyres, he offers us £3,750 and we accept, without hesitation. Because we have accepted his offer, the buyer feels morally obliged to complete the transaction. He pays us the £3,750 and drives away. But, while he is driving home, he has more time in which to reflect upon his own negotiating ability. He may ask himself why he did not beat us down even further. After all, we accepted his opening offer, without hesitation. Or, indeed, he may become very **suspicious** of us, and may wonder whether something is possibly wrong with the car. He may even feel **angry** with himself for not having 'screwed' us down even lower than his offer of £3,750.

Perhaps there is no such thing as a 'fair' deal. We may be convinced that what we accepted for our car was fair, but fair to whom – the buyer or the seller?

We may even convince ourselves that, because the buyer readily offered us £3,750, we might have been able to squeeze another hundred or so out of him. Having such thoughts, after concluding the deal, may cause us to feel **frustrated**.

Approaching negotiation

While we assume that every negotiation that takes place is 'unique', in other words, no two meetings are ever alike, there are no actual ground rules that we can observe before negotiation takes place. Unless we have a fully scripted version of what the other party will say or throw at us, how can we possibly prejudge the outcome? Basically, each person will play their part according to their own instincts.

Obviously, we will come to that meeting well prepared, and will do our best to negotiate terms and conditions that will suit us best. But will our preconceived terms and conditions meet with the full acceptance of the other party? After all, they will, quite naturally, want to secure the best possible deal for themselves, and will have little regard for our feelings. Or, indeed, for whether or not they can give us everything that we ask for.

The whole purpose of negotiating is simply to reach a **compromise** whereby all parties believe they have got what they came for – and go back satisfied.

However, because I mention that there are no basic ground rules, that does not imply that both parties start off the negotiations on an equal footing. If neither party is equal to each other, then obviously someone has the advantage over the other.

Let us assume that this advantage is '**power**', which is held by the party to whom you are endeavouring to sell your concept.

Firstly, we must ask ourselves why it is that they have all the power and we have none. We are the sellers, and therefore this puts us at the disadvantage. Let us assume that we have a wonderful new invention which could make us millionaires. But what would happen if we offered it to a couple of dozen companies, and they all rejected us? All we have is a dream of making a million, and a nightmare if we have not got the capital with which to manufacture the invention ourselves!

We must, therefore, always be aware that, despite our invention being wonderful, unless we can negotiate successfully with others, we are not likely to achieve our own aspirations. However, we can turn this situation around, whereby we end up with the power, and the others begging to negotiate with us. This is rare, but certainly not unrealistic, even in this modern age. If you have invented a new product or concept that somebody wants, then it must have a value! And, if several companies want your new product or concept, then the power is shifted in your favour! This will, in turn, give you added confidence whenever you are negotiating the terms and conditions that you want, rather than the terms and conditions that others may offer you!

Perhaps the most difficult part of your task will be to determine the value of your invention. The other party will also have some difficulty in assessing the true worth of what you have on offer, and therefore we come back to the old negotiating table! I have endeavoured to give you some idea of how to assess the value of your invention or concept in this book. Obviously, without having a crystal ball, and not knowing what it is you have invented, I can offer nothing more than a guide. The true worth of your invention will be known only after your successful negotiation.

Although there are many people who claim to be specialists at negotiating, I can say with some conviction, that most of us are no better than average, particularly whenever we have to negotiate our own goods. Unlike an auction of fine antiques, where perhaps we can get carried away in an atmosphere of desire, negotiating in a large clinical boardroom, in unfamiliar surroundings, and with several pairs of eyes observing our every twitch, can be very daunting and intimidating, to say the least.

The key to any successful deal is having the **confidence** to handle all aspects of any situation. Always be alert and prepared with offers or counter-offers. Perhaps not always dealing for an immediate settlement, but planning your strategy so that you get what you want over a longer period, which may suit the other party, especially if they need their capital to set up the operations themselves. It is a question of 'give and take'. Never be the one to want to 'take all'. Remember that negotiating is all about concessions and conciliation, with each party having a common aim. No inventor can stand alone – they need to share before they receive!

Our confidence is as fragile as our ego which can often be shattered by a cutting remark that brings us down to earth. Our confidence can also be shattered in several other ways. The following illustration is a true account of what once happened to me. Perhaps it was meant to happen, to bring me down to earth.

During the early seventies I was involved in negotiating an industrial development site in the south of England. It was important to my future that I obtained the best possible deal, and much was at stake. I had a couple of potential buyers who had expressed keen interest in the site which gave me confidence, placing me in a position of power. After all, I had the land, and others had expressed interest in wanting it. My secretary had arranged a day and a time for, say, Mr X to meet me on the site. The arrangements were made between my secretary and Mr X's secretary.

After the appointment had been made, and perhaps unwisely, my secretary told me that whilst speaking to Mr X's secretary, she had told her that I was not the kind of guy to wait around for anyone, should they be more than ten minutes late, after the appointed time. I'm afraid either I had over-impressed my secretary, or indeed, if that is how I conducted my business affairs in those days, then I must have been extremely arrogant or full of over-confidence, and some of my true friends may say I was both. I am however, pleased to say that, over the years, many have 'knocked me down to size', as I slink into obscurity!

I recall the appointment was set for 11 am. It had been and still is my policy never to be late for any appointment, and I arrived, well before the due time, and parked my Jensen Interceptor car, which was my 'prop' and possibly my 'status symbol' in those days, and ambled about the site. By about 11.30 am I was getting quite restless, and possibly thinking the worst of this 'sod' who dared to keep me hanging about like this. Suddenly there was a great deal of noise, appearing from nowhere and my car was enveloped in dust.

When all the dust had settled, I was astonished to see a helicopter had landed a few yards away. From the helicopter, out jumped a well-groomed man who introduced himself as being Mr X.

After we had exchanged the usual courtesies, the first thing he said to me was, 'I'm very sorry for being late . . . my secretary told me that if I was more than ten minutes late, I may not find you here' (he gave no reason why he was late at this stage). Then he added salt to my wounds by saying, 'I'm very sorry about this, as I have been told you are an extremely busy chap'.

Witnessing his highly original entrance, in his superb 'prop', I was slightly lost for words, not on account of being envious of his 'props' but in admiration of his 'style'. However, I did manage to mutter something like, 'That's quite OK, I have had problems in starting my car' which was a bare-faced lie. To which he replied,

'Here, let me have a try: I believe my wife has a car like this' acting as though Jensen Interceptors were on-par with Skodas. Upon turning the key the engine roared into life (as I knew it would) finally shattering any illusion I may have had of myself being a high-powered executive!

Fortunately for me, we concluded an equitable deal. However, later on, when I got to know him better, he told me that his secretary had formed the impression that I was a 'right pompous bastard' and between them, had decided to 'test a theory' and I was going to be their victim. Mr X purposely arrived half an hour late, because he was convinced that as I was the seller I would be waiting for him much longer than ten minutes.

His theory proved correct; in fact, I may have still been there, some twenty years later! Obviously, the impression that was created via my secretary, that I was some kind of high powered 'wheeler-dealer', who wouldn't give anyone more than ten minutes of my time, certainly cut no ice with Mr X who proved his own theory, at my expense.

Reflecting on the way I may have behaved in my business dealings, I do have to say that if I was as bad as this example portrays, I wholly deserved to have my ego deflated by Mr X who obviously had a lot more business 'wisdom' than I possessed at that time! Needless to say, I had been subtly taught a lesson by a more experienced 'stage manager', which made me realize that the seller is by no means not always in the 'commanding' position of having all the power!

I should qualify the following bold statement when I say that the buyer is always in the more commanding position than the seller. In theory this is true, but in practice there are many times when the power remains in the hands of the seller. For example, if you are fortunate enough to own a priceless art collection, or maybe a Picasso that a dozen collectors are eager to buy, then, obviously the seller is in the commanding position.

The inventor could also find himself in a similar position, should he be fortunate enough to have invented a product that could have worldwide sales potential. But, even if he can identify the sales enormity of his invention, he will still have to negotiate, or convince others to take on the commercial risks of producing, marketing and promoting a new product, which is, as yet, untried and untested on the consumers. Our friend, who owns the priceless collection of art has the advantage over potential buyers simply because he has something concrete to 'show' the buyer who, being aware of its value would be willing to pay the asking price, should he be desperate enough to want it!

Recognizing 'props' and tactics

The word 'props' has been mentioned several times in this chapter. It is an accepted fact that props, or images play an important role in the structure of any business enterprise. From, say, a small car sales firm who may have a grandiose sounding name, thus giving the impression of being larger than they really are, to a multinational corporation, whose props include marble foyers the size of Jumbo Jet hangars, with their image being Rolls Royces for their executive directors.

The use of props may well be a form of deception and psychologists may tell us that we all suffer from some kind of 'delusion paranoia'. But, any projected image is better than having no image at all! Also props, whether they are a genuine part of an organization or not, do serve a very useful purpose. That purpose gives us, the general public, an indication of whether we want to do business with that company or not. (Of course, not always to our advantage.)

For example, let us assume that you have inherited the sum of £15,000, and you meet a guy in the pub who tells you that he is a financial consultant, and that he would be willing to invest your capital in the best possible way, producing the best possible return.

He gives you his card. You, naturally, ask around, and everyone you speak to confirms that Mr Financial Consultant is considered to be good at investing other people's money, though none has actually dealt with him personally.

You telephone him and make an appointment. Should he have said, 'Don't come to my office, I'll come and see you', you may have had reason to be **suspicious**. But, let us assume, he agrees to see you at his office and gives you his address.

You arrive at the entrance to a run-down building, situated in a second-rate, commercial area of the city, where it is well known that all kinds of 'spivs' thrive. In the grubby entrance-way you see a business card indicating that Mr Financial Consultant's office is situated on the top floor or, indeed, in the 'attic'!

Would you be suitably impressed to hand over your fifteen grand to him? I bet my last fiver you wouldn't! On the other hand (because I have a nature that likes to analyse most things or situations), could you not be over-reacting, assuming the worst simply because of his down-market props?

It is possible that he may be completely honest in his dealings and, not having the wealth or inclination to pay extortionate office rents, had chosen to lease this particular office. Perhaps he may be unaware that his office location is doing nothing for his professional image! Now, if that were the case, I would say that he may well be quite genuine – unless he asks you to pay him in cash – in which case, beat a hasty retreat!

Now, let us look at the other side of the coin. Same man in pub, with same profession. However, on the day of the appointment, you arrive at his office which is situated in a much sought-after part of the city, known by all to be the area favoured by bankers and financial 'whiz-kids'.

You are immediately impressed with the surroundings and enter the palatial foyer. The concierge descends upon you, saying, 'Can I help you, Sir?' in a well-cultured, military voice that you identify as being of a rank no less than a colonel. You ask him for directions to the financier's office. Before getting into the lift, you say to the concierge, 'I have to shift some funds about . . . How I wish life could be easier than this!', thus trying to impress upon him that you are some big-time business tycoon!

The lift takes off like grease lightning. So much for modern technology, you murmur to yourself. Eventually, you find yourself timidly tapping on a solid oak, ornate door, the size of which compares favourably with a cricket pitch.

You are warmly greeted by an attractive lady called Penelope. You know this because it says so on her identity badge. Penelope escorts you into another enormous office where you come face-to-face with the 'big cheese' sitting at a desk so large it makes him look like a midget!

However, by this time, you are really impressed and, boy, do you want to invest with this company. He manages to extricate his backside from a two foot deep, leather chair, and greets you with a smile, saying, 'Hello, want to make an investment, do we?' You say, 'Well, I do', and within a few minutes you are fifteen grand lighter, and back in the entrance foyer, persistently trying to give the concierge ten pence for calling a taxi to take you to the main bus depot! The concierge is resisting all temptation to take your last ten pence. Finally, you put it back in your pocket saying 'Thanks, I won't forget you'. To which he replies, 'And I won't forget you, Sir', in a voice now more reminiscent of a drill sergeant!

Just before you are about to get into the taxi, you look back to admire the fine office façade. You notice a sign etched in granite, above the entrance-way, and situated between an impressive pair of gargoyles. It is written in Latin, a subject you attempted to learn at college. You are somewhat puzzled because you are almost convinced it reads, 'Here comes another sucker'!

Some months later, you receive a letter from a firm of accountants stating that they are the appointed receivers of the company with which you made your investment. You subsequently find out that the company had not been paying the rent on their impressive offices, and had 'gone down the swannee' – taking your fifteen grand with them!

Now you are bound to say, 'What the hell has all this props business got to do with me? I haven't got fifteen grand to invest, so this hardly applies to me'. Perhaps you haven't got fifteen grand to invest, but could your invention be worth more than fifteen grand? Perhaps it could be worth twenty times more! If so, you could be visiting quite a number of prestigious offices in your quest to sell your invention.

Regardless of whether or not any of these examples apply to your particular circumstance, it does no harm to be aware of the ploys individuals and companies take merely to impress upon those who deal with them that they are, in fact, worth dealing with! The props that are displayed before you are not there to provide a better working atmosphere for their employees. Indeed not, they are there simply for the benefit of the customers.

It is unfortunate, yet quite usual for us to judge or be judged by our lifestyle and visible trappings. No one is likely to be very impressed to hear how successful a person may be, if that person is living in 'slum' conditions. Therefore, we all try desperately to improve our standard of living, even if it means 'living beyond our means'. There are always a number of people who would condemn such 'vulgar' behaviour. But more often than not, they can be the 'losers' in life, and perhaps it is far easier for them to criticize those who display their success in this way, than make efforts to become part of it themselves. There are also many who have no desire whatsoever for any material wealth, just as long as the 'State' is taking good care of their needs!

I know of one close friend whose philosophy in life is, 'If I don't try, I cannot possibly fail!' I wish I had the courage to tell him that his so-called philosophy is indeed the philosophy of a born loser! But why should I be the one to pour scorn on his philosophy; perhaps he may have the 'wisdom' that could work for many of us too in some situations.

Intimidation is used through all kinds of ploys, often as a tool to make us feel inferior – thus having the effect of losing our self-confidence, whenever we are about to enter negotiations. How many of us feel the under-dog whenever we have to negotiate with large impressive companies, that we secretly would like to become a part of? We can all be intimidated in lots of different ways. Some companies will deliberately keep us waiting, long after the appointment time which is bound to increase the tension and anxiety we are under. Quite often a secretary will come along and say 'I'm sorry about this delay, Mr Y is in a *very* important conference. What this is likely to mean is 'The bastard is still having his coffee and doughnuts, so you will just have to wait until he has finished'. Have you noticed, it is always a *very important* meeting that is taking place? This is yet another form of intimidation to make us feel that they do not regard our meeting with them as being of high priority!

Furthermore, **WE** often have to travel to negotiate with **THEM**, rather than the other way around, thus indicating their importance over us. Often we have to sit and wait outside their office long after the time for the appointment has past. However, it is an accepted fact that the longer they keep us waiting, the more eager they probably are to deal! So use their ploy to bolster your own confidence. Better still (and only do this if you are *really* confident that others are interested in your invention), when they keep you waiting, call the receptionist over and say to her, 'Look, I know your boss is a very busy man, but so am I. Please go into his office and tell him that I am only prepared to wait another five minutes'. I would bet they soon drink up their coffee, and usher you in before those five minutes are up. If they do not, then carry out your threat and do not give them another second. Should they materialize within your specified time, this will serve to strengthen your own 'power', and they may be reluctant to 'pussy-foot' around further with your feelings.

All these tactics are designed to reduce our confidence, and lower the perception we may have regarding the high value of our concept, thus further reducing our negotiating expectations. Some people also have the ability of making us feel that they are doing us a great favour by giving us their valuable time. Some may not be concerned that we may have had to travel overnight to keep the appointment, so long as we turn up on time.

Now, you are sure to say, 'How will I know when all this is happening to me?' Quite frankly, if you were not aware of these ploys before, then it is quite possible you may assume that the treatment you receive is normal business practice. It is maddening when we are aware of what these 'sods' are doing, but, because we need the deal, we have to endure their little games!

You may then go on to say, 'When does all this start?' It starts from the moment you make contact! **WE** usually make contact by letter. When **THEY** reply (most do not) it will only be a couple of lines, written on impressive, embossed letterheaded paper, listing branches throughout the world, and possibly with a head office either in London, Paris or New York. Oh boy, when we receive this letter, do we want to do business with them! Even though the letter may only state a suggested time for us to meet! If their letterhead is enough to impress you then you are going to be an easy victim for what will follow!

Around the negotiating table

Let us now assume that we finally get around the negotiating table. Everyone is observing one another, each waiting for the other to 'set the ball in motion'. Before you reach this stage, make quite sure that you have first done your homework on the company. For instance, what concepts have they handled in the past? Try and obtain a copy of their last year's accounts. Some will happily give you a set of accounts upon request. Everything that you can find out about them will be an advantage. They may even be impressed with your obvious knowledge of their product successes. Do not bother to mention their failures – they know them too well already!

It is quite possible that the meeting will be very relaxed. After all, they don't really want to have to do battle with you if they can make you surrender gracefully! When the tension eases, do not start getting too 'chummy', and begin calling everyone by their first names. Even if they call you 'Elvis', and your name is 'John the Baptist', don't correct them. Let them find out their own mistake, and make their own correction.

Conduct yourself in a business-like manner throughout. There is nothing wrong in chuckling along with some director who is forever making silly jokes – but don't *you* make silly jokes! Save your smiles and chuckles for when they put a deal on the table that is so silly it would make anyone around that table collapse with laughter!

They may engineer a situation designed to make you 'lose your cool'. Should this happen, do not display any signs of anger, or start grabbing at their lapels. This is perhaps, their 'try-on' period. There may be, at least, six others at that table! They will have already rehearsed their play-acting roles with each other, well before you arrived.

You may soon be informed that one of the guys at that table is a 'highly distinguished' marketing and promotion expert who knows all about just what the consumer wants. He will underplay the value of your concept. Take no notice of all this 'crap'. Remember that you have something that they may want, otherwise you would not be there in the first place!

If you believe they have all the power, then they DO! But you can shift some of that power back over to your side by the way in which you conduct your negotiations. If you are persuasive enough, this could change their whole perception of the value of your concept!

If, however, the situation reaches the stage whereby they are simply being foolish, do not be afraid to say, 'OK gentlemen, I think we are getting nowhere – thank you for your time', and get up to leave the table. This takes courage, but what have you got to lose? If they are trying to 'screw you down', do not give them the satisfaction. Leaving the table under those circumstances is not a sign of weakness, but a demonstration of strength. I would not be at all surprised if, before you get as far as the door, you are called back. But when you get up to leave, do not rush your departure. Collect all your papers and place them neatly back inside your briefcase, and do not leave without shaking their hands. (Definitely, not their necks!)

Assume that they do ask you back – perhaps unlikely, but quite possible, if they really do want your concept. You have shifted some power back on to your side. Notice I said, 'some' power. Use it wisely and to your advantage, but do not push them too far. Your leaving the table has already deflated their ego, do not try and capitalize on this too much or let this situation go to your head by trying to 'screw them down'. Be wise and give and take; perhaps taking more than they were originally prepared to give. But, at the end of the day, unless you are both happy with the deal, then there 'ain't going to be no deal'! Always allow the other side to go away believing that they have got the better deal – because many times they have!

Obviously, you must not get paranoid trying to figure out whether the other side is trying to play games with your fragile nature. If you see one of the directors scratching his nose at the meeting, do not immediately assume he is trying to transmit some secret message to his colleagues. Maybe he just has an itchy 'conk'! Don't panic also if one of the directors accidentally drops some notes on the floor and another director swoops to pick them up. It is most unlikely that they are passing any pre-arranged price guides. Perhaps the director who dropped his notes has a bad back, and the other was just doing him a favour! Supposing it is you who accidentally drops your notes. Would you expect your action to throw them into a state of confusion?

Ploys or props are nothing more than a 'psychological tactic', but if you disregard them, then they will not be intimidating.

I can well appreciate the feelings and emotions any inventor may experience, whenever faced with the prospect of selling his invention. Perhaps, after several years of disappointment and/or self-denial, he would relish the opportunity of dealing with *anyone* who may show him a way of ending his nightmare. That moment is the time when he will be most vulnerable, and will often be blind to any warning or danger signals. However, having gone through difficult times, do not be foolish enough to drop your guard. When you have a contract duly signed by the other party, and some cash in your hand, then is the time for you to relax and enjoy yourself with your close friends and family. Especially your family, who will invariably have endured the hardships, and shared all your anxieties along the way. You may have been the inventor but, without their support, you could still be struggling. So when you make it, look after them well!

Although I may have strongly given you the impression throughout this book, and in particular this chapter, that all companies you may deal with are just waiting to 'rip you off', and may use every conceivable ploy to achieve their objectives, this may not always be the case. Indeed, many companies will prove to be straight and honest in their dealings with you. But, be on your guard.

Let's ignore the ploys for a moment and take a closer look at yourself, and your own business ethics to establish whether or not, given the chance, you would take advantage of anyone. For example, assume you have a very plausible and persuasive manner, one which encourages others to invest in your 'mad-cap' idea. Later on, everyone loses their investment. When tackled about it, you would probably show regret, but would also probably say, 'Well, you took a commercial risk, and that's business, I'm afraid'! Yes, quite so, and your sentiments will also be shared by those who are after *your* concept!

It's a 'dog-eat-dog' situation. Therefore, never tangle with dogs bigger and more powerful than yourself, unless you have stamina! Naturally, you have to trust in your own instincts as to whether or not others may be taking advantage of you. But, as I have mentioned several times, if you have well-protected the rights to your concept, then you have little to worry about. In fact, all you have to worry over is being clever enough to appreciate the full potential of your invention, and being able to value its worth – well before you enter into the arena of negotiation!

The following list of 'pre-flight' checks, which should be carried out before you start negotiating, may be useful. However, they are not in any sequence of importance, nor are they to be regarded as being definitive. They are a guide only – one which may, hopefully, generate enough 'thrust' to enable you to achieve 'lift-off'!

Ground rules for business meetings
Never

- **Never**: travel long distance to any negotiation arranged for the same day – stay overnight, and arrive fresh and relaxed

- **Never**: let them see that you are impressed by their props or palatial surroundings

- **Never**: make comments about the size or strength of their organization

- **Never**: show too much gratitude whenever your demands or terms are met

- **Never**: give too much away – without wanting something in return

- **Never**: display anger or lose your cool, whatever the

circumstances

- **Never:**   park your bike in the director's car space!

- **Never:**   expect to conclude a deal at the first meeting: several meetings may be necessary

- **Never:**   be intimidated by being outnumbered at any meeting – remember they may all want to learn from you!

- **Never:**   be vulgar, even if they are

- **Never:**   insult their intelligence

- **Never:**   say how clever you are; allow them to judge for themselves

- **Never:**   forget that you may need them – more than they may need you!

- **Never:**   get too smart if you want to deal

- **Never:**   relax your guard over lunch or drinks

- **Never:**   be late for any appointment

- **Never:**   boast of having dozens of potential buyers, even if you have, or have not!

- **Never:**   go to any meeting without knowing *exactly* what your full objectives are

- **Never:**   be torn between 'need' and 'greed'

- **Never:**   discuss your business or get too familiar with their receptionist or secretary. Get as familiar as you like – after the deal!

- **Never:**   interrupt their conversation

- **Never:**   smoke at any meeting, unless they fully approve (but never smoke until they do themselves)

- **Never:**   eat sweets or chew gum at any meeting
- **Never:**   do a deal without a written contract!
- **Never:**   display any signs of emotion whenever you believe you are pitching too high: the other party maybe amazed that you are pitching so low!

Always

- **Always:**   arrive at any meeting well-groomed
- **Always:**   remain in full control of all your objectives
- **Always:**   be a good listener
- **Always:**   remind yourself why you are negotiating in their office – and not yours
- **Always:**   remember it may be your first deal – but not theirs
- **Always:**   leave something in the 'pot' for others also!
- **Always:**   retain your humour, even if they lose theirs
- **Always:**   negotiate to win. But don't encourage intransigence
- **Always:**   pitch high – you can always reduce gradually
- **Always:**   know what you are after – and go for it!
- **Always:**   be honest; don't make statements that you cannot substantiate
- **Always:**   listen to sound reasonings
- **Always:**   record the names of everyone you negotiate with, and note down all that was said or negotiated

- **Always:** be willing to compromise
- **Always:** write a letter of thanks after the conclusion of negotiations – whatever the outcome!

'The longer they keep you waiting . . . the
more they want to deal!'

HC

CHAPTER 23

How to sell your concept and negotiate a fair deal

Inventors will have to overcome many obstacles in their inventive lives, not least in showing some common sense as to the value of their concept.

Many inventors genuinely believe that their invention must be worth a fortune, simply because they conceived it. Anyone who invents for the first time is bound to feel this emotion, which can often be the cause of wasted opportunities.

It is an accepted fact that assessing the value, or being able to quantify the worth, of an invention is going to be difficult. How can anyone place a value, with any degree of accuracy, upon a product that is 'new', and which has never been subjected to the testing ground of the marketplace?

In the end, it comes down to commercial guesswork, with the buyer of your concept doing the guesswork. Unfortunately, there are not many inventors who can accept that their invention is only a small part of the elaborate marketing plan that usually follows the launch of a new product. The inventor has only provided the 'tool' for that marketing strategy, and will have to rely on team-work.

The inventor provides the initiative for others to take the commercial and financial risks and, therefore, those taking all the financial risks will be looking for a large slice of the action also. The inventor will need this teamwork, unless he proposes to self-manufacture, or become his own marketing and promotion expert, prepared to employ a large sales force to sell his goods. This is not advisable as it takes time to establish your network (and you may not have the time or the money).

Perhaps the most daunting task for any inventor will be in finding buyers for his concept. Even more daunting will be the difficulty in negotiating a reasonable deal. Many you deal with will not give a damn for your feelings of being the inventor. Even less importance will be placed on your valuation which could be emotionally inflated to match your self-esteem attached to being the inventor. Now, if all this sounds tough, and you think you don't want to hear any of this nonsense, simply because you think it will not apply in your circumstances, then I hope your circumstances will place you among the 5% of inventors who come through to make their millions. But the sad fact is that it is estimated that 80% of inventors lose a small fortune, and the remaining 15% may be lucky enough only to recover their investment. Nevertheless, as inventors are born optimists, who is to say that you will not be among the 5%? Therefore, never give up – the time to give up is when you know that you are beaten!

The object of any successful deal will depend upon several factors, not least getting out of the deal what you expect. That principle applies to all parties, but each party may have different motives and, therefore, will endeavour to negotiate an agreement to suit their own circumstances. All parties around a negotiating table must be flexible, and willing to be reasonable to the demands and conditions put forward by the other side, otherwise the end result will be nothing achieved other than time wasted.

Flexibility is probably the keyword to any successful negotiation. However, this does not imply that you must be the one to be flexible all the time. But if you are inflexible all the time, this will only create an atmosphere of discontent, and the discussions are likely to break down.

Having confidence in one's concept must be matched with having self-confidence in being able to negotiate the best possible deal for yourself. If you appear to be confident, this will be noted by the other party who may realize that you are not going to be a 'push over'. Once they realize this, and they usually do within the first five minutes of the meeting taking place, they will show you a little more respect. But this will not prevent them from 'screwing' you into the ground, if you allow them to.

The value that you put on your invention is not likely to match the worth others place on it, therefore there must always be scope for compromise on both sides. If you think that others are wasting your time by not putting forward a deal that you want, have regard for their time also being wasted by your unwillingness to see reason. You may think that you are the only person who knows the value of your invention, but you may be the only person that doesn't.

Basically, unless you have decided to self-manufacture, you will only have two options open to you to sell your concept.

Option 1 – Patent Pending

Will deal with selling off your concept as soon as you have received your priority date.

Option 2 – Patent Granted

Will deal with the sale of your invention after you have received a patent grant.

Option 1

This option is available to any person who has an idea for which he considers he could obtain a patent but does not have the time or resources to get too concerned with its development. And, providing he is practical and extremely lucky, he may still earn a fortune by simply filing a patent application that would cost him only £15 (if he files the application himself).

Let us assume that you have done just that, and you are now in possession of a priority date. As you may be aware from reading Chapter 6 on the Patent System, you have **twelve months** in which to develop your concept further, or withdraw from the arena. Assume you utilize this twelve-month period in developing your invention (should it need developing), or, indeed, start contacting various companies with the intent of selling off your invention.

Now I shall emphasize again that, if you have come up with a wonderful invention that is original and not obvious, you do not need to obtain a patent to start manufacturing. And, if it is your intention to market your invention in the UK only, then you can legally do so, but you would have very limited rights against infringers, whereas a patent will give you **twenty years** monopoly rights. Nevertheless, it would be advisable to file a patent application simply because of other benefits that may come along whilst you are dealing with others.

A great benefit of filing a patent application is that you do not have to be so cautious whenever you reveal your idea to any company that you write to. I know throughout this book I am always sounding off about dealing in a cautious manner, and **that is still my advice**. But, if you have filed your patent application and received a priority date, you can, if you choose, dispense with the formality of receiving back your form of Non-Disclosure of Confidential Information, before you reveal your 'secrets'. Obviously, it would still be wise to mention in all your correspondence, that your dealings with the company are to be conducted in a confidential manner, and that they are not to disclose any source of information that you impart, without your written consent. You will find that those you deal with will invariably need to seek the opinion of 'experts', simply so that they can assess the commercialization of your concept. Therefore, the chances are quite a number of people will learn of your invention and, as I've stressed throughout, **ultimately you will have to rely upon their integrity**.

Another benefit on filing an early application, and getting your invention known to several companies, is that some companies may see the full potential of your invention, that may have European or world sales appeal. Therefore, if they like what they see, they may be willing to tie-up a deal quickly, providing they may still have time in which to file either an EPC or PCT (see Chapter 7).

Therefore, it is in your best interest to introduce and market your concept as from the day you receive your priority date, and get those letters out to as many companies as may be interested in your concept. Don't bother to give any company several weeks before you contact another. Get those letters out, and be prepared to have several meetings, thereby being in a position to choose the best deal for yourself. Once you have filed your application, you will be under a deadline of twelve months, which means you will not have much time to conclude a deal. OK, I accept that you can still conclude a deal after the twelve months, but what kind of deal are you going to make for yourself if you have lost the opportunity of obtaining protection in other countries? Losing your monopoly rights in other countries could mean losing out on a big deal! And some companies may not be making 'big' offers, so it is up to you!

By adopting **Option 1** you minimize your **capital risk**, simply because many of the larger companies would prosecute their own patent applications and, therefore, you will be relieved of this huge expense, yet may derive the benefits of a better deal, should your patent be granted.

If your patent is not granted, then all you have lost is the £15 fee, plus all the running around expenses. However, even though you may not obtain a patent, for any amount of reasons, that does not prevent you from exploiting your invention, providing you would not be breaching someone else's copyrights.

Deal structured on hope value

Now, let us look at the possibility of concluding a deal that is based upon nothing more than 'hope' value. In other words, everyone will hope you get your patent, but just how can you structure an agreement on the hope factor? It is not going to be easy to get a company to pay you huge sums on this basis. Nevertheless, a good deal can still be negotiated.

All those you deal with are bound to use this hope business as a lever to 'screw' you to the boards. I accept the chances of walking away from the negotiating table with a 'fist full of money' is slim, but not impossible, and much will depend upon two main factors:

Factor 1

Have you done your homework and checked out the originality of your concept? In other words, will it be new?

Factor 2

Even if you have a new invention, is it going to be a marketable product with great sales potential, and also a long shelf-life, rather than a 'one minute wonder' or fad?

Obviously, there will be many other factors to consider, but they will not necessarily concern you, as the other party will be taking everything else into consideration well before they invite you around the table.

Even if both factors are acceptable on both sides, it does not take a scholar to realize who is likely to get the better deal for himself. Obviously, the other party will be saying things like, 'We like your invention, but so far you haven't got a patent for it'. Why they say the obvious, I'll never know, but they do! Then they will say things, like, 'What happens if you don't get a patent?' Tell them that you have others interested, but that you haven't quite worked out a deal yet!

Then they are likely to say, 'Well, as you can appreciate, if we buy your concept, our company would be taking a high commercial risk, you know that, don't you?' You reply, 'Not necessarily so', and let them advance the next line of questioning. Most probably, they will say, 'Well, what figures are we talking about here?' or 'What are you looking for?' Then, obviously, after all the 'fore-play' is over, you both have to get into the spirit of 'seduction', or maybe 'screw' each other to the wall!

If you have reached the stage whereby you get around the table, what you may not be aware of is that, before your appointment, the other party would have certainly instructed a patent agent to carry out an extensive search, and would rely heavily upon the agent's professional opinion as to what your chances of getting your patent grant are. But, like 'honest' businessmen, they are unlikely to reveal the patent agent's opinion to you if, indeed, it proved to be very favourable. If it was not favourable, they may take some delight in telling you just to dampen your spirits, even though they may still wish to deal with you.

You are bound to say to yourself, 'Well, how can I be sure just what their patent agent came up with?' You can't, unless you, yourself, commissioned your own patent agent to carry out a search on your behalf, which would be most advisable. For the cost of a couple of hundred pounds, you will strengthen your own bargaining power. But, of course, being the 'honest' inventor, you conveniently forget to reveal that you have found out that your chances are excellent. (Reveal your patent agent's opinion only at the very last moment, when you simply cannot convince them that your chances are good.) The point of that deception is to see who's deceiving who!

However, let us assume for one moment that they know your chances are good, and that is why you have been invited to meet with them. If your chances were risky, they would know this, bearing in mind that it only takes a couple of days to carry out patent searches, and therefore, if yours were unfavourable, they would not have made any arrangement to meet you, as this would only be wasting their time! So bear this little point in mind whenever you are called to negotiate a deal which is based on 'hope' value.

To be fair, although you may well have been informed that you have an excellent chance of getting your patent, that is not the same as actually having it to negotiate with. Therefore, the company that you may be negotiating with is bound to want to capitalize on this fact because of the associated commercial risks including, perhaps, the costs related to additional patent protections in other countries. All this is bound to place you under some pressure to get rid of your worries and take what is offered. I would not recommend that you think, or even deal, in this way.

The fact is, you may be the one holding all the 'trump' cards. Firstly, let us weigh up all the associated risks that these companies are ramming home to you. Well, perhaps they may have to fork out a thousand or two in prosecuting further applications in other countries. But, you didn't insist that this would form part of your deal, did you? Also, if they want to file in other countries, they certainly want to deal!

Consider also that most major companies are not likely to drop all other production, simply to take on your invention immediately. Therefore, maybe waiting a couple of years until you receive your grant will be more beneficial to them. By that time, they may have exhausted other lines and can 'slot' your invention on to their production line. So there may be a dozen good reasons why it would suit them to negotiate a deal with you now!

As I mentioned, no one in industry is likely to want to start manufacture tomorrow; it takes some time to get organized. Maybe your invention requires further development, and they have the capital resources and the technical skills available. Therefore, everyone will be making commercial judgements on your invention.

Although the inventor may be somewhat restricted in selling his invention on a 'hope' situation, he does not have to conclude any deal that does not interest him, and would be free to walk away from the negotiating table at any moment. But if you are satisfied with what you have been offered, then take it. Any deal is better than no deal at all, and it is quite possible that you would have gained invaluable experience of just what companies are looking for and are prepared to pay. Therefore, it is not impossible, to use that experience, should you have other product lines, to sell to the same company.

Let's get down to the deal

Let us assume that you have a willing party, who is prepared to negotiate with you, on the basis that all you have to offer is a filed patent application. Let us forget all the nonsense about everyone trying to out-wit one another, and also assume that all talks will be conducted in an atmosphere of mutual trust and goodwill which you will find is the way most negotiations are conducted.

As I have mentioned several times before, never even consider conducting your own negotiations, if you do not have much experience, or you feel you would not be emotionally strong enough to cope on your own.

If we are totally honest with ourselves, we are lousy negotiators when it comes to dealing with something that we are personally involved with. For example, the sale of our house or even our own business can present us with problems, especially if the buyer has little regard for our feelings and starts to criticize our taste of decoration!

If you choose to appoint a better negotiator to handle your deal, then you must have the courage to stay away from the negotiating table, and not to interfere too much. In other words, no one can give their best performance while being watched over by their client. We all operate and negotiate in different ways. It would be too restraining to have your client by your side during intense negotiation, so, if you want the best deal, you would be wise to stay away from the table, unless you have full confidence in your own ability (and therefore should choose to handle it yourself).

If you go for Option 1 that is not to say that you have to sell off your exclusive rights for a 'one-off' payment. Obviously, there are many companies who would much prefer to buy the exclusive rights to your invention because, on many occasions, they can pick up a bargain for a song. But, more often than not, most companies like to be in full control of their products, and the less involvement with the inventor the better.

Naturally, if you are offered a handsome price, it would be extremely difficult to resist and cash in your hand now is perhaps better than having to wait several years, possibly for the same amount, should things not go according to everyone's expectations. You will have to accept that, once you have tied a deal, it may be several years before the fruits of that deal materialize. Many inventors do not start receiving their royalties until three to five years (possibly more), after they have concluded the deal.

If you do have a concept that everyone accepts will have great selling potential, then you can rest assured the offer you receive will reflect the market potential of your concept and, at the end of the day, you either take what's on offer, or you seek a better deal for yourself. But, even if you were to negotiate an offer which was ten times better than the last, keep praying the company has the resources to fulfil their obligations and remain in business, long enough to honour your contract!

Option 2

The principles of negotiating your deal will be exactly the same as negotiating with a patent pending. But, this time, your odds of getting a better deal for yourself would have increased considerably over Option 1, simply because you have your patent to negotiate with. It is not always practicable to go for this option but, of course, it is preferable – as I have stressed, it is the only real way you can guarantee protection of your Intellectual Property Rights and reduce the chances of your being ripped off.

Word of caution

I should warn you, however, that despite the apparent advantages of Option 2, such advantages may, in some circumstances, prove to be commercially disastrous.

For example, assume that you did not bother to contact any companies until you were in possession of your UK patent grant; assume also that, because of your cautious nature and limited finances, you sought protection in the UK and didn't bother to file applications in other countries. What kind of deal are you likely to negotiate for yourself, having now lost the opportunity of obtaining patent grants in any other country?

Therefore, you may find that the larger industrial companies, whose trading activities are either European or international, may not be interested in your invention, simply because of your limited protection. Unfortunately, the patent system can bear a striking resemblance to a game of roulette – you throw your money into the system and spin around for nearly four years until the croupier reveals your fate!

'Negotiating a contract is the inventor's ultimate aim: getting no contract is the inventor's ultimate pain!'

HC

CHAPTER 24

The contract is more important than the deal!

It is important to realize the full significance of being able to negotiate an equitable deal, but it is even more important to ensure that any deal is incorporated into a legal contract which would give you a measure of protection, should things go wrong at some later stage.

Let us firstly establish just what a contract is, and the important details you should look for, whenever you reach this stage.

A **contract** is the embodiment of the spoken and agreed word that is usually transposed into a written document, which records the terms and conditions of an **agreement** made between **two or more parties**.

Despite what you may hear to the contrary, I do not believe that there is such a thing as a watertight contract. Most contracts have some flaws or other and, therefore, you will be wholly reliant upon the professional skills and competency of your lawyer.

What must a contract contain?

This is not intended to be a book on law, therefore your lawyer would be the expert to consult when the time comes. When you have concluded your successful negotiations, your lawyer will deal with the legal ramifications by incorporating every little detail into contract form. Therefore, it is absolutely essential that you provide your lawyer with **accurate** details of the deal that you have successfully negotiated.

Depending upon the nature of your deal, and how complex it is, there could well be several dozen clauses in your contract. But for the moment, this will not concern you. Therefore, not having a crystal ball, I can only outline what I consider to be the most important details which you should immediately hand over to your lawyer once you have concluded successful negotiations (assuming your lawyer will not be by your side at the meetings). Basically, these are:

(1) The full names and address of the person/s or company with whom you have negotiated your deal.

WHY?

This must be obvious but, if it is not, please get some medical help as quickly as possible.

(2) If dealing with a limited or public liability company (PLC), make sure you obtain their Registered Office address.

WHY?

The address where you negotiated your great deal may not be standing tomorrow. Or indeed, the liquidators may be ready to pounce on them as soon as you have passed over your life's work! Do not be alarmed – I will outline your safeguards against this happening to you later on. Meanwhile, the registered address is required in order for your lawyer to carry out a search of the company, prior to you concluding your deal. Or, perhaps your lawyer may need to serve a notice upon the company at some later stage.

(3) The full names of the directors with whom you negotiated the deal.

WHY?

Apart from the fact that you should always be aware of those you are dealing with, if you need to contact them again, you will be familiar with their names. Some directors are only called upon to negotiate deals, and therefore you may never see them again. But, more importantly, they may perhaps become a party to the contract, or may be needed as a witness to that contract. Whatever the case, be sure you know their names!

(4) The name and address of their company bankers (endeavour to obtain these in a discrete manner).

WHY?

So that your lawyer can take up financial references. After all, just because they may have offered you a million, they may, in fact, not be worth a bean. Safeguard yourself against wasting your valuable time and resources.

(5) The full terms and conditions of the deal that you have successfully negotiated, subject to contract.

WHY?

So that you can provide your lawyer with as many details as possible, enabling him either to prepare a draft contract, based upon what you have told him, or approve a draft contract that may have been sent to him from the other party. Also, you may find that some people have short memories, especially after having had the time to reflect on what they have offered you! This could also apply to yourself. So make a note of all terms and conditions – no matter how insignificant or unimportant they may seem. Your lawyer should be the sole judge of what is relevant and what is not.

(6) Finally make quite certain just what it is you have agreed.

WHY?

Well, you do not want to be told by your lawyer that you have agreed to sell your exclusive rights, when you thought you had only agreed to sell the UK rights. This is another good reason why you should always negotiate, subject to contract. It is your safeguard against falling into such traps!

Obviously, other important issues not mentioned above will be dealt with by your lawyer – that is what you pay professionals for! At least you can sue them for professional negligence, should he or she not provide the usual standard of care and attention to protect your interest while acting for you.

I advise you never to enter into negotiations, unless you do so **'Subject to Contract'**. That principle should apply even if you are dealing with the Pope who may be trying to sell you the Vatican. Make it known from the off-start (usually in your correspondence), that all talks, discussions or negotiations will be 'subject to contract', which means that, although you may end the discussion in full agreement, neither party will be under any legal obligation until both sides have 'exchanged' contracts. Therefore, if you are happy with the deal, then get your lawyer to draw up the contracts as quickly as possible, just in case a party is given more time to reflect. When they reflect, it is usually not under the pressure of a negotiating table, but in the comfort and quietness of their own home, when the reality of what they have done hits them! The value of dealing **'Subject to Contract'** is equitable on both sides; therefore no party is disadvantaged by negotiation in this fair manner.

You are bound to say, Well, if I am happy with the deal, and they are happy with the deal, what is this big deal you are making about the deal being subject to contract? You may then go on to say, After all, a deal is a deal – and I have successfully negotiated mine, so what's your problem? Let me first assure you that it is not *my* problem but could well be *yours,* if you do not heed this advice, or the advice of your lawyer.

Therefore, do not blow your chances. You may never reach this stage in your life again and, having overcome impossible odds, do not go giving it all away to the first bidder who offers you an easy way to pay off your overdraft! I know from personal experience just what it feels like to reach a stage whereby everyone you negotiated with is ecstatic with the deal on the table. They start hugging you, and all those around you. The champagne flows like Victoria Falls, and the directors are falling over themselves to shake your sweaty hand, telling you all the while that you are some real hard cookie to deal with, and saying things like, With your business brain, you are bound to go far! Yes, they could well be right! If you have not exercised caution, as previously mentioned, furthest you'll be going is to the nearest 'Loony-bin', or if it is full (of inventors) you may join a squadron of 'lemmings' who are throwing themselves off cliffs when you find out that all those very nice guys, who heaped praise upon you, and even wined and dined you with pheasant breasts and brandy, have also taken you to the cleaners!

So be warned! Try and rise above all the adulation, and stick to the issue of negotiating a good and equitable deal for yourself. Remember that nobody deals with anyone unless it is in their **best** interest to do so.

If you are negotiating royalties or licences or even your exclusive rights to your invention all terms and conditions of that deal will form the basis of the contract. If you are dealing with a limited liability company or a public liability, they will have to use their company seal on all documents relating to the deal. Obviously, if you are also trading as a limited company, and you have negotiated the deal through your company, as opposed to being a sole operator, then you will need your company seal.

All contracts are basically unique, or at least they should be, in that they should contain every detail of what you have given, and what you expect in return! There are, of course, some contracts that are already prepared in standard form. Never be foolish enough to sign one of these documents, <u>under any circumstances</u>, without consulting your lawyer first.

Despite the fact that I have mentioned that every contract is unique, you may assume from their appearance that this is not the case, as indeed contracts tend to look alike and can seem as though they are drawn up by one and the same lawyer. The uniqueness applies to the terms that you have agreed, and the conditions upon which both will be fulfilled (by all parties to that contract). Hence the terminology **terms and conditions** which is the basic meat of any deal!

Although you will have to rely totally upon the expertise of your lawyers either in drawing up the agreement or approving an agreement drawn up by the other party's lawyer, it is always wise to check everything out yourself, and ensure that everything you agreed, or everything that you gave away in return, has been incorporated within the framework of that contract. Observe *every other* clause, if only to safeguard your meat from being gobbled up by some greedy bastard (later on in the life of your contract)!

Your lawyer will also deal with **penalty** and **default** clauses that would safeguard your interest in the event of the other party being in breach of that contract. For example, your royalty payments may not arrive at the due time. Or maybe the other party has sold off additional licences to your invention, conveniently forgetting to inform you of your entitlements (if any).

A contract can be simple or complicated. Much will depend upon the nature of the deal, and the eloquence of the legal draftsman (lawyer). However, eloquence is of little value if your contract is not valid in a court of law.

Naturally, whenever we negotiate with others, there must always be a strong element of trust and goodwill on both sides. It is counter-productive to thrash out a deal in a battleground atmosphere. Your contract with others will have to be played out to its full extent, therefore do not try to be too clever and walk away from the table having got everything you asked for, but having given little in return. That's not negotiation – that's thuggery!

Whenever you have thrashed out a deal, no matter how long it takes, make every effort to keep to the initial agreement. That is, do not go looking for more afterwards. This can only lead to bad feelings between parties, and others will naturally distrust you in any future dealings they may have with you. Show everyone that you are a man of your word. If you are happy with the terms, why bother to change them? Should your lawyer say you could have achieved more, why did he not have the courtesy to handle the negotiations on your behalf? Everyone is the world's best negotiator *after* the event! Instead of looking at the short-term gains, look at the long-term prospect of having future deals with the same company.

Be flexible with regard to the needs of others – the chances are your deal may tie in with their prosperity and you all will benefit. However, if you try to be a greedy negotiator, and take pride in screwing them down, or squeezing the last cent out of the deal, this will only breed discontent. The next thing you may hear is that they are trying all ways and means of terminating the contract – without you receiving any damages. So play fair, and reap the rewards!

'Breach of Contract' and legal action

There are many times when it would be wise not to form yourself into a limited liability company, but to negotiate your deal as a sole trader. My reasons are quite simple. For example, say you have negotiated your deal and the other party welch on their obligations. Naturally, after trying every other passive method to redress the situation, you are left with little choice but to take legal action.

It is a well-established fact that courts tend to favour the underdog, especially in cases where larger companies are trying to rip the small man off.

Furthermore, should you become a **litigant,** the chances of getting legal aid would be enhanced if you are a sole trader, (or individual), rather than being a director of a company. However, much would depend upon the expectations of your proposed financial dealings, and you may wish to raise this issue, whenever your accountant suggests that you trade under a limited liability company. There are merits in both, but the advantages of one may outweigh the other!

You should also consider the place where you actually negotiate your agreement, or indeed, perhaps more importantly, in what country that agreement will be signed and sealed.

For example, if you negotiate your deal in the UK, then the contract would be interpreted in accordance with English Law. Basically, this would mean that, even though you may have sold your concept to, say, an American company, any problems arising out of **Civil tort** (or legal actions, arising out of contractual disputes), would be heard in the English courts (and not American).

There are some benefits of having the English Judicial System on your side. I do not imply that the English courts would be an easier option, but certainly less costly than perhaps engaging in legal battle in America or another foreign country.

Therefore, if you are planning to get into the big league by entering into dozens of licences, make quite sure that your agreements are drawn by English lawyers, or if that's not possible, make sure the contracts will be interpreted in accordance with English law. Obviously, it will not always be possible to dictate every deal that you enter into or dictate whether the contract will be interpreted by English law or a foreign country – in which case, try to make sure that you are always represented by an English lawyer. When dealing on an international scale, you may find it necessary to have both English and foreign lawyers.

Nobody (apart from the lawyers themselves) ever benefits from litigation. Even if you win the case, you will be almost drained of human emotion, or indeed, although you may have won the case, you may not always recover your full costs. Therefore, legal action is to be avoided, unless you have absolutely no other way of protecting your rights.

The lawyer will be a master of stalling situations. Some stall a case simply to enhance the size of their fee. How many clients are going to argue over a lawyer's fees when it has taken some five years or more to resolve a legal wrangle? Any person with 'business expertise' would have solved the problem in a matter of days or even hours, whereas lawyers have the instinctive ability of being able to fool their clients into believing that the case in hand is one of the most difficult ones they have ever encountered. Yet, to you or me, most problems could be resolved if the parties only got around the table with their respective lawyers, and thrashed out the problems before more problems are created by the lawyers!

Before you instruct your lawyer to take legal action to redress a problem, ask yourself the following questions:

(1) Could I possibly resolve the issue by passive means, even if it means having to bend a little?

(2) If litigation appears to be the last resort, could I possibly afford to lose the case?

(3) If I enter into the legal arena, could there be any benefits to me, if the case was not heard within a reasonable time?

(4) If my lawyer was honest with me and told me it could take up to five or ten years to resolve, should I think twice before giving the go-ahead?

(5) Even if I win the case, have I any guarantees that the person or company will still be in business, and have the capital to pay the court award?

(6) What happens if my lawyer tells me I have a fifty-fifty chance of winning, and that he wants a couple of thousand up-front in fees?

(7) Do I really need to take legal action, or am I doing so either to get even or to seek revenge?

(8) Even if I win the case, will I recover all my costs and incidentals for my valuable and wasted time?

(9) Will my business reputation be tarnished, or my business
connections damaged?

All these questions, and lots more, will need clarification before
you decide on taking action against anyone. Do not expect your
lawyer to provide you with all the answers. Why should he hold
your hand? Your lawyer makes his living from the law, even if that
means creating business for himself!

How to conclude your contract

Let us assume that you have arranged to meet some directors of a
large organization who have expressed keen interest in your concept.

You arrive on the appointed day, probably tired after a long journey
on your motorcycle combination. You endeavour to park next to a
Rolls Royce, presumably belonging to one of the directors. The
doorman is giving you unwelcome looks and waving furiously,
indicating to you that you cannot park your bike there. Your confidence is such that you give him a V sign and continue to place a
lock and chain around your bike wheels, just in case some bastard
steals it! You remove your helmet and leather jacket and make
your way towards the impressive entrance. You hand them over to
the doorman saying, hang on to these mate – and don't run off with
them, will you?

The directors welcome you with open arms. You, by this time, are
feeling slightly over awed by your surroundings. However, the way
in which the directors are fussing over you, and making nice comments about your inventive abilities, assures you that the long

journey you have had to get there may very well have been worth-while.

During the course of the meeting you negotiate like a demon, which brings gasps of amazement from the directors. Finally the deal is struck!

It's now lunchtime, and the directors suggest that you join them for lunch at their club. They make it clear, thank the Lord, that the meal will be on them, which means you can now eat your sand-wiches on the way home. While you are knocking back the brandies, in the same way as you drink your Vimtos, everyone is being extremely nice to each other. Julian (that's the name of one of the directors) recommends that you help yourself to a few more breasts of pheasant, while he tucks into a steak the size of your garage door!

By now, you are singing like an overfed canary. Both directors seem great guys, and you are stunned by what they tell you they earn from their company.

During the course of all this chit-chat, Julian is casually enquiring into your well-being and background. You assume that he is just being friendly. Julian then says, 'I bet Harry – may I call you Harry?' 'Call me what you like', the brandy replies. And Julian continues to say, 'I bet you and your good wife take your holidays on the Bahamian Islands'. Then he adds, 'Babs, or Barbara, that's my lovely wife, and I will be going back there again this year'. You'd hate to tell him that you have already booked Bed and Breakfast in Skegness, so you say, 'Well actually Julian – may I call you Julian? Pat, Patricia, that's my lovely wife, and I hope to travel extensively this year', thereby giving him the impression that you're a real jet setter, and just praying that he did not see you arrive on your bike, your sole means of transport!

While you are having liqueurs and coffee in the lounge you hear a telephone ring. Simon (that's the name of the other director) swiftly pulls out his personal pocket telephone. 'It's our American head office, I'm afraid', he says. 'Our attorney wants me over there within twenty-four hours to sort out a few problems. I'm sorry Harry, I'll have to dash'. He then adds, 'I'm quite sure Julian will take great care of you – won't you Julian?' Julian assures Simon that he will do just that, but before Simon leaves, he says to Julian, 'Don't forget to talk to Harry about what we discussed, will you?'

Despite a slight deafness in one ear, and the alcohol playing merry hell with your liver, your inquisitive mind becomes instantly activated and you ask, 'What did Simon mean?' 'Oh, it's nothing really, Harry. Just that Simon and I plan to start our own company'. Then he stops – he is saying no more, so you are compelled to say, 'So what's that got to do with me?' 'Nothing really', he replies.

By this time you are getting excited, but you don't know just what about. You are forced to ask, 'OK Julian, what did Simon mean?' 'Well Harry, Simon and I wondered whether or not you would be interested in joining our company', he replies. He then goes on to outline the deal!

It would appear from this scenario that Julian and Simon have seen the potential of your invention, and have obviously discussed the possibility of setting up their own company, hoping that you will go along with their plans by negotiating a contract with their newly-founded company instead of signing a contract with the company whose car park your motorbike combination still graces!

QUESTION

Do you go along with Julian and Simon's plans and join their organization, knowing what you know about their limited resources? Or do you say, sorry gentlemen, I'd love to do business with you both, but not before you are more established?

ANSWER

Complete your contract with the established company. Perhaps join Julian and Simon at some time in the future, when you come up with another invention. By that time Julian and Simon may be more established, or you may be too old to care!

The above illustration may never arise in any of your dealings. Nevertheless, there is no harm in thinking about it on occasions – especially when someone offers you pheasant breasts and brandy!

I would stress that no one is under any legal obligation to use lawyers in drawing up any contracts. In fact, should you and the other party wish to, you could write your agreement to whatever on the back of a condom. That may be downright irresponsible but, if signed and witnessed, it would, in theory, be legal: both of you would, therefore, be under some contractual obligation. However, if you only have a condom upon your person, make damn sure that it is watertight and not full of holes, and doesn't F --- you up at some later stage! Pray also that, should litigation be the only alternative to enforce your agreement, that the judge is not a practising Roman Catholic! I would, however, strongly advise against doing any deals of this nature, even if it means saving a packet on legal fees!

Although I am reasonably well travelled, I have never visited Bonnie Scotland. I am told by every Scottish person I meet that Scotland is a wonderful country, and I am very tempted to spend some time there to find out for myself. I am also told that a **verbal agreement** made between two people in Scotland could constitute a legal binding agreement. Check this out before you have any dealings with these canny Scots. Or, better still, negotiate in sign language; preferably with both of your hands under your own kilt, rather than under theirs! I do hope I am able to visit Scotland before they exchange places with us Southerners!

Chapter 22 outlined some tricks people get up to whenever they are negotiating for something worthwhile. Both these chapters are directly linked: note down every detail that you find informative. When you have compiled a list, read it with some regularity so that many of the issues stick in your mind, rather than reading the entire chapters over and over again.

Before I proceed too far, and in order that you can fully understand related chapters, I would like you to assume that you have already reached a successful conclusion to the negotiation of your deal. (Not contract stage.) There are sound, logical reasons why I ask you to assume that the deal has already been struck, and these will become apparent in due course. However, let us assume that you have now reached **stage one** (deal agreed).

You now have to consider **stage two** (the final stage). Believe me, nothing would give me greater pleasure but to be able to tell you that, by reaching stage one, all of your problems are over. But I would not be doing you any service whatsoever if I did not take you through to the final stage.

Let us now assume that you have just left the company's palatial negotiating offices. You are feeling extremely pleased with yourself, and not without good reason. The negotiations went like a dream, and you exercised negotiating skills that impressed all the directors at the meeting. You even surprised yourself as, moments before you went into their office, you were shaking like a jelly baby; almost giving the game away whilst shaking the directors' hands.

On your way home, you are grinning like a Cheshire Cat and reflecting on how well you handled the negotiations, despite being faced with strong opposition. You decide to stop *en-route* and telephone your wife. Your wife is naturally delighted to hear the good news, and you fully expect that, by the time you arrive back home, the whole village will be out to greet you!

Arriving at your home, you are rather disappointed to note that your village appears deserted. And, to crown your disappointment, some inconsiderate sod has parked their vehicle, thereby blocking the entrance to your driveway. However, you convince yourself that it would be best if you maybe kept a low profile, as becoming a village celebrity would doubtless impose a great strain upon your valuable time. However, you wouldn't mind signing the occasional autograph – even if only to prove your own existence!

Although you have completed stage one, wait a while longer before you start booking that over due cruise on the Queen Elizabeth. Wait until such time as all the clever strokes, that both of you pulled on each other, are in contract form!

The contract must now be thrashed out between both your respective lawyers. Therefore, as mentioned before make quite sure you have noted every detail of what was **given** and **received** at the negotiating table. Pass every bit of the deal over to your lawyer. Most lawyers will be able to grasp the full significance, and be able to formulate a contract, based upon the information received.

It is therefore imperative that you have confidence and can trust your lawyer to deal with the contract. Most lawyers are well trained in this area, but I have to say that some lawyers are bloody incompetent, and can soon cock-up a deal made by their clients. Either they pussy-foot around not getting on with it, or they may act over-cautiously on matters that require nothing more than sound business judgement, which can often lead to the other party pulling out of a deal especially if they may have been trying to find a reasonable excuse to do so. If therefore, you have any reservations regarding the ability of your lawyer, then just keep him for writing out your will and find another to deal with the action!

The next stage will be the true test of your endurance.

Let us now examine exactly what you are bringing home, after concluding your successful deal. Well, for a start, I doubt that it will be a bankers-draft!

All you have so far achieved is an agreement in **principle** which means that you are well on your way but that the deal is still subject to the signing of formal contracts.

Warning

Should, however, at the conclusion of your business meeting, the directors offer you a 'payment' of any kind, (purely as an act of good faith on their part), do not accept one penny! Even if you have to nail both of your greedy hands to the desk.

Now you are bound to say just what kind of idiot would be foolish enough not to accept their offer of part-payment? You have posed a very fair question. I have to admit that whenever I am offered any money, I would most probably bite their fingers off with gratitude! However, just because I may be bloody greedy, that is no reason for you to adopt my weakness!

So what are the reasons for making you starve a few more weeks? We are now well aware that you have shaken hands on a successful deal – each party having tried to outmanoeuvre the other, which is acceptable business practice. The reason why I warn you against accepting any kind of advance payment is simply to protect you against yourself! Because once you have accepted a cash or cheque payment, regardless of whether it is only an insignificant part of the actual payment due to you, by accepting such payment, you have effectively **agreed** the contract. Therefore, as of that date, a legally binding agreement **exists** between both parties.

Let us assume the worst

At the negotiating table, the other side is probably far more experienced at negotiating deals than you would ever be. From the moment you set foot in their office, your behaviour becomes the focal point of their attention. They would be noting your various facial expressions, whenever they put business questions to you. They would already know something of your background, simply because you may have already revealed everything they need to know at a previous business lunch. They may be aware that you are strapped for cash, which may be obvious should the directors notice you arriving on your motorcycle combination.

Not only our inexperience but sometimes our desperation to conclude a deal will be noted by the other party, and may dictate the eventual outcome. I have, however, endeavoured to give you some useful tips on how to conduct yourself during the course of negotiating in general, through other chapters. Meanwhile, the dangers of accepting any pre-payments, before contracts are exchanged, could undermine the whole deal which you thought you had concluded, while shaking their hands at the end of the meeting.

With their cheque safely tucked inside your wallet, they may probably say, 'Well Mr Cole, it was a pleasure doing business with you'. Note that suddenly it is not Harry any more, but 'Mr Cole'! Do not read too much into this – perhaps they are genuinely being polite, or appreciate your business acumen and wish to show you some respect. They may go on to say, 'Our lawyers will be in contact with yours very shortly'. You take your leave, and that appears to be the end of it.

Well, not quite, I'm afraid. When you get back home, at the earliest opportunity, you make an appointment with your lawyer. The earliest that your lawyer can see you is in a week's time. You arrive for your appointment, full of enthusiasm. Your lawyer greets you with the words, 'Well done, I believe you have sold your invention'.

This statement takes you back a little, simply because you haven't even told him anything yet! Your lawyer explains that he has received a contract in the post yesterday and, although he has not had time to look it over, now would be a good time to do so. As he goes through the contract, you interrupt him at least a dozen times, saying things like, 'Christ, I never agreed to this', and 'I never agreed to that'. By now it has become clear that the agreement stated in the contract sadly resembles nothing like the one you thought you had struck. When you inform your lawyer that you have accepted a pre-payment, his silence becomes obvious. Then he says, 'Oh dear, oh dear, oh dear'. You now realize that something has gone very wrong!

If the contract your lawyer received is not what you agreed, you will have some difficulty in proving it. Litigation is costly and time-consuming. Naturally, you are in a right fix, and it may take far more than a clever lawyer to put matters right!

It is remotely possible that your lawyer may be able to extricate you from this serious situation, should it be proved that your contract is unconscionable. In other words, if the other party had acted unscrupulously, or took unfair advantage of you.

Litigation, in such matters, could take several years, with the legal costs far beyond the average person's capability to pay. Perhaps your lawyer could reach some compromise with the other party. But, whatever the outcome, this situation could well have been avoided by not going ahead and acting as your own lawyer!

I would recommend that you ask your lawyer to go with you whenever you arrange a business appointment that is likely to reach a successful conclusion.

I do not advise anyone to negotiate any such deals all on their own: everyone needs some moral support. The great advantage of having your lawyer by your side, apart from the professional back-up, is that he may be able to deal with a draft contract on their territory, even if it means staying overnight.

Your lawyer should be able to agree a clause in that contract whereby you receive a part-payment, which could be released to you immediately, pending the full **engrossment** of the final contract. If you find yourself in this situation, then do not be afraid to discuss the implication of getting a pre-payment on exchange of contracts.

Naturally, if all parties wish for a quick settlement then it's down to the lawyers to 'process' the deal as quickly as possible. The quicker the deal is completed, the quicker the other party can begin to exploit your concept, and the quicker you start receiving those royalties should that form part of your deal.

It is, therefore, imperative that you choose a lawyer who would give you every support when needed – a lawyer who will see the difficulties you may be facing, and possibly volunteer to take time off from his office to come along to the negotiating table with you. Lawyers of this calibre are a rare species these days; but if you don't ask them, they certainly will not suggest going themselves.

Should, however, your lawyer be unable to accompany you, do not be too smart and go it alone.

I would recommend that you go and see your nearest Chamber of Commerce. Explain to the secretary or president exactly what your intentions are, and ask them if they could recommend one of their members to accompany you. Better still, engage the professional services of a member of the Institute of International Licensing Practitioners or indeed a member of the Licensing Executive Society. Both addresses are listed in the Appendix. Both are professional associations, whose members are trained in the area of negotiating licenses, royalties or general exclusive sell-offs of their clients' Intellectual Property Rights. They offer impartial advice which means that if you are their client, they will take over all your worries and will endeavour to obtain the best possible deal for you!

Furthermore, engaging a professional to negotiate on your behalf will certainly pay dividends. You may find that most of the companies that you negotiate with will prefer to deal in this way, rather than with novices! It simply saves a lot of time. Therefore, it takes a professional to engage a professional.

Even if the other side is not represented by a member of one of these associations, that will not necessarily mean that your negotiator will wipe the floor with the other side. It will demonstrate that you are acting in a professional manner, and the chances are, a deal will evolve to your mutual benefit. There will obviously be costs involved, and it would be wise to get in writing exactly what they are, before engaging anyone.

You must remember that you have now reached the critical stage of your journey and it would be utter foolishness even to think that because you have battled through so far, the negotiating part will be a piece of cake.

In fact, I have to make a public confession and tell you that despite my own useful knowledge on this subject, I would have serious doubts as to whether I could pull off the best deal for myself, assuming I had reached your stage of the game. Indeed, the more I think about it the less likelihood I would have of concluding a successful deal in this way, simply because I would have too much emotional connection with my concept, and we all know that innovators often mislead themselves into believing that their invention must be 'priceless' and worth a fortune, because they invented it. However, without wishing to demote my own negotiating abilities, I would certainly achieve a better deal for someone else, should they engage my services, and became my client. It would be a completely different emotional experience as one could deal in an impartial way, and fully detached from emotional restraints.

I suspect that many licensing agents would agree an initial time fee, and commission based upon what they actually have achieved for you. In any event, contact the office to get more details. Incidentally, and as a last thought on this particular issue, although you will have to pay professional fees, most professionals aim to recover all the fees they charge their clients, by way of getting that bit extra out of the deal! Therefore, it will cost you nothing if they can get more than you ever expected.

Useful clauses for your licence

Prior to your granting another party a licensing agreement on your patent or whatever it is you are negotiating to license out, the following clauses should be incorporated into your agreement (they are not in any form of sequence neither are they exhaustive as every contract or agreement will slightly vary, according to the actual deal that you are negotiating or have negotiated). Your lawyer will no doubt complete the picture, but these may serve to stimulate your mind):

- The agreement to be **subject to contract**
- Full names and addresses of company that you are dealing with
- Whether licence is exclusive or non-exclusive
- State whatever is being licensed
- Terms and conditions of grant
- Define: manufacturing or marketing licence
- If territorial licence: define territory
- Clause also not to 'exceed' boundary limits
- Limitations as to patent permitted use
- Licensee to give undertaking not to exceed permitted use
- Licensee to give undertaking not to disclose terms of agreement to third parties
- Specify payment dates, i.e. when royalties are paid
- Clause: failure to maintain production quality
- Licensor to retain full rights upon insolvency of licensee
- Not to assign (without licensor's consent)
- Licensee not to modify or alter specifications
- Licensee to maintain sales records
- Licensor (or advisers) to audit sales records
- Specific date to commence production
- Acknowledge licensor's rights in all licensee's promotion or sales literature
- Licensee to indemnify licensor against all claims arising or pursuant to licensee's use

- Licensee to use best endeavours to promote product(s)
- Clause: stating reasons for termination of agreement
- Damages for licensee's breach of agreement
- Expiry of licence
- License's right to renew (after expiry date)
- Clause: stating minimum of sales to be achieved
- All payment to be net (no deductions of any kind)
- Notice of licensee's intending to 'wind-up' company
- Limitations of period for completion of contracts made prior to termination
- Delivery-up to licensor of all confidential or technical information upon termination
- Licensee to pay patent annuity fees and insurance (if applicable)
- Licensee to register licence and at own expense with patent office
- Clause: stating that you retain your full ownership to your Intellectual Property, irrespective of whether the other party gives an undertaking that they will provide further technology or develop your concept. Much will depend upon the advance stage of your own development prior to negotiating licence agreements: therefore you may have to compromise, by sharing your Intellectual Property Rights. (Even if you do share your rights this would not necessarily mean that you have to share half the royalties or reduce your monetary expectations – neither of you has anything without the other, so don't get greedy!
- Registered address of company, in order to serve any notices upon them

- All agreements to be interpreted in accordance with English Law (whenever possible) or Scottish Law (if appropriate)

- Any disputes between parties will be dealt with by arbitration procedures as laid down by either the English or Scottish Law Societies

Obviously, your lawyer may include a dozen or more clauses within your agreement, and will 'expand' upon each clause because one day your agreement may have to be interpreted in a court of law. Therefore, never be foolish enough to act as your own lawyer – even if you are a trained lawyer always get further legal advice!

A final word

Let me finish by giving you one final example as to why I urge you to be cautious in every aspect of your dealings. It may make you more aware as to why you should protect your rights well before you enter into negotiations with anyone, regardless of whoever they are.

Never be fooled by the size of the company or conglomerate that you are dealing with. I know you must trust someone in this life, but don't automatically trust anyone whenever you are dealing with your invention. Perhaps you may understand my concern when you read the following true facts.

An American inventor, by the name of Mr Robert Kearns, who also happens to be a University Professor, invented a new kind of vehicle windscreen wiper. It would appear that in the mid-sixties, Professor Kearns took his invention to the Ford Motor Company in America, hoping to sell the rights to his invention. Ford Motors stopped dealing with him and, in 1969, they introduced a new wiper on all their cars, one which was based on Professor Kearns own principles. Ford Motors claimed the rights for themselves. In other words, they stole his idea!

Professor Kearns took Ford Motors to court and he won his case. The courts ordered the Ford Motor Company to pay the Professor a royalty of about ten pence (UK currency) per unit, back-dated from 1969.

Additionally, the courts awarded Professor Kearns substantial damages of about £2.9 million. It is also estimated that his royalty payment alone from Ford Motors will exceed £600,000 per year, so you can imagine the many millions he will make each year from other car manufacturers who are using his invention.

Now all this may not have been possible if indeed Professor Kearns had not been able to satisfy the courts that this simple yet brilliant idea was his creation! Therefore, I have mentioned it time and time again throughout this book, and I shall mention it for the last time: **Never expose your idea or concept to anyone, without first taking out precautions to protect your Intellectual Property Rights!**

The illustration of Professor Kearns may serve to prove two vital points that I have endeavoured to preach throughout this book.

(1) Mr Ron Hickman and indeed Professor Kearns, and a great many others, made their millions from having an ingenious yet simple idea! Therefore, you have the same chances in life to equal their success.

(2) Regardless of the size of the company that you may be doing business with, still exercise some caution. Therefore, before you start singing like a canary or indeed, accepting lunches of pheasant breasts and brandy, make quite certain that you have taken every precaution, as outlined in this book, to protect and safeguard your Intellectual Property Rights.

GOOD LUCK!

Glossary

ABSTRACT: A summary of words that describe your idea or invention. Denoting art in which the subject is represented by shapes and patterns, rather than by a realistic likeness.

AGREEMENT: A name for a contract, which is made between two or more parties; a settlement of terms or conditions associated with any business transaction, or arrangement made privately between two or more people.

APOLLO: First space craft to land men on the moon. On 21 July 1969, US astronauts Neil Armstrong and Edwin (Buzz) Aldrin first stepped out of 'Apollo' on to the surface of the moon. The mission had lasted eight days in all, of which twenty-one hours and thirty-six minutes were spent on the moon's surface.

ASSET: A thing or person that is valuable or useful; usually associated with property or a person's worth. His assets are quite considerable. Used in the context of this book, it means that the holder of a patent or other registrations can effectively trade them.

ASSIGNED: To transfer one's rights over to another person; I am the copyright owner, but I propose to assign my work over to the publisher; I have assigned my lease of my shop. To vest your whole interest in whatever, over to someone else.

AXIOM: A self-evident statement, usually intended by the author to express some words of wisdom.

CAPITALIZE: To take advantage of; now that I have my patent, I can capitalize on my good fortune and endeavour to sell to the highest bidder.

CERTIFICATE OF REGISTRATION: A document confirming that you have submitted an application for whatever – or obtained registration for whatever.

CIVIL TORT: A legal jargon usually associated with a civil 'wrong' or 'injury' for which action for damages may be instituted, (arising out of contractual disputes).

CLONE: A person that closely resembles another usually in having the same facial features. A twin duplicate of a person.

CONCEPT: An idea usually to an advanced stage.

CONCIERGE: The head doorman of hotel or office commercial buildings; usually wears a uniform and found lurking in the foyer.

CONTRACT: A verbal or written agreement made between two or more parties.

COPYRIGHT: The exclusive legal right to reproduce and control an original literary, musical or other form of artistic work. Copyrights are not registrable, but legally protectable in cases of infringement. Copyrights can be assigned over to another by the owner of the original works: I am the author of this book, therefore no person shall breach my copyrights by reproducing or copying it without my written authority to do so.

COUNTERFEITING: Illegally producing a copy from the original: usually associated with forgeries of stamps, passports or money: an imitation designed to deceive or defraud. The flagrant abuse and infringement of a person's Intellectual Property Rights.

CRITERIA: Standards by which something can be judged or decided upon. The basic criteria for obtaining a patent would be, it must be new, it must not be obvious and it must be capable of industrial application.

DAMAGES: Used in the legal sense: should you be in breach of contract, I shall sue you for damages; seeking a monetary solution in a court of law. Or should you slander my good name, I shall sue you for damages.

DATABASE: Stored information, usually on a computer disc and quickly retrievable. Used widely by the Patent Office in their Search and Advisory Division.

DEFAULT: Implied in legal context meaning that a party to an agreement has not observed the terms or conditions of the agreement and is, therefore, in default (presumably a penalty would follow).

DESIGN (Registered): A monopoly right giving you protection of your design, for a specific period and granted by the Patent Office. A registered design can be bought, sold or licensed.

DESIGN (Right): Design right is a new Intellectual Property Right which applies to original, non-commonplace designs of a shape or configuration of articles. Design right is not a monopoly right, nor registrable, but it gives the owner the right to prevent copying and lasts until ten years after first marketing articles made to the design. A design right can be bought, sold or licensed.

DESIGNATE: To select specific names of countries in which you wish to file your patent application, which would be applicable to European Patent Convention (EPC) or Patent Cooperation Treaty (PCT).

DESIGNER (Stubble): A day or two's growth of hair on a man's face: Those types with the stubble, believe it makes them more 'macho', the reverse is often the case.

DISCLAIMER: A word usually associated in the legal framework of contracts, which denotes a repudiation or denial; not accepting any liability for whatever eventualities occur after a transaction.

EUROPEAN PATENT CONVENTION (EPC): Several European countries, including the UK, subscribe to this Patent Convention. Means that the person wishing to have patents in several European countries, need only file one application. But in doing so, the applicant must 'designate' and name the countries that he wishes to obtain protection of his invention. Although you file only one application, you still pay the appropriate fee of each chosen country.

EXCLUSIVE RIGHTS: Granting a person or company sole rights to manufacture or exploit your invention or copyrights.

FAIR DEALINGS: This will apply more to the infringement of an author's work: for example, the Copyright, Designs and Patents Act 1988 deals with exceptions to infringements. The Act provides for a large number of exceptions to the rules of infringement, some examples would include literary, dramatic, musical or artistic works for the purpose of research, private study, criticism or review.

FRANCHISING: The grant of a licence to operate an already established business, with a proven track record, in areas agreed by the franchiser. The buyer or franchisee, will use the same trade name and operate the new business in accordance with the established business. It is customary in many agreements of this nature for the operators to pay an agreed percentage of either their turnover or profit to the franchise or parent company and purchase all goods for resale through the main parent company, despite each operator being the owner of his establishment. For example, McDonalds, Kentucky Fried Chicken and Dyno-Rod are all franchised operations.

GOVERNMENT INNOVATIVE CENTRE: A kind of business 'workshop' set up by the government to offer assistance and training to all individuals and small businesses. The centres are regionalized and staffed by business and professional personnel with special training in the field of helping people to 'start up' businesses, which include assistance for the innovators, and assisted government grants.

IDEASMAN: A person of either gender who is forever creating inventive ideas.

IMPUNITY: To commit an uncivilized act against society which would be exempt from punishment or unpleasant consequences: a criminal may be offered impunity of the law, to act as a witness for the prosecution.

INDEMNIFY: To insure against loss or damages, perhaps arising out of the company that you deal with going out of business (obtaining protection against eventualities).

INFRINGEMENT: When a person copies your Intellectual Property Rights, without your authority. Normally associated with the reproduction of a person's copyrights without their authorization.

INTELLECTUAL PROPERTY RIGHTS: Can include copyrights, patent grants, registered designs, design rights; those rights which are applicable to the owner's original works that have a measure of protection in law.

INTERLOCUTORY: A legal injunction to prevent infringement of a person's rights.

LEGAL AID: To assist persons who are unable to afford the full cost of legal representation.

LICENSING: The owner may grant a licence to another to exploit the right, whilst retaining overall ownership and can either negotiate a 'one off' payment or agree royalty payments. Licences are usually granted to cover specified territorial areas or separate countries. Licence agreements will usually specify when that agreement expires with possible provisions of renewal. Licence agreements can be complex documents and legal advice should be sought at all times. (A licence can be granted orally, but this is certainly not advised.)

LITIGANT: A party involved in a law suit.

LITIGATION: The process of bringing or contesting a law suit.

LOONY-BIN: A slang name for a lunatic asylum where some inventors may end up if they aren't careful!

MONOPOLY: Trader with no competition: exclusive rights to exploit your patent for twenty years.

NON-DISCLOSURE OF CONFIDENTIAL INFORMATION: An expressed agreement (preferably in writing) indicating that your trade secrets will be safe with those who are a party to signing that paper document. The recipient undertakes to treat your discussions or information that is supplied to him in confidence, and will not disclose that information to a third party without your authorization. Another method of trying to protect 'ideas' which cannot be protected by legal process.

PATENT AGENT: A person professionally trained in all aspects of the patent laws and systems. A person to engage whenever you wish to file for a patent or other forms of design registrations.

PATENT COOPERATION TREATY (PCT): Also referred to as International Patent Application. An applicant who wishes to file a patent or registered designs on an international scale need only file one application, but will have to designate and specify the countries that form part of this treaty. There are 39 countries that subscribe to this treaty, including the USA and the UK; applicants will pay the appropriate patent fees of their designed country: it is a saving on time and general administration. (Similar procedure to filing a European Patent Convention (EPC)).

PATENT COUNTY COURTS: The revised Copyright, Designs and Patents Act 1988 makes provision for cases of infringement of those rights to be now heard in a Lower Court known as a Patent County Court. This is a great benefit both in obtaining an earlier court date and allows huge savings on legal costs, at least a fraction to that of a High Court hearing. There are, however, certain provisions of using these courts which are outlined in this book. For the first time in legal history, chartered patent attorneys are able to represent you in these courts, thus eliminating the need for expensive barristers and their entourage.

PATENT GRANT: Another term indicating that a person has now obtained their patent.

PATENT SYSTEM: Appertaining to the rules, regulations and laws and procedures of seeking protection for your Intellectual Property Rights.

PENALTY: In the context of contracts or agreements, when you are in default of an agreement, you will suffer a penalty. (A penalty clause in contracts usually defines the nature of the penalty).

PLAGIARIZE: To steal a person's Intellectual Property Rights, for the purpose of reproducing or selling those goods without any payment of royalties: more associated with literary, musical or artistic works.

PLOY: A crafty manoeuvre designed to take the advantage of another. For example, you may be negotiating your deal with a beautiful lady who displays her charms enough to distract your concentration on the deal. A company may keep you waiting well after the due appointment, to express to you that they have the power to keep you waiting until they are ready to see you.

PRIORITY DATE: When you have filed your application to the Patent Office, they will acknowledge receipt of your filed application. This acknowledgement is your 'priority date' which implies that you now have a priority date over any other person who may file an application on the same invention. (After your own application). A priority date does not imply or guarantee that you will eventually obtain a patent.

PROPS: Usually associated with property to support your image: can at times be used in a deceptive manner to make people believe you are rich when you're not. Spacious marble clad office foyers, giving you the impression of corporate strength and importance. Props can apply to stage or theatre scenery, probably inter-connected to increase your visual impression.

PROTOTYPE: Generally associated with a two- or three- dimensional model of your invention. A working model to show potential customers how your invention works.

QUIA TIMET: A legal injunction to prevent an infringement of your copyright before it happens. If you hear that a company is about to launch a product which would infringe your rights, you can apply to the courts and put a stop to it.

REGRESSION: To go back in time to when you were a child: behaviour more appropriate to a child.

RENEWAL FEES: Once you have obtained a patent grant or other forms or registered rights, you still have to pay a yearly registration fee to the issuing Patent Office, until the date of expiry of your registered rights.

REVOKED PATENT: Occasionally, patent grants can be revoked by the issuing Patent Office for several reasons. For example, you may have published details of your invention in a trade magazine or publicly revealed details of your invention before the Patent Office does so; you may not have paid the renewal fees. But in some cases, a claim to originality by another inventor may be upheld in a court of law, possibly by another country; therefore, this may give grounds for your patent grant to be revoked!

RIPPED OFF: Slang for being taken advantage of. Someone who has 'taken you for a ride' over some business transaction. This quite often happens to innovators so read this book thoroughly.

ROYALTIES: They are a form of payment that is given to the inventor by the buyer or licensee of his invention for the right to manufacture or commercially exploit the inventor's idea or concept. The basis of payment is a percentage of the manufacturer's selling price (over and above the manufacturing cost). Other methods of calculating royalties is defined in Chapter 17.

SCEPTICS: Person(s) who seriously doubt the abilities of their fellow man: pessimistic types, always prepared to look on the downside of things. The world is full of sceptics when it comes to evaluating an innovator's dream.

SEARCH AND EARLY PUBLICATION: An applicable term associated with the Patent Office, which denotes that they have carried out their usual searches and now propose to publish (or expose to the general public) full details of the invention that you claim a patent or monopoly rights thereon.

SEIZURE (of goods): Usually a measure taken by persons involved in defending their rights against counterfeiting or the reproduction of goods for resale without the authority of the copyright owner. For example, designer goods, perfume, talcum powder, brand goods that are protected by their copyrights or trade marks. The Port officials have the power to seize such goods to prevent them coming on to the market.

SERVICE MARK: It is an identification symbol which is used in the course of trade to enable the consumer to distinguish one trader's service from a similar service. It is a registrable right and must be distinguishable from any other service mark symbol.

SEMICONDUCTOR CHIPS: Similar in process to silicone chips. A kind of microchip that has increased technological advancements.

SUBSTANTIVE EXAMINATION: This is a Patent Office term to denote your application is now in the final stages. The patent specification is now examined to see that it meets all relevant requirements of the patent law. All searches previously carried out will be thoroughly examined to establish whether your invention is new and not obvious. Once these requirements have been met, your patent is then granted.

SPIVS: An assumed shady character who thrives on small time wheeling and dealing. Many times unkindly associated with used car dealers. George Cole, actor, celebrity and star of the TV series 'Minder' and I are not related – but I'm sure his character-part could teach us all a thing or two!

TECHNOCRAT: A person of either sex who deals in the field of science and technology or research (a scientist).

TECHNOLOGY TRANSFER AGENTS: Person(s) or companies who specialize in marrying the inventor with industries. Can often offer in house project development and deal with all licences of your invention. They work on a percentage of what they can sell your invention for. Many offer a fine professional service, but there are some who are in business just to rip off the innovator by charging high fees to cover their administration. Check them all out first before committing yourself to their service.

TRADE MARK: It is an identification symbol which is used in the course of trade to enable the consumer to distinguish easily one trader's goods from another trader who is selling the same goods, but not necessarily the same quality product. Usually carries the initials TM on the products. It is a registered right and is, therefore protected in a court of law against infringement. Trade or service marks are now regarded as a company asset and high values can be placed upon them whenever disposing of a company. They can also be sold or licensed and, in some cases, can be used as collateral for a bank loan.

TRADE MARK AGENTS: A person(s) who deals specifically in the area of trade or service marks. They will give you advice and prosecute your application for registration. Specialist in the field of trade or service marks.

VALIDITY: Having some foundation which is based on the truth; legally acceptable licence or registration. Having substance to your claim for monopoly rights to your invention.

VERBAL AGREEMENT: An agreement that is done verbally and not recorded into a written contract. Difficult to prove in a court of law and, therefore, not wise to enter into if you are dealing with your invention. It is believed that a verbal agreement in Scotland is enforceable in law. Scottish Law is distinguishable from English Law: so be careful what you say, should you deal in Scotland.

VOID: In the context of contracts that are rendered ineffectual or invalid. For example, I could not obtain a patent on my invention, therefore, the conditional contract (conditional upon me getting my patent grant) now becomes void: it ceases to be valid any more.

WHIZ-KID: A term of endearment we often give to anyone we assume is likely to reach great heights in their career. A go-getter, usually associated in the finance industry.

'WORKMATE': Registered trade mark name of a work bench designed and invented by Mr Ron Hickman for all DIY enthusiasts and tradesmen. Over twenty-five million units sold universally at the time of this book's publication.

Appendix of useful addresses

The Patent Office operates departments from both London and Gwent. If in any doubt about which division you need, contact the main office in Gwent:

The Patent Office
Concept House
Tredegal Park
Cardiff Road
Newport
Gwent NP9 1RH
Tel: 0633 814000

The Designs Registry
The Patent Office
Chartist Tower
Upper Dock Street
Newport
Gwent NP9 1DW
Tel: 0633 814000
General Enquiries ext 5162

Queries on copyright should be addressed to:

Industrial Property and Copyright Department
Copyright Enquiries
Hazlitt House
45 Southampton Buildings
Chancery Lane

London WC2A 1AR
Tel: 071 438 4778
Search and Advisory Service
The Patent Office
Hazlitt House
45 Southampton Buildings
Chancery Lane
London WC2A 1AR
Tel: 071 438 4747/8

Marketing and publicity enquiries, requests for free literature, and general enquiries relating to the services of the Patent Office, are dealt with on 071 838 4747

The European Patent Office
Erhardtstrasse 27
D 8000 Munchen 2

The Department of Trade and Industry
Consumer Affairs Division
Millbank Tower
Millbank
London SW1P 4QU
Tel: 071 211 3000

Or:

(Name of Country, i.e. Germany)
Overseas Trade Division
Department of Trade and Industry
1 Victoria Street
London SW1H 0ET
Tel: 071 215 7877

Or:

HM Customs and Excise
General Customs Division B
Kent House
Upper Ground
London SE1 9PS
Tel: 071 928 0533

Chartered Institute of Patent Agents
Staple Inn Buildings South
High Holborn
London WC1V 7PZ
Tel: 071 405 9450

Institute of Trade Mark Agents
Suite 3
Panther House
38 Mount Pleasant
London WX1X 0AP

Scottish Woollen Trade Mark Association Ltd
45 Moray Place
Edinburgh EH3 6EQ

Trade Marks Patents & Designs Federation
5th Floor
Henrietta Place
London W1M 9AG

Trade Mark Consultants Co
54 Hillbury Avenue
Harrow
Middlesex HA3 8EW
Tel: 081 907 6066
Fax: 081 907 0743
(contact George Myrants)

The Law Society
The Law Society's Hall
113 Chancery Lane
London WC2 1PL
Tel: 071 242 1222 (England and Wales)

The Incorporated Law Society of Northern Ireland
Law Society House
90–106 Victoria Street
Belfast BT1 3JZ
Tel: 0232 231614

The Design Council
28 The Haymarket
London SW1Y 4SU
Tel: 071 839 8000

Chartered Society of Designers
29 Bedford Square
London WC1B 3EG

European Business & Innovative Centre (BIC)
205 Rue Belliard
2nd Floor
B1040 Brussels
Tel: 32 2 23 10747
Fax: 32 2 23 11016

The Anglo-Taiwan Trade Committee
4th Floor
Minster House
272–274 Vauxhall Bridge Road
London SW1V 1BB
Tel: 071 829 9167

Anti-Counterfeiting Group (ACG)
c/o Quilthorn Ltd
2 Lewins Yard
Market Square
Chesham
Bucks HP5 1ES
Tel: 0494 449165

British Technology Group
Information Division
101 Newington Causeway
London SE1 6BU
Tel: 071 043 6666

Database
Director of Marketing
Longman Cartermill Ltd
Technology Centre
St Andrews
Fife KY16 9EA
Tel: 0344 77660

The Engineering Council
10 Maltravers Street
London WC2R 3ER
Tel: 071 240 7891

British Institute of Management
Management House
Cottingham Road
Corby
Northants N17 1TT
Tel: 0536 204222

Institute of Management Consultants
5th Floor
32–33 Hatton Garden
London EC1N 8DL
Tel: 071 242 2140

MOD New Supplies Services
(Small Firms Group)
Room 318
Lacon House
Ministry of Defence
Thelbalds Road
London WC1X 8RY
Tel: 071 430 5851

Technology Transfer Agents
The Director
H Room E/601
Training Agency
Moorfoot
Sheffield
Tel: 0742 307740

British Franchising Association
Franchise Chambers
75a Bell Street
Henley-on-Thames
Oxon RG9 2BD
Tel: 0491 578 049

Small Firms Division
Department of Employment
Steel House
Tothill Street
London SW1H 9NP
Freefone Enterprise
Dial: 0800 222999

The Institute of Purchasing & Supply (IPS)
Easton House
Easton on the Hill
Stamford
Lincolnshire PE9 3NZ
Tel: 0780 56777

NSP Group Limited
NSP House
211 Lower Richmond Road
Richmond
Surrey TW9 4LN
Tel: 081 878 9111
Fax 081 878 9582

Further Sources:

The Institute of Patentees and Inventions
Suite 505a
Triumph House
189 Regent Street
London W1R 7WF
Tel: 071 242 7812

Offer an invaluable and comprehensive service to their members,
therefore if you have a patent or have filed for a patent, then don't
hesitate to contact the Secretary, to find out what they can do for
you!

Licensing Agents

It is essential to have a professional to negotiate your deal on your behalf: too much is at stake to try and go it alone! Contact:

Institute of International Licensing
Practitioners
Suite 78 Kent House
87 Regent Street
London W1R 7HF
Tel: 071 439 7097

Or:

Licensing Executives Society Ltd
c/o Borax Research Ltd
Cox Lane
Chessington Surrey KT9 1SJ
Tel: 081 397 5141

BP Innovation LINC
Gatekeeper Agencies
General enquiries: 071 920 3079

Ogwr Partnership Trust
Enterprise Centre Bryn Road Tondu
Bridgend CF32 9BS
Tel: 0656 603871

Cambridge Enterprise Agency
71a Lensfield Road
Cambridge CB2 1EN
Tel: 0223 323553

SCOPE
Scope House
Western Road
Crewe CW1 1DD
Tel: 0270 589 569

DONBAC
19–21 Hallgate
Doncaster DN1 3NA
Tel: 0302 340 320

Design Works (Gateshead)
William Street Felling
Gateshead NE10 0JP
Tel: 091 495 0066

Entrust
Portman House
Portland Road
Newcastle upon Tyne NE2 1BL
Tel: 091 261 4838

Glasgow Opportunities
7 West George Street
Glasgow G2 1EQ
Tel: 041 221 0955

Kettering Business Venture Trust
Doublas House
27 Station Road
Kettering N15 7HH
Tel: 0536 513840

London Enterprise Agency
4 Snow Hill
London EC1A 2BS
Tel: 071 236 3000

Manchester Business Venture
Manchester Chamber of Commerce
56 Oxford Street
Manchester M60 7HJ
Tel: 061 236 0153

Milton Keynes Business Venture
Civic Office
1 Saxon Gate East
Milton Keynes MK9 3JH
Tel: 0908 660044

Enterprise Plymouth
Somerset Place
Stoke
Plymouth PL3 4BB
Tel: 0752 569211

Sandwell Enterprise
Sandwell Business Advice Centre
Victoria Street
West Bromwich B70 8ET
Tel: 021 500 5412

Innovation Centres

All these are members of AICE, the Association of Innovation Centre Executives, and provide a wide range of support and assistance:

North East Innovation Centre
Saltmeadows Road
Gateshead NE8 3AH
Tel: 091 490 1222

Industrial Development Unit
Strathclyde Regional Council
20 India Street
Glasgow G2 4PF
Tel: 041 227 3861

Merseyside Innovation Centre
131 Mount Pleasant
Liverpool L3 5TF
Tel: 051 708 0123

South London Innovation Centre
1-4 Brixton Hill Place
London SW2 1HJ
Tel: 081 671 4055

Centre for Product Development
The Lenton Business Centre
Lenton Boulevard
Nottingham N47 2BY
Tel: 0602 78200

Business Development Centre
Welsh Development Agency
Treforest Industrial Estate
Pontypridd CF37 5UT
Tel: 0443 841777

Cornwall Innovation Centre
Camon Wilson Way Pool
Redruth TR15 3RS
Tel: 0209 717111

Somerset Innovation Centre
Rural Development Commission
3 Chartfield House
Castle Street
Taunton TA1 4AS
Tel: 0823 276905

Industrial Development Unit
Telford Industrial Centre
Stafford Park 4
Telford TF3 3BA
Tel: 0952 290329

The Design Council

The Innovation Centre
The Design Council
28 Haymarket
London SW1Y 4SU
Tel: 071 839 8000

Development Agencies

These support and encourage new and existing businesses in their regions by varied means, including financial and marketing help.

Scottish Development Agency
Rosebery House
Haymarket
Edinburgh EH12 5EZ
Tel: 031 337 9595

Welsh Development Agency
Business Development Centre
Treforest Industrial Estate
Pontypridd CF37 5UT
Tel: 0443 841 777

Rural Development Commission
141 Castle Street
Salisbury
Wiltshire SP1 3TP
Tel: 0722 336255

Patent Libraries

Patent Department Central Library
Birmingham B3 3HQ
Tel: 021 235 4537

Science & Technology Department
Mitchell Library
Glasgow G3 7DN
Tel: 041 221 7030

Patents Information Unit
32 York Road
Leeds LS9 8TD
Tel: 0532 488747

Patents Department
Central Library
Liverpool L3 8EW
Tel: 051 225 5442

British Library
25 Southampton Buildings
London WC2A 1AW
Tel: 071 405 8721
Patent services Tel: 071 323 followed by:

UK and EPO patent enquiries: 7919
Express photocopy service: 7927
On-line patent search service: 7903

Science Museum Library
South Kensington
London SW7 5NH
Tel: 071 589 3456

Patents Department
Central Library
St Peter's Square
Manchester M2 5PD
Tel: 061 236 9422

Commercial Department
Central Library
Newcastle upon Tyne NE99 1DX
Tel: 091 261 0691

Science & Technology Library
Central Library
Sheffield S1 1XZ
Tel: 0742 734 742

Patent Information Centres

These hold patent indexes and guidance material only

Commercial Department
Central Library
Aberdeen AB9 1GU
Tel: 0224 634 811

Commercial Department
Central Library
Bristol BS1 5TL
Tel: 0272 299 148

The Library
Lanchester Polytechnic
Coventry CV1 2HF
Tel: 0203 838448

Reference Department
Central Library
Plymouth PL4 8AL
Tel: 0752 264 675

Reference Department
Central Library
Portsmouth PO1 2DX
Tel: 0705 819311

Commercial Department
Central Library
Belfast BT1 1EA
Tel: 0232 243233

Licensing Agents

Institute of International
Licensing Practitioners
Suite 78
Kent House
87 Regent Street
London W1R 7HF
Tel: 071 439 7091

Licensing Executives Society Ltd
c/o Borax Research Ltd
Cox Lane
Chessington
Surrey KT9 1SJ
Tel: 081 397 5141

Lawyer for Enterprise

Lawyers offering the LE scheme: offer a free consultation to discuss your business. For a list contact:

The Law Society
113 Chancery Lane
London WC2A 1PL
Tel: 071 405 905

Information for market/product research etc.

Your local reference library

This could be a central public library with a commercial section; or a college, polytechnic or University library. As a member of the public you can usually use all of them. Many have on-line access to UK and international commercial/technical databases.

The British Library
Business Information Service
25 Southampton Buildings
London WC2A 1AW
Tel: 071 323 7454

For Free, quick enquiry service:
071 323 7979 for fee-based research service
including on-line searching

Sources of all UK companies' information including annual reports. Comprehensive collection of market research reports and journals, directories, trade, business and product literature.

Companies House
England and Wales: Crown Way
Cardiff CF4 3OZ
Tel: 0222 388 588

Scotland: 100–102 George Street
Edinburgh EH2 3DJ
Tel: 031 225 5774

Export Market Information Centre

Department of Enterprise

1 Victoria Street
London SW1H 0ET
Tel: 071 215 5444

Market Research Society
15 Northburgh Street
London EC1V 0AH
Tel: 071 490 4911

British Standards Institution
BSI Linford Wood
Milton Keynes MK14 6LE
Tel: 0908 220022

UK Science Parks Association
44 Four Oaks Road
Sutton Coldfield
West Midlands B74 2TL
Tel: 021 308 8815

Chartered Institute of Marketing
Moor Hall Cookham
Maidenhead
Berkshire SL6 9QH
Tel: 0628 524 922

British Venture Capital Association
1 Surrey Street
London WC2R 2PS
Tel: 071 836 5702

Project Extra

GKN Technology Limited
Birmingham New Road
Wolverhampton WV4 6BW
Tel: 0902 334361

Greater London Enterprise Kickstart
63-67 Newington Causeway
London SE1 6BD
Tel: 071 403 0300

Investors in Industry (3i)
91 Waterloo Road
London SE1 8XP
Tel: 071 928 7822

BP Innovation LINC
c/o General Manager LINC
London EC1A 2BS
Tel: 071 236 3000

NatWest/BP Awards for Technology
Room 2539
The British Petroleum Company PLC
Britannic House
Moor Lane
London EC2Y 9BU
Tel: 071 920 3079

Small Firms Merit Award for Research and Technology
(SMART)

Contact any Department of Enterprise Regional Office

Open to firms of fewer than twenty-five employees with a business idea involving technological innovation. Stage 1 offers up to £37,500 towards a feasibility study; Stage 2 offers up to £50,000 for implementation.

Honeywell/Sunday Times
British Innovation Awards
c/o Quentin Bell Organisation plc
22 Endell Street
Covent Garden
London WC2H 9AD
Tel: 071 379 0304

British Association for the Advances of Science
Fortress House
23 Savile Row
London W1X 1AB
Tel: 071 494 3326
Fax: 071 734 1658

G. A. Richards & Co
Solicitors
Premier House
8-10 Portland Terrace
Southampton
Hampshire SO1 0EG
Tel: 0703 211600
Fax: 0703 236437

Reddie & Grose
Chartered Patent Agents
16 Theobalds Road
London WC1X 8PL
Tel: 071 242 0901
Fax: 071 242 3290

International Technology and Innovation
Technology House
Risborough Road
Stoke Mandeville
Aylesbury
Bucks HP22 5UT
England
Contact:
Mr Nick Bartman
(Managing Director)
Tel: 0296 614040
Fax: 0296 612174

Index